Lecture Notes in Computer Science 4408

Commenced Publication in 1973
Founding and Former Series Editors:
Gerhard Goos, Juris Hartmanis, and Jan van Leeuwen

Ricardo Choren   Alessandro Garcia
Holger Giese   Ho-fung Leung
Carlos Lucena   Alexander Romanovsky (Eds.)

Software Engineering for Multi-Agent Systems V

Research Issues
and Practical Applications

 Springer

Volume Editors

Ricardo Choren
PUC-Rio, Rio de Janeiro, Brazil
E-mail: choren@les.inf.puc-rio.br

Alessandro Garcia
Lancaster University
United Kingdom
E-mail: garciaa@comp.lancs.ac.uk

Holger Giese
University of Paderborn
D-33098 Paderborn, Germany
E-mail: hg@uni-paderborn.de

Ho-fung Leung
The Chinese University of Hong Kong
Hong Kong, China
E-mail: lhf@cse.cuhk.edu.hk

Carlos Lucena
PUC-Rio, Rio de Janeiro, Brazil
E-mail: lucena@inf.puc-rio.br

Alexander Romanovsky
University of Newcastle
Newcatle upon Tyne, UK
E-mail: Alexander.Romanovsky@newcastle.ac.uk

Library of Congress Control Number: 2007931241

CR Subject Classification (1998): D.2, I.2.11, C.2.4, D.1.3, H.3.5

LNCS Sublibrary: SL 2 – Programming and Software Engineering

ISSN   0302-9743
ISBN-10   3-540-73130-X Springer Berlin Heidelberg New York
ISBN-13   978-3-540-73130-6 Springer Berlin Heidelberg New York

Springer is a part of Springer Science+Business Media

springer.com

© Springer-Verlag Berlin Heidelberg 2007
Printed in Germany

Typesetting: Camera-ready by author, data conversion by Scientific Publishing Services, Chennai, India
Printed on acid-free paper   SPIN: 12078462   06/3180   5 4 3 2 1 0

Preface

Software is present in every aspect of our lives, pushing us inevitably towards a world of distributed computing systems. Agent concepts hold great promise for responding to the new realities of large-scale distributed systems. Multi-agent systems (MASs) and their underlying theories provide a more natural support for ensuring important agent properties, such as autonomy, environment heterogeneity, organization and openness. Nevertheless, a software agent is an inherently more complex abstraction, posing new challenges to software engineering. Without adequate development techniques and methods, MASs will not be sufficiently dependable, thus making their wide adoption by the industry more difficult.

The dependability of a computing system is its ability to deliver a service that can be justifiably trusted. It is a singular time for dependable distributed systems, since the traditional models we use to express the relationships between a computational process and its environment are changing from the standard deterministic types into ones that are more distributed and dynamic. This served as a guiding principle for planning the Software Engineering for Large-Scale Multi-Agent Systems (SELMAS 2006) workshop, starting with selecting the theme, "building dependable multi-agent systems." It acknowledges our belief in the increasingly vital role dependability plays as an essential element of MAS development.

SELMAS 2006 was the fifth edition of the workshop, organized in association with the 28th International Conference on Software Engineering (ICSE), held in Shanghai, China, in May 2006. After each workshop edition, it was decided to extend its scope, and to invite several of the workshop participants to write chapters for books based on their original position papers, as well as other leading researchers in the area to prepare additional chapters. Thus, this volume is the fifth in the *Software Engineering for Multi-Agent Systems LNCS* series.

In planning this volume, we sought to achieve both continuity and innovation. The papers selected for this volume present advances in software engineering approaches to develop dependable high-quality MASs. In addition, the power of agent-based software engineering is illustrated using actual real-world applications. These papers describe experiences and techniques associated with large MASs in a wide variety of problem domains.

This book brings together a collection of 12 papers addressing a wide range of issues in software engineering for MASs, reflecting the importance of agent properties in today's software systems. The papers in this book describe recent developments in specific issues and practical experience. At the end of each chapter, the reader will find a list of interesting references for further reading. The papers are grouped into five categories: Faulty Tolerance, Exception Handling and Diagnosis, Security and Trust, Verification and Validation, and Early Development Phases and Software Reuse. We believe that this carefully prepared volume will be of particular value to all readers interested in these key topics, describing the most recent developments in the field of software engineering for MASs.

The main target readers for this book are researchers and practitioners who want to keep up with the progress of software engineering in MASs, individuals keen to understand the interplay between agents and objects in software development, and those interested in experimental results from MAS applications. Software engineers involved with particular aspects of MASs as part of their work may find it interesting to learn about using software engineering approaches in building real systems. A number of chapters in the book discuss the development of MASs from requirements and architecture specifications to implementation.

We are confident that this book will be of considerable use to the software engineering community by providing many original and distinct views on such an important interdisciplinary topic, and by contributing to a better understanding and cross-fertilization among individuals in this research area.

Our thanks go to all our authors, whose work made this volume possible. Many of them also helped during the reviewing process. We would also like to express our gratitude to the members of the Evaluation Committee who were generous with their time and effort when reviewing the submitted papers. In conclusion, we extend once more our words of gratitude to all who contributed to making the SELMAS workshop series a reality. We hope that all of us will feel that we contributed in some way to helping improve the research on and the practice of software engineering for MASs in our society.

February 2007   Ricardo Choren
                                                              Alessandro Garcia
                                                                  Holger Giese
                                                                Ho-fung Leung
                                                                 Carlos Lucena
                                                          Alexander Romanovsky

Foreword

Although agent-based systems originated in the artificial intelligence community, they have become, over the past decade, an important topic for software engineering research. The reason for this is quite simple; the agent paradigm is extremely useful, if not essential, for solving many problems in software construction in the modern world of highly distributed, service-oriented, telecommunications and Internet-based systems. In many senses, there is nothing all that new about agents. After all, learning, goal-based behavior, planning and so on have been the subject of study for decades. Basic definitions of agents always include the concept of autonomy, defined (usually by example) as the ability to decide whether to accept a communication or not. But this ability is inherent in all software. Just look at operating systems or any reactive system! The idea of an open system also predates agents, e.g., actor systems, the Internet, etc. What is different about agents is the novel combination of these ingredients 'in one package' and the degree to which characteristics such as autonomy and being open are driving forces in the construction of these systems.

In this sense, it is quite natural to ask questions about agent system construction from the point of view of software engineering. As with any piece of software, we would expect that the software will be properly engineered, and not developed according to the paradigm described by the old joke about AI: How does an AI programmer develop software? He begins with the empty program and debugs until it works!

We know a lot about properly engineering software systems, even if this knowledge is not always deployed, but is there anything new that needs to be added in order to adapt the existing techniques and tools to support the construction of agent systems? As an example, Jean-Pierre Briot notes in the foreword of the 2004 SELMAS volume that the FIPA Agent Communication Language standard is an extension of the middleware idea inherent in CORBA to support the kind of communication requirements of business systems. There has been much discussion in the literature of platforms for agent-based systems, such as JADE, Grasshopper, JACK, Zeus, etc. In my view, these are middleware proposals, analogous to CORBA. Of course, they are more structured than CORBA and support more multidimensional interaction. But they are still middleware concepts. (Unfortunately, they are often referred to as 'architectures', leading to confusion when discussing *software architectures*. See below.) The past volumes of SELMAS and the current volume address issues in software engineering that investigate how standard ideas in software engineering apply to the construction of agent-based systems and the extent to which they have to be adapted.

What seems remarkable to me is the robustness of existing software engineering techniques with respect to this change in domain of application. One only has to peruse the section titles in the present volumes to see this historical resonance: 'Fault Tolerance', 'Exception Handling and Diagnosis', 'Security and Trust', 'Verification and Validation', 'Early Development Phases and Software Reuse'. Of course, the papers might thus be uninteresting to the wider community if the change in domain, to multi-agent systems, did not require substantial work in adapting and extending these techniques. This is certainly what made the papers in the volume of great interest to me.

In my own area of interest, software architecture, I noted above a confusion that has crept into the agent literature. There is much discussion about architecture, but it seems to relate to the internal architecture of the middleware component of relevant platforms. There is very little discussion of software architecture, per se, in relation to the application itself, other than at the gross level of components. One of my own students is doing 'archaeology' on multi-agent system designs in the literature to determine what the software architecture of these designs might be. Initial investigation would seem to indicate that most such applications have an implicit software architecture and it is a standard one from the software architecture literature. Layered architectures and blackboard architectures are common. Against our expectations, it is hard to spot any new software architectures emerging from the agent world. This is extremely surprising and might be a fruitful topic for further investigation and discussion at a future instance of SELMAS!

Tom Maibaum
McMaster University

Organization

Evaluation Committee

Natasha Alechina
Mercedes Amor
Carole Bernon
Rafael Bordini
Jean-Pierre Bnot
Giacomo Cab~i
Grui a Catalin-Roman
Mehdi Dastani
Mark Greaves
Zahia Guessoum
Giancarlo Guizzardi
Alexei Iliasov
Christine Julien
Rogerio de Lemos
Michael Luck
Viviana Mascardi
Haralabos Mouratidis
Andrea Omicini
Juan Pav6n
Gustavo Rossi
John Shepherdson
Viviane Silva
Danny Wcyns

Additional Reviewers

Juan Botia
Davide Grossi
Yuanfang Li

Table of Contents

On Fault Tolerance in Law-Governed Multi-agent Systems

Maíra A. de C. Gatti[1], Gustavo R. de Carvalho[1], Rodrigo B. de Paes[1],
Carlos J.P. de Lucena[1], and Jean-Pierre Briot[2]

[1] Software Engineering Laboratory, PUC-Rio,
Rio de Janeiro, Brazil
{mgatti, guga, rbp, lucena}@les.inf.puc-rio.br
[2] Laboratoire d'informatique de Paris 6 (LIP6),
Universit´e Pierre et Marie Curie, Paris, France
Jean-Pierre.Briot@lip6.fr

Abstract. The dependability of open multi-agent systems is a particular concern, notably because of their main characteristics as decentralization and no single point of control. This paper describes an approach to increase the availability of such systems through a technique of fault tolerance known as agent replication, and to increase their reliability through a mechanism of agent interaction regulation called law enforcement mechanism. Therefore, we combine two frameworks: one for law enforcement, named XMLaw, and another for agent adaptive replication, named DimaX, in which the decision of replicating an agent is based on a dynamic estimation of its criticality. Moreover, we will describe how we can reuse some of the information expressed by laws in order to help at the estimation of agent criticality, thus providing a better integration of the two frameworks. At the end of the paper, we recommend a means to specify criticality monitoring variation through a structured argumentation approach that documents the rationale around the decisions of the law elements derivation.

Keywords: Multi-Agent Systems; Open Systems; Law-Governed Approach; Dependability of Open Systems; Fault Tolerance; Requirements; Criticality; Availability, Reliability.

1 Introduction

There are many definitions in the literature for agents and, consequently, multi-agent systems. And despite their differences, all of them basically characterize a multi-agent system (MAS) as a computational environment in which individual software agents interact with each other, in a cooperative manner, or in a competitive manner, and sometimes autonomously pursuing their individual goals. During this process, they access the environment's resources and services and occasionally produce results for the entities that initiated these software agents [1]. As the agents interact in a concurrent, asynchronous and decentralized manner, this kind of system can be categorized as a complex system [2].

R. Choren et al. (Eds.): SELMAS 2006, LNCS 4408, pp. 1–20, 2007.
© Springer-Verlag Berlin Heidelberg 2007

The absence of centralized coordination data makes it hard to determine the current state of the system and/or to predict the effects of actions. Moreover, all of the possible situations that may arise in the execution context led us to be uncertain about predicting the behavior of agents. However, in critical applications such as business environments or government agencies, the behavior of the global system must be taken into account and structural characteristics of the domain have to be incorporated [10].

A particular issue that arises from this kind of software is: how we can ensure their dependability (which is the ability of a computer system to deliver service that can justifiably be trusted [3]) considering the reliability of critical applications and availability of these agents. There are some proposals to address such problem ([3][4][5][6], for instance, for fault tolerance and [7][8] for reliability) which have been proposed in the last few years using different approaches; each one solved a restricted problem involving dependability.

In this paper we propose an approach to increase the availability of multi-agent systems through a technique of fault tolerance known as agent replication, and to increase its reliability through a mechanism of agent interaction regulation called law enforcement mechanism. Therefore, we will combine two frameworks. The first framework, named XMLaw, manages law enforcement to increase reliability and correctness. The second framework, named DimaX, manages adaptive replication of agents in order to increase fault-tolerance. In DimaX, the decision of replicating an agent is based on a dynamic estimation of its criticality given by a criticality monitoring strategy. The agent criticality defines how important the agent is to the organization and consequently to the system. The estimation of the criticality of an agent can be based on different information, as the messages it sends or receives, or the role it plays, etc. In this paper, we will describe how we can reuse some of the information expressed by laws, and supported by XMLaw, in order to further contribute to the estimation of agent criticality, thus providing a better integration of the two frameworks. The novelty of this contribution is in the proposed combination of law-based governance and replication-based fault-tolerance, rather than in specific contributions in law-based governance or in fault-tolerance.

We also propose a means to specify the criticality monitoring strategy through a structured argumentation [24] that documents the rationale around the decisions of the law elements derivation. However, it will not be detailed in this paper. Moreover, we also provide a framework that implements the criticality monitoring variation behavior specified.

The subsequent sections are organized as follows: Section 2 presents an introduction to the agent replication-based fault tolerance for multi-agent systems, and Section 3 presents the law enforcement approach for increasing the reliability of these systems. Section 4 states a scenario for the problem description. Section 5 details the proposed solution for the problem as an integrated architecture. This architecture is the integration of both approaches presented in Section 2 and 3. Section 6 presents one of the case studies implemented to validate the concepts and the architecture. And finally, Section 7 concludes this paper and presents future works.

2 Fault Tolerance in Multi-agent Systems: Agent Replication

The multi-agent systems deployed in an open environment, where agents from various organizations interact in the same MAS, are distributed over many hosts and communicate over public networks, hence more attention must be paid to fault tolerance.

Several approaches ([4][14][15]) address the multi-faced problem of fault tolerance in multi-agent systems. Some of them handle the problems of communication, interaction and coordination of agents with the other agents of the system. Others address the difficulties of making reliable mobile agents, which are more exposed to security problems. Some of them are based on replication mechanisms [9], and as mentioned before they have solved many problems of ubiquitous systems.

Agent replication is the act of creating one or more replicas of one or more agents, and the number of each agent replica is the replication degree; everything depends on how critical the agent is while executing its tasks. Among the significant advantages over other fault-tolerance solutions, first and foremost, agent replication provides the groundwork for the shortest recovery delays. Also, generally it is less intrusive with respect to execution time. And finally, it scales much better [9]. There is a framework, named DimaX [6], that allows dynamic replication and dynamic adaptation of the replication policy (e.g., passive to active, changing the number of replicas). It was designed to easily integrate various agent architectures, and the mechanisms that ensure dependability are kept as transparent as possible to the application. Basically, DimaX is the integration between a multi-agent system called Dima and the dynamic replication architecture for agents called DarX.

There are two cases that might be distinguished: 1) the agent's criticality is static and 2) the agent's criticality is dynamic. In the first case, multi-agent systems have often static organization structures, static behaviors of agents, and a small number of agents. Critical agents, therefore, can be identified by the designer and can be replicated by the programmer before run time.

In the second case, the agent criticality cannot be determined before run time due to the fact that the multi-agent systems may have dynamic organization structures, dynamic behaviors of agents and a large number of agents. Then it is important to determine these structures dynamically in order to evaluate agent criticality. The approach detailed in [16] proposes a way of determining it through role analysis. It could be done by some prior input from the designer of the application who specifies the roles' weights, or there would be an observation module for each server that collects the data through the agent execution and their interactions. In the second approach, global information is built and then used to obtain roles and degree of activity to compute the agent criticality.

Another way of dynamically determining these structures to evaluate agent criticality is to represent the emergent organizational structure of a multi-agent system by a graph [6]. The hypothesis is that the criticality of an agent relies on the interdependences of other agents on this agent. First, the interdependence graph is initialized by the designer, and then it is dynamically adapted by the system itself. Some algorithms to dynamically adapt and describe it are proposed in [6].

We will present here an enhancement of these approaches and it will be further described in Section 5. Basically, we improved the agent criticality calculation through dynamic elements present during interactions with other agents. These elements will be described in the next section while the law enforcement approaches, especially the one that was chosen, are exposed.

3 Law-Governed Interaction

In open multi-agent systems the development takes place without a centralized control, thus it is necessary to ensure the reliability of these systems in a way that all the interactions between agents will occur according to the specification and that these agents will obey the specified scenario. For this, these applications must be built upon a law-governed architecture.

In this kind of architecture, enforcement that is responsible for the interception of messages and the interpreting of previously described laws is implemented. The core of a law-governed approach is the mechanism used by the mediator to monitor the conversations between agents.

Note that law-governed approaches have some relations with general coordination mechanisms (e.g., tuple-space mechanisms like Tucson [26]) in that they specify and control interactions between agents. However, the specificity of law-governed mechanisms is about controlling interactions and actions from a social (social norms) perspective, whereas general coordination languages and mechanisms focus on means for expressing synchronization and coordination of activities and exchange of information, at a lower (not social) computational level.

Among the models and frameworks that were developed to support law-governed mechanism (for instance, [7][8][17][18]), XMLaw [7] was chosen for three main reasons. First, because it implements a law enforcement approach as an object-oriented framework, which brings the benefits of reuse and flexibility. Second, it allows normative behavior that is more expressive than the others through the connection between norms and clocks. And finally, it permits the execution of Java code through the concept of actions. Thus, in this section, we explain the XMLaw description language [7] and the M-Law framework [19].

M-Law works by intercepting messages exchanged between agents, verifying the compliance of the messages with the laws and subsequently redirecting the message to the real addressee, if the laws allow it (Figure 1). If the message is not compliant, then the mediator blocks the message and applies the consequences specified in the law.

This infrastructure, whenever necessary, can be extended to fulfill open system requirements or interoperability concerns. M-Law architecture is based on a pool of mediators that intercept messages and interpret the previously described laws.

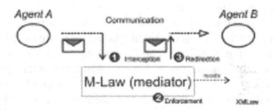

Fig. 1. M-Law Architecture

M-Law was built to support law specification using XMLaw. XMLaw is the description language used to configure the M-Law mediator by representing the interaction rules of an open system. These rules are interpreted by M-Law that analyzes the compliance of software agents with interaction laws at runtime. Basically, interactions should be analyzed and subsequently described using the concepts proposed in the model during the design phase. After that, the concepts have to be mapped to a declarative language based on XML. It is also important to point out that agent developers from different open MASs must agree upon interaction procedure. In fact, each open MAS should have a clear documentation about the interactions' rules. By doing that, there is no need of agent developers' interaction.

Interaction's definitions are interpreted by a software framework that monitors component interaction and enforces the behavior specified by the language. Once interaction is specified and enforced, despite the autonomy of the agents, the system's global behavior is better controlled and predicted. Interaction specification of a system is also called the laws of a system. This is because besides the idea of specification itself, interactions are monitored and enforced. Then, they act as laws in the sense that they describe what can be done (permissions), what cannot be done (prohibitions) and what must be done (obligations).

Among the model elements, the outer concept is the LawOrganization. This element represents the interaction laws (or normative dimension) of a multi-agent organization. A LawOrganization is composed of scenes, clocks, norms and actions. Scenes are interaction contexts that can happen in an organization. They allow modularizing interaction breaking the interaction of the whole system into smaller parts. Clocks introduce global times, which are shared by all scenes. Figure 2 summarizes the XMLaw conceptual model, its concepts and their relations.

Norms capture notions of permissions, obligations and prohibitions regarding agents' interaction behavior (as mentioned before). Actions can be viewed as a consequence of any interaction condition; for example, if an agent acquires an obligation, then action "A" should be executed.

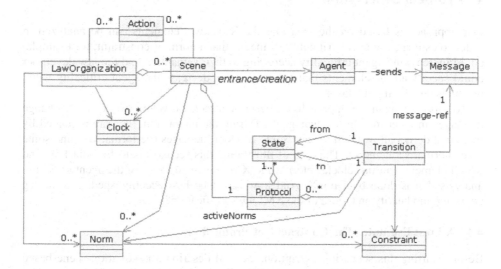

Fig. 2. Partial View of XMLaw Conceptual Model

Scenes define an interaction protocol (from a global point of view), a set of norms and clocks that are only valid in the context of the scene. Furthermore, scenes also identify which agents are allowed to start or participate in the scene.

Events are the basis of the communication among law elements; that is, law elements dynamically relate with other elements through event notifications. Basically, we can understand the dynamic of the elements as a chain of causes and consequences, where an event can activate a law element; this law element could generate other events and so on.

Furthermore, laws may be time sensitive, e.g., although an element that is active at time t1, it might not be active at time t2 (t1 < t2). XMLaw provides the Clock element to take care of the timing aspect. Temporal clocks represent time restrictions or controls and they can be used to activate other law elements. Clocks indicate that a certain period has elapsed producing clock-tick events. Once activated, a clock can generate clock-tick events. Clocks are activated and deactivated by law elements. Both are referenced to other law elements.

Constraints are restrictions over norms or transitions and generally specify filters for events, constraining the allowed values for a specific attribute of an event. For instance, messages carry information that is enforced in various ways. Constraints can be used for describing the allowed values for specific attributes. Constraints are defined inside the Transition or Norm elements. Constraints are implemented using Java code. The Constraint element defines the class attribute that indicates the java class that implements the filter. This class is called when a transition or a norm is supposed to fire, and basically the constraint analyzes if the received values are valid. For instance, a constraint can verify if the date expressed in the message is valid; if it is not, the message will be blocked.

The proposal here is not to detail the framework or the language, so further details can be found in [7] and [19]. The next sections will address both DimaX and XMLaw and how their integration works.

4 Problem Description

Our approach is based on the idea that the XMLaw's elements can be analyzed in order to estimate the agent criticality. It means that a norm or constraint, for example, could increase the agent criticality according to their semantic. And the law developer could specify all the elements that can increase or decrease the agent criticality while he/she is developing the laws.

To further explain our approach, we describe a scenario where two agents exchange messages in order to achieve their goals. During the interaction, they are regulated by rules that do not allow them to send some types of messages (performatives) and some other normative elements. The idea of illustrating this scenario is to find out how and which elements (norms, clocks, etc.) of the XMLaw could improve the agent criticality analysis that is done by DimaX. And how can it be best accomplished, considering coupling, modularity and reuse of the XMLaw specification?

4.1 A First Example: The Contract Net Protocol

Before starting this scenario description, we will describe a negotiation scene based on FIPA-CONTRACT-NET protocol [21]. The goal is to map a FIPA compliant protocol into a state machine protocol and discover (through this illustration) the rationale around the XMLaw protocol specification. And then, we will present the XMLaw final protocol state machine for the scenario that will be soon detailed.

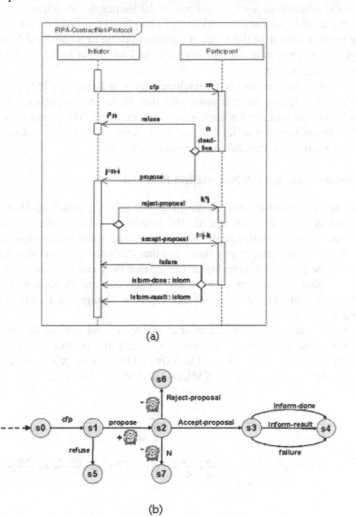

Fig. 3. a) FIPA-CONTRACT-NET protocol [21], b) FIPA Protocol State Machine

In the FIPA-CONTRACT-NET protocol, basically, the Initiator requests m proposals from other agents by issuing a call for proposals (*cfp*) act, which specifies the task. Participants receiving this message are viewed as potential contractors and are able to generate n responses. Of these, j are proposals to perform the task, specified as propose acts. The Participant's proposal includes the preconditions that the Participant is setting out for the task, which may be the price; the time when the task will be done, etc. Alternatively, the $i=n-j$ Participants may refuse to propose. Once the deadline passes, the Initiator evaluates the received j proposals and selects agents to perform the task; one, several or no agents may be chosen. The *l* agents of the selected proposals will receive an accept-proposal act and the remaining *k* agents will receive a reject-proposal act. The proposals are associated with the Participant, so that once the Initiator accepts the proposal; the Participant acquires a commitment to perform the task. Once the Participant has completed the task, it sends a completion message to the Initiator in the form of an inform-done or a more explanatory version in the form of an inform-result. However, if the Participant fails to complete the task, a failure message is sent.

Now, suppose the protocol state machine shown in figure 3, where *si* represents the protocol's states during its execution and the clocks' representation are the clocks activation and deactivation for each + or -, respectively. The protocol starts with the state s0 when the Initiator solicits m proposals from other agents and it ends with the states s4, or s5, or s7, it depends on the protocol's flow.

4.2   A Second Example: A Negotiation Protocol

Considering this rationale for developing the protocol state machine, imagine a scenario where there are two agents: the customer and the seller of an institution. Suppose that an open multi-agent system exists where the agents that want to buy a product may enter or leave at any time, and that there are sellers in this institution that want to sell the product for the highest price that they can achieve. Then, we have a negotiation scene where each agent wants to succeed and there is a protocol in this scene that represents all the messages that can be exchanged and all the rules that rule this scene and the participants.

At any time, any agent can enter into the scene and initiate the protocol. If we specify this scene in XMLaw, we have to specify the protocol as a state machine, where each transition of the protocol is activated by a message sent by an agent and it can activate the other elements of XMLaw, as clocks and norms.

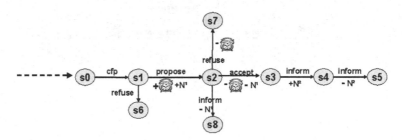

Fig. 4. Protocol State Machine Representation of the Scene Negotiation

Basically, the negotiation proceeds as follows: a customer initiates a negotiation by sending a proposal for a book to a seller. It informs the maximum price that he will pay for the book. The seller can accept the proposal or can refuse it. If he accepts, it can send proposals with lesser or equal price informed by the customer. When the customer receives the proposal, it has 2 minutes to decide if he will accept it or not. After 2 minutes, if the customer hasn't answered the seller, it can sell the product to another customer. Otherwise the seller is not allowed to sell it to anybody else. If the customer accepts it, the seller informs the bank where the payment must be made. Then the customer has the obligation of paying for the product and of informing the number of the voucher to the seller. The scene ends then when the customer informs that he paid it with the proof of payment (figure 4 and table 1).

If we consider that when an event (such as clock activation/deactivation, norm activation/deactivation, etc.) occurs during the scene execution, the agent criticality could increase or decrease, since the agent becomes more or less important; thus, each element should be taken into account in order to calculate the agent criticality in the best way. Moreover, other elements and events that might not be handled by XMLaw should be analyzed in order to evaluate how they could influence the agent criticality analysis. For instance, when an agent starts playing a role its criticality may increase or decrease.

Table 1. Protocol State Machine Description

State		Message	Description	Event
Initial	Final			
s0	s1	Cfp	The customer starts a negotiation sending a proposal to a seller.	
s1	s1	propose	The seller accepts the customer's proposal. He sends proposals with lesser or equal price informed by the customer.	Clock activation Norm activation
s1	s6	Refuse	The seller refuses the customer's proposal and the protocol ends.	
s2	s3	Accept	The customer accepts the seller's proposal before 2 minutes.	Clock deactivation
s2	s7	Refuse	The customer refuses the seller's proposal before 2 minutes.	Clock deactivation
s2	s8	inform	The customer doesn't answer the seller and the seller informs him that he can offer the book to another customer.	Norm deactivation
s3	s4	Inform	The seller informs the customer the bank where he has to pay for the book and he has the obligation to pay in order to receive the book.	Norm activation
s4	s5	Inform	The customer informs the voucher and has the permission to receive the book.	Norm deactivation

In the context of the negotiation scene, when the customer must answer the seller if he will accept his proposal or refuse it since the clock activation event will be fired, his criticality should increase, since the seller cannot sell the product while the customer doesn't answer him. Thus, the customer is very important to the seller at this time and should not crash. Then, when the clock deactivation is fired, the customer criticality should decrease. Another situation would be the payment for the product. Since the customer has the obligation of paying for the product when he accepts the price, his criticality should also increase. Those variations are shown in figure 5.

We can see the protocol execution on the left side of the picture. Next to it is a draft of the main criticality variation. This main result is based on the criticality variation that

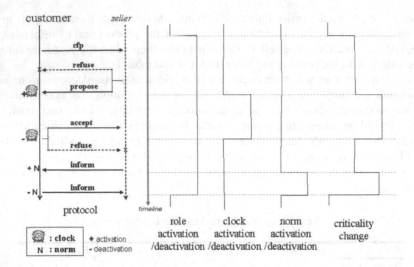

Fig. 5. Criticality variation for customer role

occurs as a result of each event, as previously mentioned. The clock's picture represents the clock activation/deactivation event and the letter N represents the norm activation/ deactivation event during the protocol execution, according to the plus or minus sign that comes before the picture or letter. For instance, in an analogous manner, if we analyze the seller criticality during the scene execution, his criticality should increase when the customer proposes a price for the product because he has the obligation to answer him.

That said, it is important to highlight that the goal of this work is to combine the law-based governance with a replication-based fault-tolerance technique. This combination will improve the agent criticality estimation. This, by its turn, improves the agent replication technique of open multi-agent systems. Our proposal is that the agent criticality estimation will be done also through the events generated by the law elements. Those events may be fired during a protocol execution and can increase or decrease the agent criticality according to the type of the event and to its semantic. It could be a norm/clock/role/transition activation/deactivation event or even a message arrival event.

In the next section, we will explain how we extended both XMLaw and DimaX to attempt both the design strategies of estimating the agent criticality and its execution at runtime. We also will describe the integrated architecture developed.

5   Proposed Solution: The Integration

In this section we will present the integrated architecture and we will describe the proposed solution, first from the XMLaw and M-Law point of view, second from the DimaX point of view. At the end, we conclude describing how to use the mechanism and instantiate the resultant framework.

5.1 The Proposed Architecture

A sample scenario was created in order to illustrate the integrated architecture of both M-Law and DimaX framework (figure 6). Considering two agents: Agent A and Agent B, each one has its monitor agent called, Agent A's Monitor and Agent B' Monitor, respectively. Suppose that both are running in the same machine (host) and that each monitor will register itself in a communication port through a socket communication channel when it starts its execution.

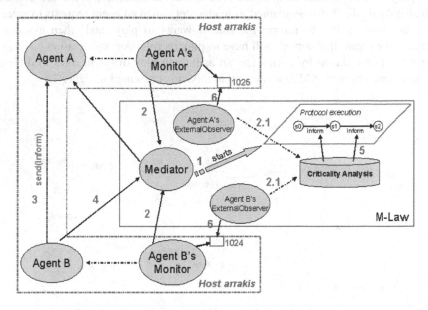

Fig. 6. The Integrated Architecture Mechanism Overview

The following flow will be executed when the agents are created and, for instance, when an interaction scene between both is started:

0. DimaX Server is started;
1. M-Law Server is started and the XMLaw file is loaded
2. DimaX monitors the agent interactions
3. The Agent B sends a message to the Agent A
4. M-Law mediator applies the enforcement
5. The criticality analysis module monitors the events and recalculate the agent's criticality. This module fires an event to be sensed by the ExternalObserver of each agent
6. The ExternalObserver listens to the events and opens a socket to send the information to the (DimaX) monitor of the agent.

Therefore, during the M-Law enforcement, whenever the component of criticality of M-Law detects to recalculate the agent criticality, it fires an event of type *update_criticality* in the scene context. The *ExternalObserver* that is listening for that event and for that agent in this scene context will send a message through socket communication to the address and port number where the monitor of that agent is listening.

5.1.1 XMLaw Extensions

We have extended XMLaw through two ways: first we added more expressivity and functionality to the Role element (Figure 7). It defines the organization's and scene's roles, and is important because the agent behavior is regulated also through the role that it plays in an organization or scene. And the second extension is the new element: CriticalityAnalysis. With the adapted Role element, when an agent requests to enter in an organization, it has to inform the role it wants to play; and when a scene is executed, the agent, if accepted, will have to play its role. An organization has one or more roles to be played by agents and an agent can play different roles in different organizations. The new XMLaw conceptual model is presented in figure 7.

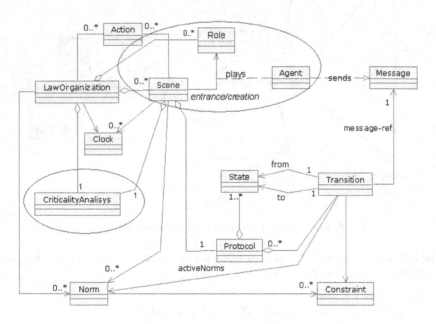

Fig. 7. XMLaw Conceptual Model

Considering the new element *CriticalityAnalysis*, it can be added in the organization or scene level. Thus, there would be a criticality analysis module for each scene in a way that, for instance, if an agent is interacting with other agents in two different scenes, and if those scenes have their criticality analysis module specified, the agent resultant criticality will be composed by the criticality variation of the scenes currently running.

The *CriticalityAnalysis* element has three elements: *Weight*, *Increases* and *Decreases*. The first one defines the weight that each event type contributes to the monitoring. Those events are the ones that increase or decrease the agents' criticality and will be referenced in the other two elements. The *Weight* element is optional because the system assumes some values to the event types that may occur. It only should be specified if the designer wants to give more or less importance to an event type than it was defined. For instance, if the law designer doesn't want to monitor the message arrival event, he should specify its value as zero.

The other two elements (*Increase* and *Decrease*) specify the necessary information for the detection and handling of the specified event by the monitoring module in order to recalculate the criticality of a given agent. The *Increases* element contains the list of events that contribute to increasing the agent criticality. And the *Decreases* element contains the list of events that contribute to decreasing the agent criticality.

Both *Increase* and *Decrease* elements are specified through three attributes and the *Assignee* element. The *event-id* attribute specifies the identification of the event to be sensed, the *event-type* attribute specifies the event type of the event defined by the *event-id* attribute, and the *value* attribute represents the associated value that the event contributes to the increasing or decreasing of the agent criticality. And, finally, the *Assignee* element contains the agent information: the agent role and a variable with the agent instance.

Table 2. Criticality specification in XMLaw

```
<CriticalityAnalysis>
  <Weight ref="role" value="0.2"/>
  <Weight ref="message" value="0"/>
  <Increases>
    <Increase event-id="customer" event-type="role_activation"
        value="0.3">
      <Assignee role-ref="customer"
          role-instance="$customer.instance"/>
    </Increase>
    <Increase event-id="seller" event-type="role_activation"
        value="0.7">
      <Assignee role-ref="seller"
          role-instance="$seller.instance"/>
    </Increase>
    <Increase event-id="time-to-decide"
        event-type="clock_activation" value="0.5">
      <Assignee role-ref="customer"
          role-instance="$customer.instance"/>
    </Increase>
    <Increase event-id="customer-payment-voucher"
        event-type="norm_activation" value="0.8">
      <Assignee role-ref="customer"
          role-instance="$customer.instance"/>
    </Increase>
  </Increases>
  ...
  </Decreases>
</CriticalityAnalysis>
```

Considering the sample scenario presented in the problem description section, table 2 shows the resultant specification to the criticality monitoring of the specified scene as an example of XMLaw specification using the described elements. For instance, notice that the message arrival events will not be monitored. On the other hand, the role activation/ deactivation event will be monitored with a different value (0.2).

Basically, the specification shows that, when an agent starts playing the customer role, its criticality has to be recalculated and updated by a weight of 0.3. The same happens when an agent starts playing the seller role, its criticality has to be updated by a weight of 0.7. Those actions are executed when the role activation event is fired.

5.1.2 M-Law Framework Extensions

This section presents the extensions developed in M-Law in order to implement the behavior of the criticality's monitoring module added to the XMLaw language. And it also presents the mechanism that implements this behavior.

As the M-Law is an event based framework where the protocol state moves forward through event notification, the new element *CriticalityAnalysis* had to be implemented like the other elements. Doing it by this way, it would generate and sense the system events and would minimize any overhead to the system.

That said, the *CriticalityAnalysisExecution* class implements the *IObserver* interface (figure 8). The *IObserver* interface defines the behavior of the events consumers. The consumers subscribe their interests in some event type using the *attachObserver* method. Thus, when the *CriticalityAnalysisExecution* class is instantiated, it subscribes itself for each specified event in the *Increases* and *Decreases* lists of the *CriticalityAnalysis* element, and for the event of message arrival if specified.

When the instance of the *CriticalityAnalysisExecution* object is executing and receives an event, it checks if the event data match with the specified data concerning the agent that will have its criticality updated. To this end, the *RoleReference* received is compared to the expected assignee *RoleReference*.

Once the event that occurred is the expected one, the *updateAgentCriticality* method is executed. This method receives the agent identification, the event weight value, the event value, the operation and the additional information about the event to be written by the agent monitor in the log.

This method doesn't update the criticality of the agent, it calculates the new value based on the collected data and sends to the agent monitor running in DimaX. Then, the monitor will apply one of its strategies for updating the agent criticality with the received value, combining or not with other strategies, and will set the finally criticality value which, by its turn, will be used to calculate the agent number of replicas.

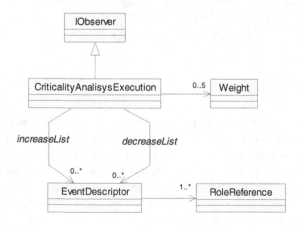

Fig. 8. Partial View of the Criticality Module Class Diagram

5.1.3 DimaX Framework Extensions

In this work we rely on the design decisions of DimaX. The model of failure considered is crash and the number of replicas depends on the criticality. However, DimaX also assumes that resources for replicas may be bounded. Furthermore, the mechanism is dynamic. That is resources for replicas may be redistributed dynamically depending on the evolution of the relative criticalities of the agents.

We extended DimaX through the same extension reasoning used to estimate through the role analysis [16][23] approach for updating the agents' criticality.

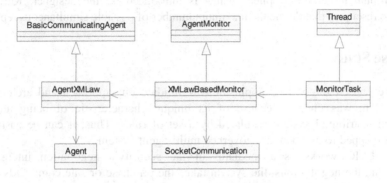

Fig. 9. DimaX Extensions Class Diagram

Figure 9 shows the class diagram of the extensions. The *BasicCommunicatingAgent* and *AgentMonitor* classes there were already in the DimaX framework. And the *Agent* class there was already in the M-Law framework. Finally, the *Thread* class is a *Java* class. We created the *XMLawBasedMonitor* class which extends the *AgentMonitor* class and implements the agent monitor behavior. It has a reference to the *AgentXMLaw* class, which is the class that implements the agent behavior and delegates the law-enforcement tasks to the *Agent* class in a transparent way. Moreover, the *MonitorTask* is a thread that listens for the messages sent through the socket communication channel and, when a message arrives, starts the mechanism of updating the agent criticality implemented by the agent monitor through the *computeCriticalityFromXmlaw* call method.

The message received contains the agent identification, the criticality value calculated by XMLaw, the operation to be performed and the additional information about the event generated. The criticality value is the event type weight value (ae) multiplied by the event weight value (ve). Let the $w_i(t)$ the agent i's criticality in the instant t, the final criticality value varies according to the following criteria:

- If it was generated by a Increase element:

$$w_i\ (t) = w_i\ (t) + ae*ve\ .$$

- If it was generated by a Decrease element:

$$w_i\ (t) = w_i\ (t) - ae*ve\ .$$

The result of those expressions would be combined with others results derived from criticality estimation and the degree of activity of the agent would be considered in this estimation. Finally, the calculation of the number of replicas nbi of Agent i, which is used to update the number of replicas of the domain agent, is determined as the same as before:

$$nbi(t) = \text{rounded}(rm + wi(t) * Rm/W) .$$

Where wi is the agent criticality, W is the sum of the domain agents' criticality, rm is the minimum number of replicas which is introduced by the designer, Rm is the available resources that define the maximum number of possible simultaneous replicas.

6 Case Study

We have chosen the SELIC application to validate our approach and architecture. This system was chosen because of its unique characteristic of being an open governed distributed system regulated by a set of rules. Thus, it can be easily and directed mapped to an open law-governed multi-agent system.

The SELIC works as a mediator of the security's negotiation interactions. Concerning the negotiations, the system takes the purchase or sale commands in full or part, definitive or committed, by the necessaries proceedings to the financial movement and of custody related to the settlement of those operations, which are done one by one in real time.

We choose to implement a committed operation. There are several requirements that rule the interaction on behalf of all institutions in a committed operation, as the several types of messages that could be sent and the several behavioral that should be implemented according to the messages specified, including norms and constraints. We choose a scenario that encloses all the law elements necessary to theconcepts proven. Figure 10 shows this scenarios and below there is an example of interaction.

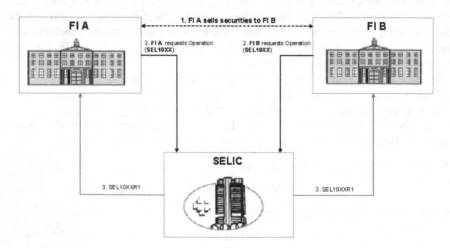

Fig. 10. SELIC Example

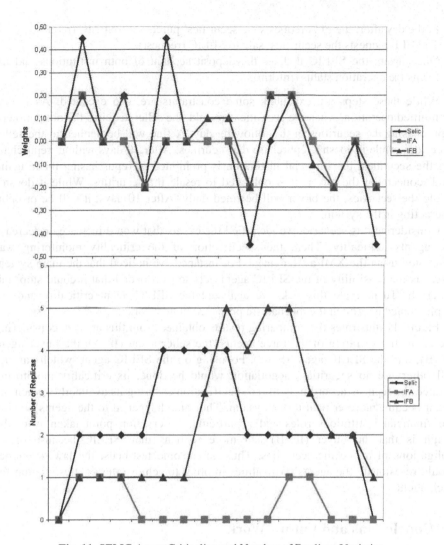

Fig. 11. SELIC Agent Criticality and Number of Replicas Variation

The financial institution A (FI A) needs to sell securities to the financial institution B (FI B) and takes the commitment of repurchasing them in the following day. It works like if FI A was taken a loan from FI B for a day.

- The SELIC notifies the financial institutions that the operations are open for negotiations (inform);
- The FI A requests the securities' sale to SELIC (request);
- The FI B request the securities' purchase to SELIC (request);
- The SELIC updates the deposit account of both institutions and informs the operation status (inform);

- In the day after, the FI A requests the securities' purchase to SELIC (request);
- The FI B requests the securities' sale to SELIC (request);
- Once again, the SELIC updates the deposit account of both institutions and informs the operation status (inform).

While those steps are executed, some constraints are also executed. As it is a committed operation, when the securities are sold, the seller acquires the obligation of repurchasing the securities in the following day. A fine will be applied to the seller every day while it doesn't repurchase the securities. After 10 days without repurchasing the securities, the financial institution is prohibited of repurchasing them again. And, concerning the buyer, it is obligated to resale the securities. While it doesn't resale the securities, the buyer will be fined daily. After 10 days, it will be prohibit interacting in the system.

Considering this scenario, we identified the events that would increase or decrease the agents' criticality. Then, the specification of the criticality monitoring was generated using the XMLaw language. For instance, we noticed that the main system threat is the possibility of the SELIC agent gets so overloaded that it could stop, fail or crash. To mitigate this risk, we analyzed the SELIC agent criticality and we implemented it through the mechanism proposed in this work.

Figure 11 illustrates the comparing results obtained from this analyze considering the criticality variation of the three agents: the seller agent (IF A), the buyer agent (IF B), and the SELIC agent (Selic). Focusing on the SELIC agent, which can not fail otherwise no securities' negotiation would be done, its criticality monitoring created the replicas accordingly to the specification ensuring its availability when the agent became more critical to the system. The same happened to the agents playing the financial institutions roles and a particular observation point taken from the graph is that the buyer (IF B) had more replicas than SELIC because of its obligations of resale the securities. Thus, after some test-beds, the law developer would re-estimate the agents' criticalities in order to achieve the right estimation for each agent.

7   Conclusions and Future Work

This work proposed a pragmatic mechanism of estimating agents' criticality in law-governed multi-agent systems. We proposed the integration of two frameworks (M-Law and DimaX) to achieve dependability in open multi-agents system through fault tolerance and we evaluated this architecture through a real case study. During the development of this work, some initial approaches were proposed [25] and improved in order to achieve an efficient one.

We presented an extension of the XMLaw conceptual model described in Section 3 and we proposed to use new elements that help specifying the attributes concerning the agent criticality during its interaction with other agents.

We extended XMLaw with the new *CriticalityAnalysis* element. And we extended the M-Law framework to implement the monitoring of the events that should improve the criticality analysis done by DimaX. Any event considered important by the designer of the application while specifying its law can be taken into account. Finally, we extended DimaX and we integrated it with M-Law, providing another algorithm for calculating the agent's criticality.

Therefore, along these works, an important issue arose: how do we know that the criticality analyzes specification implements the real expected monitoring? Thus, we proposed the use of Law Cases [24] to help on this task and we used it on the case study presented as an evaluation of this proposal in Section 5. The Law Cases approach help to derive the law elements through a rationale that could be documented. Basically, a Law Case is a structured argument providing evidence that an open multi-agent system meets its specified dependability requirements through the rationale around the law elements derivation.

An issue to be considered is about the centralized nature of current XMLaw mediator. We are aware that it is a limitation for scalability. Hence, there is currently ongoing work to design and implemented a new distributed version.

References

1. http://agtivity.com/agdef.htm, accessed in Oct/2005.
2. Jennings, Nicholas R., An Agent-Based Approach for building Complex Software Systems, Communications of the ACM, 44(4), 35-41, April 2001.
3. Peng Xu, Ralph Deters. "Using Event-Streams for Fault-Management in MAS," IEEE/WIC/ACM International Conference on Intelligent Agent Technology (IAT'04), 2004, pp. 433-436.
4. A. Fedoruk and R. Deters. Improving fault-tolerance by replicating agents. In AAMAS2002, Boulogna, Italy, 2002.
5. Fedoruk, A. and Deters, R. 2003. Using dynamic proxy agent replicate groups to improve fault-tolerance in multi-agent systems. In Proc. of the Sec. int. Joint Conf. AAMAS '03. ACM Press, New York, NY, 990-991.
6. Guessoum, Z., Faci, N., Briot, J.-P., Adaptive Replication of Large-Scale Multi-Agent Systems - Towards a Fault-Tolerant Multi-Agent Platform. Proc. of ICSE'05, 4th Int. Workshop on Soft. Eng. for Large-Scale Multi-Agent Systems, ACM Software Engineering Notes, 30(4) : 1-6, July 2005.
7. Paes, R., Carvalho, G. R., Lucena, C.J.P., Alencar, P. S. C., Almeida H.O., and Silva, V. T.. Specifying Laws in Open Multi-Agent Systems. In: Agents, Norms and Institutions for Regulated Multi-agent Systems (ANIREM), AAMAS2005, 2005.
8. Murata, T. and Minsky, N. "On Monitoring and Steering in Large-Scale Multi-Agent Systems", Proceedings of ICSE 2003, 2nd Intn'l Workshop on Software Engineering for Large-Scale Multi-Agent Systems (SELMAS 2003).
9. Guerraoui, R. and Schiper, A. Software-based replication for fault tolerance. IEEE Computer Journal, 30(4):68--74, 1997.
10. Vázquez-Salceda, J., Dignum, V., and Dignum, F., Organizing Multiagent Systems, Autonomous Agents and Multi-Agent Systems, 11, 307-360, 2005.
11. Lussier, B. et al. 3rd IARP-IEEE/RAS-EURON Joint Workshop on Technical Challenges for Dependable Robots in Human Environments, Manchester (GB), 7-9 September 2004, 7p.
12. Laprie, J. C., Arlat, J., Blanquart, J. P., Costes, A., Crouzert, Y., Deswarte, Y., Fabre, J. C., Guillermain, H., Kaâniche, M., Kanoun, K. Mazet, C., Powel, D., Rabéjac, C. and Thévenod, P. Dependability Handbook (2nd edition) Cépaduès – Éditions, 1996. (ISBN 2-85428-341-4) (in French).

13. Avizienis, A., Laprie, J.-C., Randell, B. Dependability and its threats - A taxonomy. IFIP Congress Topical Sessions 2004: 91-120.
14. Decker, K., Sycara, K. and Williamson, M. Cloning for intelligent adaptive information agents. In ATAL'97, LNAI, pages 63–75. Springer Verlag, 1997.
15. Hagg, S. A sentinel approach to fault handling in multi-agent systems. In C. Zhang and D. Lukose, editors, Multi-Agent Systems, Methodologies and Applications, number 1286 in LNCS, pages 190–195. Springer Verlag, 1997.
16. Guessoum, Z., Briot, J.-P., Faci, N. Towards Fault-Tolerant Massively Multiagent Systems, Massively Multiagent Systems n. 3446, LNAI, Springer Lecture Note Series, Verlag, 2005, pg. 55-69.
17. Minsky, N.H., Ungureanu, V., Law-governed interaction: a coordination and control mechanism for heterogeneous distributed systems, ACM Trans. Softw.Eng.Methodol. 9 (3) (2000) 273-305.
18. Esteva, M., Electronic institutions: from specification to developement, Ph.D. thesis, Institut d'Investigació en Intelligència Artificial, Catalonia - Spain (October 2003).
19. Paes, R., Alencar, P., Lucena, C. Governing Agent Interaction in Open Multi-Agent Systems. Monografias de Ciência da Computação nº 30/05, Departamento de Informática, PUC-Rio, Brazil, 2005.
20. Weinstock, C.B., Goodenough, J.B., Hudak, J.J., Dependability Cases, Technical Note, CMU/SEI-2004-TN-016, 2004.
21. FIPA – The Foundation for Inteligent Physical Agents - Contract Net Interaction Protocol Specification http://www.fipa.org/specs/fipa00029/
22. XML Schema. http://www.w3.org/XML/Schema, last accessed in Aug, 2006.
23. Guessoum, Z., Briot, J.-P., Marin, O., Hamel, A., and Sens, P.. Dynamic and Adaptive Replication for Large-Scale Reliable Multi-Agent Systems. Software Engineering for Large-Scale Multi-Agent Systems, No 2603, p. 182–198, LNCS, Springer, 2003.
24. Gatti, M.A.C, Carvalho, G. R., Paes, R., Lucena, C.J.P, Briot, J.-P.. Structuring a Law Case for Law-Governed Open Multi-Agent Systems. Monografias em Ciência da Computação, PUC-Rio, n. MCC27/06, p. 1-34, 2006.
25. Gatti, M. A. C., Lucena, C.J.P. de, Briot, J.-P. On Fault Tolerance in Law-Governed Multi-Agent Systems. In: 5th International Workshop on Software Engineering for Large-scale Multi-Agent Systems, 2006, Shanghai. 28th International Conference on Software Engineering. New York, NY, USA : ACM Press, 2006. p. 21-27.
26. Omicini, A. and Zambonelli, F.. TuCSoN: A Coordination Model for Mobile Information Agents, *Proc. First Int'l Workshop Innovative Internet Information Systems,* June 1998.

On Developing Open Mobile Fault Tolerant Agent Systems

Budi Arief, Alexei Iliasov, and Alexander Romanovsky

School of Computing Science, University of Newcastle upon Tyne,
Newcastle upon Tyne NE1 7RU, England
{L.B.Arief, Alexei.Iliasov, Alexander.Romanovsky}@newcastle.ac.uk

Abstract. The paper introduces the CAMA (*C*ontext-*A*ware *M*obile *A*gents) framework intended for developing large-scale mobile applications using the agent paradigm. CAMA provides a powerful set of abstractions, a supporting middleware and an adaptation layer allowing developers to address the main characteristics of the mobile applications: openness, asynchronous and anonymous communication, fault tolerance, and device mobility. It ensures recursive system structuring using location, scope, agent, and role abstractions. CAMA supports system fault tolerance through exception handling and structured agent coordination within nested scopes. The applicability of the framework is demonstrated using an ambient lecture scenario – the first part of an ongoing work on a series of ambient campus applications. This scenario is developed starting from a thorough definition of the traceable requirements including the fault tolerance requirements. This is followed by the design phase at which the CAMA abstractions are applied. At the implementation phase, the CAMA middleware services are used through a provided API. This work is part of the FP6 IST RODIN project on Rigorous Open Development Environment for Complex Systems.

Keywords: Mobile agents, exception handling, system structuring, coordination, middleware, Linda, ambient lecture.

1   Introduction

The mobile agent paradigm is now used in developing a variety of complex applications as it supports systems structuring using decentralised, distributed and autonomous entities cooperating to achieve their individual aims. These applications include smart house, urban traffic management, information search and retrieval, Internet trading, network monitoring, load balancing, healthcare systems and enterprise quality management. The mobile agent paradigm promotes system openness, flexibility and scalability, and naturally supports mobility of code and devices. Very often the applications developed using agents must meet various dependability requirements. This, in particular, includes various business (money, information) and safety critical applications. This is why ensuring system fault tolerance is becoming imperative for successful deployment of

R. Choren et al. (Eds.): SELMAS 2006, LNCS 4408, pp. 21–40, 2007.
© Springer-Verlag Berlin Heidelberg 2007

modern agent applications. Although there have been a number fault tolerance frameworks developed for agent systems, we have found that they have limited applicability due to several reasons. First of all, they typically focus on tolerating hardware faults, which, as a matter of fact, is not the main source of modern system failures. Secondly, they often provide means which are not adequate for achieving fault tolerance as they do not take into account the defining characteristics of the agent systems: agent mobility, autonomy and asynchronous communication, and system openness and dynamicity, which create new challenges for ensuring agent system fault tolerance. A typical example here is a naive assumption that the native Java and RMI exception handling is completely adequate for developing complex agent systems.

In this work, we are focusing on *coordination mobile environments*, which have become very popular in developing mobile agent applications. These environments rely on the Linda approach to coordination of distributed processes. Linda [1] provides a set of language-independent coordination primitives that can be used for communication-between and coordination-of several independent pieces of software. Linda is now becoming the core component of many mobile software systems because it fits in nicely with the main characteristics of mobile systems.

Linda coordination primitives support effective inter-process coordination using the concepts of *tuples* and *tuple spaces*. A tuple is a data object that holds several objects; it can be seen as a vector of typed data values, some of which can be empty, in which case they match any value of a given type. A tuple space is an implementation of the content-addressable memory, providing a repository of tuples that can be accessed concurrently. It provides operations to allow processes to put tuples in it, get tuples out if they match the requested types, and test for them. Certain operations, like *get* (or **in**) can be blocking, whereas others, such as *test* (or **inp**) are non-blocking.

A number of Linda-based mobile coordination systems have been developed recently; these include Lime [2], Klaim [3], and TuCSoN [4].

Lime is one of the most developed, supported and widely-used examples of such environments. It supports both *physical mobility*, such as a device with a running application travelling along with its user across network boundaries, and *logical mobility*, when a software application changes its platform and resumes execution in a new one. To do that, Lime employs a distributed tuple space. Each agent has its own persistent tuple space that physically or logically moves with it. When an agent is in a location where there are other agents or where there is a network connectivity to other Lime hosts, a new shared tuple space can be created, thus allowing agents to communicate. If connection is lost or some agents leave, parts of the shared tuple space became inaccessible. Lime middleware – implemented in Java – hides all the details and complexities of the distributed tuple space control and allows agents to treat it as normal tuple space using conventional Linda operations.

Klaim is a Linda-based process algebra with a notion of explicit locations. Absolute or relative location addresses can be attached to Linda operations to specify the execution site of an operation. Klaim also has a type system extension used for control access. It is one of the few systems supporting strong code mobility [5].

TuCSoN [4] is another agent coordination system which is designed to be used with the existing mobile agent infrastructures. It mainly focuses on solving communication problems, but it ignores agent mobility and security. Coordination is based on the Linda tuple space paradigm. Each host provides a set of named tuple space which can be used for both local and remote coordination. A destination for a remote operation is specified using a tuple space name and a globally unique host name.

Exception handling [6] is widely accepted to be the most general approach to ensuring fault tolerance of complex applications facing a broad range of faults. It provides a sophisticated set of features for developing effective fault tolerance using handlers specially tailored for the specific exception and system state in which the error is detected. It ensures nested system structuring and separates normal system behaviour from the abnormal one. Our analysis [7] shows that the existing Linda-based mobile environments do not provide sufficient support for development of fault tolerant mobile agent systems. The real challenge here is to develop general mechanisms that smoothly combine Linda-based mobility with exception handling. The two key features of mobile agents are asynchronous communication and agent anonymity. This is what makes mobile agents such a flexible and powerful software development paradigm. However, traditional fault tolerance and exception handling schemes are not directly applicable in such environments.

In this paper, we discuss a novel framework for disciplined development of open fault tolerant mobile agent systems and show how it is being applied in developing an ambient campus application. This framework offers a set of powerful abstractions to help developers by supporting exception handling, system structuring and openness. These abstractions are supported by an effective and easy-to-use middleware which ensures high system scalability and agent compatibility. The plan of the paper is as follows. In the next section we introduce our CAMA framework in detail by describing the main abstractions offered to system developers, a novel exception handling mechanism and our current work on CAMA implementation. This is followed by a section discussing our experience in applying CAMA in the development an ambient lecture scenario as a part of our ongoing work on ambient campus applications. The last section of the paper outlines our plans for the future work.

2 Context-Aware Mobile Agents

We have developed a framework called CAMA *(Context-Aware Mobile Agents)*, which encourages disciplined development of open fault tolerant mobile agent applications by supporting a set of abstractions ensuring exception handling, system structuring and openness. These abstractions are backed by an effective and easy-to-use middleware allowing high system scalability and guaranteeing agent compatibility.

2.1 Cama Abstractions

Any CAMA system consists of a set of *locations*. A location is a container for *scopes*. A scope provides a coordination space within which compatible agents can interact using the scoping mechanism described below. *Agents* are the active entities of the system. Each agent is executed on a *platform*; several agents may reside on a single platform. A platform provides an execution environment for agents as well as an interface to the location middleware. Fig. 1 shows how these abstractions are linked.

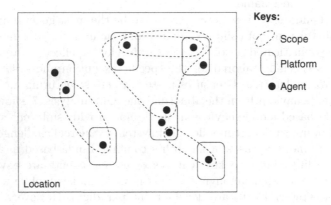

Fig. 1. Location, scopes, platforms and agents in CAMA

An agent is built using one or more *roles*. A role is a specification of one specific functionality of an agent. A composition of all agent roles forms its specification.

A location can be associated with a particular physical location (such as a lecture theatre, a warehouse or a meeting room) and can have certain restrictions on the types of supported scopes. Location is the core part of the system as it provides means of communication and coordination among agents. We assume that each location has a unique name. This roughly corresponds to the IP address of the host in a network (which are usually unique) on which it resides. A location must keep track of the agents present and their properties in order to be able to automatically create new scopes and restrict access to the existing ones. Locations may provide additional services that can vary from one instance to another. These are made available to agents within what appears to be a normal scope where some of the roles are implemented by the location system software. As with all the scopes, agents are required to implement specific roles in order to connect to a location-provided scope. Few examples of such services include printing on a local printer, accessing the internet, making a backup to a location storage, and migrating to another location.

Agent *context* represents the circumstances in which an agent find itself [8]. Generally speaking, a context includes all information from an agent environment which is relevant to its activity. The context of an agent in CAMA consists of the following parts: the state connections to the engaged locations; the names, types and states of all the visible scopes in the engaged locations; and the state of scopes in which the agent is currently participating, including the tuples contained in these scopes. A set of all locations defines global structuring of the agent context. This context changes when an agent migrates from one location to another.

Agents represent the basic structuring unit in CAMA applications. To deal with various functionalities that any individual agent provides, CAMA introduces agent role as a finer unit of code structuring. A role is a structuring unit of an agent, and being an important part of the scoping mechanism, it allows dynamic composition of multi-agent applications, as well as being used to ensure agent interoperability and isolation.

Scope structures the activity of several agents in a specific location by dynamically encapsulating roles of these agents. Scope also provides an isolation of several communicating agents thus structuring the communication space.

A set of agents playing different roles can dynamically instantiate a multiagent application. A simple example is a client-server model where a distributed application is constructed when agents playing two roles meet and collaborate. An agent can have several roles and use them in different scopes. A server agent can provide the same service in many similar scopes. In addition, it can also implement a client role and act as a client in some other scopes.

Supporting system openness is one of the top design objectives of CAMA. Openness is understood here as the ability to create distributed applications composed of agents developed independently. To this end, CAMA provide powerful abstractions that help to dynamically compose applications from individual agents, an agent isolation mechanism and a service discovery based on the scoping mechanism.

Scoping Mechanism. The CAMA agents can cooperate only when they participate in the same scopes. This abstraction is supported by a special construct of coordination space called *scope*. Scoping is a means to *structure* agent activity by arranging agents into groups according to their intentions. Scoping also allows agent communication to be configured to meet the requirements of the individual groups. Reconfigurations happen automatically, thus allowing agents (and their developers) to focus solely on collaboration with other agents participating in the same scope. There are several benefits of agent system structuring using scopes:

- scopes provide higher-level abstractions of communication structuring;
- they reduce the risk of creating ad hoc structures that maybe incorrect, malfunctioning or cyclic;
- this structuring enforces strong relationship among agents supporting interoperability and exception handling;
- scopes support simple semantics thus facilitating formal development;
- scopes become units of fault tolerant system ensuring error confinement and supporting error recovery at the scope level.

A scope is a dynamic data container that provides an *isolated* coordination space for *compatible* agents. This is done by restricting the visibility of the tuples contained in the scope only to these agents. We say that a set of agents is compatible if there is a composition of their roles that forms an instance of an abstract scope model.

Agents can issue a request to create a scope, and when all the preconditions are satisfied, a scope is atomically instantiated by the hosting location. The scope creation request includes a scope identifier (a string) and a scope requirement structure. The request returns the name of the newly created scope. The agent creating the scope can use this name to join the scope, to make the scope public (visible to other agents), to leave the scope and to delete it.

A scope has a number of attributes divided into two categories: scope *requirements* and scope *state*. Scope requirements essentially define the type of a scope, or, in other words, the kind of activities supported by it. Scope requirements are derived from a formal model of a scope activity and, together with agent roles, form an instance of the abstract scope model. State attributes characterise a unique scope instance. In addition to these attributes, scope contains *data* represented as *tuples* in the coordination space. Along with these data, there may be *subscopes* which define *nested activities* that may happen inside the scope.

Nested scopes are used to structure large multi-agent applications into smaller parts which do not require participation of all agents. Such structuring has a number of benefits. It isolates agents into groups, thus enhancing security. It also links coordination space structuring with activity structuring, which supports localised error recovery and scalability. There is no hard rule when to use nested scopes. However, for reasons stated above, any application incorporating different modes of communication or different types of activities should use subscopes. An online shop is an example of such application. A seller publicly communicate with buyers while the latter are looking around for some products. However, payment must be a private activity involving only the seller and the buyer. In addition to obvious security benefits, a dedicated payment subscope helps to determine which agents must be involved into recovery should a failure happen during payment.

Restrictions on roles dictate the roles that are available in the scope, and how many agents are allowed for any given role. The latter is defined by two numbers: the minimum number of agents required for a given role and the maximum number of agents allowed for a given role. A *scope-state* tracks the number of currently-taken roles and determines whether the scope is ready for agent collaboration or whether more agents are allowed to join.

The existing scoping mechanisms (e.g. [9,10]) are not explicitly developed to support data and behaviour encapsulation or isolation, which are crucial for error confining and recovery. None of them is directly applicable for dealing with mobile agents interacting using coordination spaces (see our analysis in [7]). Also, these schemes do not support the set of abstractions which we have identified as crucial for CAMA.

Basic Operations in Cama. In CAMA, all the communication within a location happens through a single shared tuple space. This leads to an asymmetrical design of the middleware where the tuple space operations are implemented in a *location middleware* while agents only carry a lightweight *adaptation layer*. On top of the coordination primitives derived from Linda, the CAMA middleware provides the following operations:

- engage(id) - issues a new location-wide name that is unique and unforgeable for agent id. This name is used as an agent identifier in all other role operations.
- disengage(a) - makes the issued name a invalid.
- create(a, n, R)@s $(n \notin 1.s)$ - agent a creates a new subscope within scope s called n with given scope requirements R at location l. The created scope becomes a private scope of agent a.
- delete(a, n)@l.s $(n \in 1.s \land a$ *is owner of* $1.s.n)$ - agent a deletes a subscope called n contained in scope s. This operation always succeeds if the requesting agent is the owner of the scope. If the scope is not in the pending state then all the scope participants shall receive CamaExceptionNotInScope exception notifying the scope's closure. This procedure is executed recursively for all the subscopes contained in the scope.
- join(a, n, r)@s $(n \in 1.s \land r \in n \land n$ *is pending or expanding*) - adds agent a into scope n contained in l.s with role r. This operation succeeds if scope l.s.n exists and agent a is allowed to take the specified role in the scope. This operation may cause the scope to change state.
- leave(a, n, r)@s (a *is in* l.s.n *with role(s)* r) - removes agent a with roles r from scope l.s.n. The calling agent must be already participating in the scope. This operation may also change the state of the scope.
- put(a, n)@s - agent a advertises scope n contained in scope s, thus making it a public scope. A public scope is visible and accessible by other agents.
- get(a, r)@s: enquires the names of the scopes contained in scope l.s and supporting role(s) r.

An agent always starts its execution by looking for available locations nearby. Once it has become engaged to a location, it can join a scope or create a new one. An agent needs to know the name of the scope it intends to join. It can be the name of an existing scope or the name of a new scope created by this agent. When joining a scope, an agent specifies its role in the scope. In the current implementation of the middleware, an agent can choose a role in a scope from one of the roles it implements. The join operation returns a handle for a scope, which can be used by an agent to collaborate with other agents through Linda coordination primitives. To create a scope, an agent must specify the name of the scope and the scope requirements, which define the possible roles within the scope and their restrictions.

Physical and Logical Mobility. Physical mobility allows devices carrying the agent code to move between locations. Logical mobility allows agent code and state to be moved from one location to another.

Physical mobility in CAMA is implemented using connectivity of the devices to the locations. When such a connectivity is established, the agent running on the device receives a special event notifying it about the discovery of the new location. CAMA allows any agent to access the list of active locations it is connected to at any time. An agent receives a predefined disconnection exception when the connectivity is lost. To support this functionality, the location middleware periodically sends heart-beats messages in the proximity.

The CAMA middleware does not support logical mobility as the first class concept since the CAMA architecture does not allow locations to see each other. Nevertheless, agent migration can be provided through the standard inter-agent communication. Data can be moved between locations in CAMA by agents working at both locations at the same time, or by an agent physically migrating between two locations or by using some other capability supporting data transfer between locations. In particular, we have implemented a simple proof-of-concept support ensuring weak code mobility. In this implementation, a dedicated agent provides a service of data transfer between locations using internet or LAN networking. Using this service, any agent can transfer itself or another agent to another location.

2.2 Fault Tolerance

The CAMA framework supports application-level fault tolerance by providing a set of abstractions and a supporting middleware that allow developers to design effective error detection and recovery mechanisms. The main means for implementing fault tolerance in CAMA is a novel exception handling mechanism which associates scopes with the exception contexts. Scope nesting provides recursive system structuring and error confinement. In addition to this, the CAMA middleware supports a number of predefined exceptions (such as the connection-disconnection exceptions and the violation of the scope constraints exceptions).

In developing the exception handling support for CAMA, we relied on our previous work reported in [7], in which we proposed and evaluated a novel exception handling scheme developed for coordination-based agent applications. Here we give a brief overview of our exception handling mechanism; the full description can be found in [11]. The main novelty of the CAMA mechanism is that it explicitly links nested scopes with the exception contexts.

Exception handling in CAMA allows fast and effective application recovery by supporting flexible choice of the handling scope and of the exception propagation policy. The mechanism of the exception propagation is complimentary to the application-level exception handling. All the recovery actions are implemented by application-specific handlers attached to the agents. The ultimate task of the propagation mechanism is to transfer the exceptions between agents in a reliable and secure way. However, the freedom of agent behaviour in agent-based systems does not allow any guarantees of reliable exception propagation to be given in a general case. In particular, the situations can be clearly identified when exceptions may be lost or not delivered within a predictable time period. This is the case for CAMA as well. To alleviate this, for example, in a mobile agent application requiring cooperative exception handling involving several agents, agents behaviour must be constrained in some way to prevent any unexpected migrations or disconnections. In our ongoing work we are developing techniques supporting formal analysis of exception handling behaviour of the multi-agent systems.

There are three basic operations available to the CAMA agents for catching and raising inter-agent exceptions. These functionalities are complementary and orthogonal to the application-level mechanism used for programming internal agent behaviour.

The `raise` operation propagates an exception to an agent or a scope. There are two variants of this operation:

- `raise(m, e)` - raises exception `e` as a reaction to message `m`. The message is used to trace the producer and to deliver an exception to it. The operation fails if the destination agent has already left the scope in which the message was produced.
- `raise(s, e)` - raises exception `e` in all participants of scope `s`.

The crucial requirement for the propagation mechanism is to preserve all the essential properties of agent systems such as anonymity, dynamicity and openness. The exception propagation mechanism does not violate the concept of anonymity since we prevent the disclosure of agent names at any stage of the propagation process. Note that the `raise` operation does not deal with names or addresses of agents. Moreover, we guarantee that our propagation method cannot be used to learn the names of other agents.

Two other operations, `check` and `wait` are used to explicitly poll and wait for inter-agent exceptions:

- `check` - raises exception `E(e)` if there are any pending exceptions for the calling agent.
- `wait` - waits until any inter-agent exception appears for the agent and raises it in the same way as the `check` operation.

Systematic use of exception handling should allow developers to design mobile agent applications tolerating a *broad range of faults*, including disconnections, agent mismatches, malicious or unanticipated agent activity, violations of system properties, potentially harmful changes in the system environment, reduced amount of resource available, as well as users' mistakes.

Unfortunately, there has not been much work carried out in this area. Tripathi and Miller [12] introduces a guardian model in which each agent has a dedicated guardian responsible for handling all agent exception. This model is general enough to be applied in many types of mobile systems but it does not directly address the specific characteristics of the coordination paradigm. Another relevant work is on exception handling in a concurrent object-oriented language called Oz [13]. In this system, exceptions can be propagated between the mobile callee and caller objects. The approach proposed is not applicable to the coordination- based mobile systems. Moreover, the main intention behind this work is not to support the development of open dynamic agent applications.

2.3   Cama Implementation

In the current version of the CAMA system, the location middleware is implemented in C (we call it $_c$CAMA). This allows us to achieve the best possible performance of the coordination space and to effectively implement numerous extension, such as the scoping mechanism. The location middleware implementation is quite compact - it consists of approximately 6000 lines of C code and should run on most Unix platforms. We have so far tested it on Linux FC2 and Solaris 10. The full implementation of the location middleware is available at SourceForge [14].

The CAMA middleware does not suffer from scalability problems inherent to system for distributed tuples spaces or a remote tuple access features. Due to the local nature of coordination in CAMA, the complexity of coordination rises linearly and has a small coefficient.

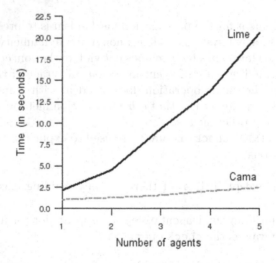

Fig. 2. The performance of Lime compared to that of CAMA

Fig. 2 compares the performance of Lime and CAMA systems. Results for both systems are given on the same scale. In each run, a given number of agents perform non-destructive read on 1000 distinct tuples (each tuple is around 1000 bytes in size). The Y-axis represents the execution time in seconds and the X-axis represents the number of agents simultaneously reading from the tuple space.

Fig. 3 presents another set of results from our experiment. Different bar shades correspond to different test cases. Test cases are made of a fixed number of out and rd operations with different tuple sizes and number of tuples. This experiment shows that CAMA performance compares favourably against several other Linda-style tuple space systems, such as LighTS [15] (which is a part of Lime), TSpaces [16] and GigaSpaces [17].

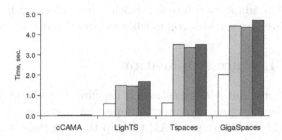

Fig. 3. Comparative performance of CAMA and other Linda-style tuple space systems

In order to use the location middleware mentioned above, we have developed a CAMA adaptation layer in Java[1] called $_j$CAMA. This adaptation layer defines several classes for representing – among others – the abstract notions of Location, Scope and Linda coordination primitives. $_j$CAMA provides an interface through which mobile agents or applications can be developed easily.

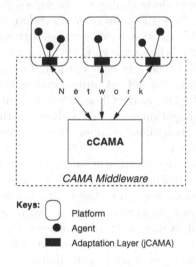

Fig. 4. CAMA architecture

A diagrammatical representation of the CAMA-based system architecture can be seen in Fig. 4. Each platform carries a copy of $_j$CAMA. Agents residing on a platform uses the features provided by $_j$CAMA to connect over the wireless or wired network to the $_c$CAMA location middleware.

It is possible to construct other adaptation layers for different platforms and languages. For now, the $_j$CAMA Java adaptation layer outlined above permits agent development for PocketPC-based PDAs. It has a very small footprint (~60Kb) and can be used with both standard Java and J2ME. In the future

---

[1] We use Java for developing the applications for PDAs.

we plan to develop adaptation layers for other languages such as Python and Visual Basic, as well as versions compatible for smartphone devices.

3   Ambient Lecture Application

This case study provides a demonstration on how the CAMA framework can be used in developing open, dynamic and pervasive systems involving people carrying hand held devices (e.g. PDAs) to help them in their daily activities.

3.1   Introduction

We focus on the activities performed by students and teachers during a lecture (the *ambient lecture* scenario – see [18] for more details) and consider a set of requirements that define this scenario. This set will be extended to cover more general *ambient campus* scenarios (i.e. location-aware activities that can be performed on campus) such as interactive/smart map, events announcer, library application and students organiser.

There are several other projects aiming to integrate software systems – including mobile applications – into education or campus domain. The ActiveCampus project [19] aims to provide location-based services such as *Map* service (showing outdoor and indoor map of the user's vicinity along with activities happening there) and *Buddies* service (showing colleagues and their locations, as well as sending messages to them). The ActiveCampus system is implemented as a web server using PHP and MySQL. ActiveClass [20] is a client-server application for encouraging in-class participation using PDAs allowing students to ask questions regarding the lecture in anonymous manner, hence overcoming the problem of shyness among many students.

Gay et. al. carried out an experiment investigating the effects of wireless computing in classroom environment [21]. Students were given laptop computers with wireless or wired connection to the internet, allowing them to use any existing tools and services such as web browsers, word processors, instant messaging software – as well as any additional software they wish to install. The results suggest that the introduction of wireless computing in learning environments can potentially affect the development, maintenance and transformation of learning communities, but not every teaching activity or learning community can or should successfully integrate mobile computing applications.

Classtalk [22] is a classroom communication system that allows teacher to present questions for small group work, collect the answers and display the histograms showing how the class answered those questions. Up to four students can be in one group, sharing one input device (a palmtop), which is wired to the central computer controlled by the teacher.

Similar to Classtalk, our system allows students to be grouped together in order to carry out some task given by the teacher. The novelty of our approach lies in the communication channel (wireless instead of wired connection) as well as in using the framework for supporting scoping and fault tolerance (the mechanisms described in Sect. 2).

3.2 Traceable Requirements

We started our work on the scenario by producing a requirements document [23], which consists of an explanatory text, diagrams, and requirements definitions. The requirements definitions are arranged using a specially-developed taxonomy which allows us to structure them according to various views on system behaviour, including: environment (EN), agent states (ST), service requirements and restrictions (SV), security (SE) and fault tolerance (FT). Each requirement is given a number within the group, for example:

```
EN 1: The scenario is composed of users, locations and ambient
computing environment (ACE)
```

```
ST 5: Lecture state has two sub-states: individual state and
group state
```

```
SV 1: For ACE-supported lecture to begin, there should be one
teacher agent and several student agents in the same location
```

```
SE 5: Each student agent belongs to only one group at any
given time during a lecture
```

```
FT 14: Migration activity must tolerate wireless disconnection
and loss of ACE support
```

At the high level, the system consists of users (people participating in the scenario, i.e. teachers and students), locations (rooms with wireless connectivity) and *ambient computing environment* (ACE). ACE is composed of wireless hotspots, software agents and computing platforms (desktop computers or PDAs) on which the agents are run.

The interactions among users are done through agents. Each location provides a CAMA location middleware through which agents exchange information. Agents connect to the location middleware using the wireless hotspot available in each room.

Each teacher and student has an agent associated with him/her and assisting his/her participation in the lecture. During a lecture, the teacher and the students can be engaged in the following activities: lecture initiation, material dissemination, organisation of students into groups, individual or group student work, and questions and answers session.

3.3 Design

The ambient lecture system is being designed to meet the requirements in [23]. In this design, each classroom is a location with a wireless support, in which a lecture is conducted. An agent can take one of the two roles: teacher or student.

The teacher agent runs on a desktop computer available in the classroom, while student agents are executed on PDAs (each student is given a PDA).

We use the scoping mechanism described in Sect. 2.1 to structure the system. The teacher agent creates the outer scope constituting the lecture which student agents join. A lecture starts when there is one teacher agent and a predefined number of student agents joining this scope.

To support better system structuring, data and behaviour encapsulation, as well as fault tolerance, all major activities during the lecture are conducted within subscopes (nested scopes). The group work is one of the activities performed as a nested scope. The teacher – through his/her agent – arranges students into groups, so that only students belonging to the same group can communicate with each other through their agent. Each group is then given a task to solve – in this case, a B specification [24]. Students within the same group work together towards a solution, using a shared editor to modify the specification, and carrying out B operations such as proving and type-checking (which are provided by the system).

At the beginning of any lecture, all agents (teacher and students alike) are placed in the main scope. The teacher agent keeps a list of all students joining the lecture, and through the application's graphical user interface (GUI), the teacher can select which students to be placed within each group.

Each group is given a unique name and the groups are mutually exclusive, i.e. a student cannot belong to more than one group. The teacher agent creates a subscope for each group, assigns a B project for this group to work on, and issues a *StartGroup* tuple to the student agents involved so that they automatically join the subscope they are assigned to. This is achieved by executing the CAMA `JoinScope` operation that uses the group name as a parameter. This structuring guarantees that while within a group, a student can send messages to other students belonging to the same group, but he/she will also receive any message sent in the main lecture scope. To achieve this, the CAMA middleware creates a separate thread for each role inside a subscope.

The full details of the operations that can be carried out by both the teacher and the student agents during the ambient lecture can be seen in [18]. Here we outline the operations for the group work:

Teacher

The teacher prepares the group work by organising the students into groups, assigning a B project for each group to work on, and monitoring each group.

– *Assigns a B project to a group*
  Each group will be given a B project to work on, which contains at least one B machine specification that the students need to edit and run B commands on.
– *Watches the activity of each student*
  This monitoring activity is useful to measure each student's participation during the group work. A passive student might require further help or different group arrangements might be needed.

– *Inspects edited files*
  The teacher can check the progress of the group work by inspecting
  the changes that the students made on the files and by checking the
  status of the B commands already issued.
– *Assists by editing files*
  The teacher may modify the B machine specification files in order
  to make it clearer for the students how to solve the problem, or to
  "reset" the file if the students made too many mistakes.
– *Takes part in a discussion*
  The teacher may help the students to understand the problem they
  are trying to solve by asking probing questions as well as giving hints
  and advice.
– *Forces unlocking of resources*
  If a student appears to hold a file for too long (this could happen,
  say if the student agent crashes), the teacher can manually unlock
  the file to allow other students to edit it.

Student
The students' actions during group work mostly concern with editing B
machine specification and carrying out the B commands such as proving
and type-checking. They can also communicate with other student agents
within their group, the teacher, as well other student agents in the global
lecture scope. We are thinking about disabling the communication with
other student agents in the global scope.

– *Chooses a file to work on within a project*
  Each project will have a list of associated files, and the student can
  choose which file to work on. This file represents a B machine specification and each student is allowed to work with only one file at a
  time.
– *Edits a file*
  There is a *shared editor* window that provides concurrency control
  (multiple readers, one writer) for editing a file. A student agent needs
  to obtain a lock before it can edit a file. We decided to use a non-
  blocking mechanism for obtaining the lock, so that the student can
  carry on with other activities if somebody else possesses the lock at
  that time. Only one agent can edit each file at any one time, although
  other agents can read the content of this file and see the update in
  real time. The lock must be released by the writing agent upon the
  completion of the editing process.
– *Proves/model checks/type-checks/does interactive proving*
  The Ambient Lecture software allows the students to carry out these
  commands on the B machine specification they are working with.
  With the current implementation, the student agents are not required to obtain the editing lock first before carrying out these commands. We agree that this is not a desirable feature, and we will fix
  this in the later implementation.

- *Takes part in a discussion*
  During the discussion, students may ask questions, and other students in the group may provide the answer. If the questions remain unanswered, the group may ask the teacher for assistance.
- *Asks teacher's assistance*
  The teacher monitors group work, and from time to time, students may ask the teacher for clarification on the task they are working at.
- *Sends messages to other students*
  Students can send messages to other students in the same group.

Students cannot explicitly leave a group; only the teacher can decide whether a student must leave a group, for example at the end of the group work. Students can leave the Ambient Lecture setting altogether though, and when this happens, they will automatically leave the group subscope as well.

Following the fault tolerance requirements, the agents handle a number of potentially erroneous conditions. Some of them are detected by the agents themselves, others are detected by the middleware which raises predefined exceptions declared in the signatures of the CAMA operations. One example of these exceptions is the `CamaExceptionNoRights` exception, indicating that the agent concerned has no right to be in a particular scope, hence it cannot send or receive messages from the tuple space.

```
try {
  // Connect to the location middleware
  Connection connection = new Connection("Teacher",
    server, portNo);
  Scope lambda = connection.lambda();

  // Create a lecture scope that allows 1 Teacher
  // agent and up to 10 Student agents.
  ScopeDescr sd = new ScopeDescr(2, "lectureScope").
    add(new RoleRest("Teacher", 1,1)).
    add(new RoleRest("Student", 0,10));
  workScope = lambda.CreateScope("lectureScope", sd);

  // Join the scope and make the scope public
  workScope = workScope.JoinScope("Teacher");
  workScope.PutScope();
}
catch(CamaExceptionInvalidReqs e) { ... }
catch(CamaExceptionNoRoles e) { ... }
...
```

Fig. 5. Sample code: scope creation by the Teacher agent

3.4 Implementation

We developed an application for the group work activity described in Sect. 3.3. There are two sets of agent software: **Teacher** and **Student**. Commands and data are passed as tuples through the tuple space provided by the location middleware.

Each agent runs at least two threads of execution: one thread handles the GUI and provides a means for sending tuples to the tuple space; another thread polls tuples from the tuple space and interprets the command contained in them. More threads are created when subscoping is used, so that an agent can also poll tuples from within the subscopes.

Fig. 5 shows a snippet of the code for the **Teacher** agent, demonstrating how the lecture scope is initiated. Agents can join as a **Teacher** or a **Student**. In this example, only one **Teacher** agent is allowed, along with up to ten **Student** agents. An exception will be raised if this restriction is violated.

Fig. 6 shows the "Lecture Overview" screen-capture of the **Teacher** agent. The icon **S** represents a student, the icon **G** represents a group, and the icon **R** represents a resource or a file containing B specification. It shows that there are three **Student** agents: "Bob" and "Alice" (these agents are run from a desktop computer) and "John" (run from a PDA).

At some stage, the **Teacher** agent places Alice and John into "Group1". Alice is shown viewing a specification file called "Chat" while John is editing it. Fig. 7 on the left shows the screen-capture of the PDA used by John as he edits the Chat specification. Alice then asks John (through the group messenger) to carry out type-checking on this specification, as can be seen on the right hand side of Fig. 7.

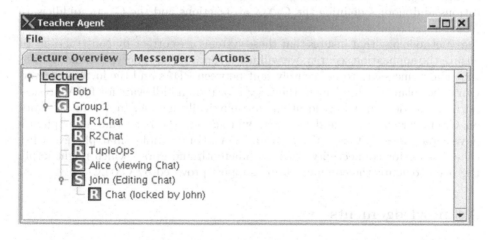

Fig. 6. Screen capture of the Teacher agent's Lecture Overview

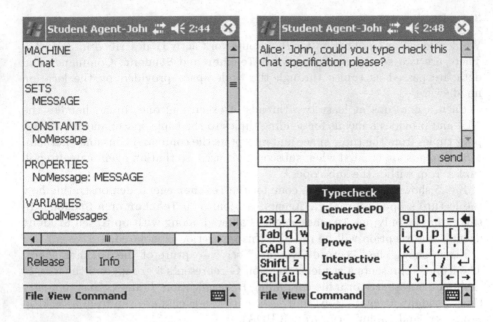

Fig. 7. Screen capture of John editing Chat specification and receiving a group message from Alice

4   Future Work

Our long-term goal is to support formal development of fault tolerant mobile agent systems. To achieve this goal, we are developing a number of formal notations and models defining the CAMA abstractions and the CAMA middleware (some initial results are reported in [25]). We are now working on a top-down design methodology that insures that these systems are correct-by-construction. To ensure the application security, we will use an appropriate encryption mechanism that allows messages to be securely sent between PDAs and the location server. Our other plan is to implement the CAMA location middleware for PDAs to support applications in which locations are physically mobile. In our future work on CAMA for smartphone devices, we will address the facts that smartphones have capabilities that are different from PDAs. For example, smartphones utilise other means for connectivity (such as bluetooth and gprs), which might imply the need to adapt the communication support provided by CAMA.

Acknowledgements

This work is supported by the IST RODIN Project [26]. A. Iliasov is partially supported by the ORS award (UK).

References

1. Gelernter, D.: Generative Communication in Linda. ACM Transactions on Programming Languages and Systems **7**(1) (1985) 80–112
2. Picco, G.P., Murphy, A.L., Roman, G.C.: Lime: Linda Meets Mobility. In: Proceedings of 21st Int. Conference on Software Engineering (ICSE'99). (1999) 368–377
3. Bettini, L., Bono, V., Nicola, R.D., Ferrari, G., Gorla, D., Loreti, M., Moggi, E., Pugliese, R., Tuosto, E., Venneri, B.: The Klaim Project: Theory and Practice. In Priami, C., ed.: Global Computing: Programming Environments, Languages, Security and Analysis of Systems, LNCS 2874, Springer-Verlag (2003) 88–150
4. Omicini, A., Zambonelli, F.: Tuple Centres for the Coordination of Internet Agents. In: SAC '99: Proceedings of the 1999 ACM symposium on Applied computing, New York, NY, USA, ACM Press (1999) 183–190
5. Bettini, L., Nicola, R.D.: Translating Strong Mobility into Weak Mobility. In Picco, G., ed.: Proceedings of 5th IEEE International Conference on Mobile Agents (MA), LNCS 2240, Springer (2001) 182–197
6. Cristian, F.: Exception Handling and Fault Tolerance of Software Faults. In Lyu, M., ed.: Software Fault Tolerance. Wiley, NY (1995) 81–107
7. Iliasov, A., Romanovsky, A.: Exception Handling in Coordination-based Mobile Environments. In: Proceedings of the 29th Annual International Computer Software and Applications Conference (COMPSAC 2005), IEEE Computer Society Press (2005) 341–350
8. Roman, G.C., Julien, C., Payton, J.: A Formal Treatment of Context-Awareness. In Wermelinger, M., Margaria, T., eds.: Fundamental Approaches to Software Engineering, 7th International Conference, FASE 2004, part of the Joint European Conferences on Theory and Practice of Software, ETAPS 2004, LNCS 2984. Springer (2004) 12–36
9. Satoh, I.: MobileSpaces: A Framework for Building Adaptive Distributed Applications using a Hierarchical Mobile Agent System. In: Proceedings of the ICDCS 2000. (2000) 161–168
10. Merrick, I., Wood, A.: Coordination with Scopes. In: Proceedings of the ACM Symposium on Applied Computing 2000. (2000) 210–217
11. Iliasov, A., Romanovsky, A.: Structured Coordination Spaces for Fault Tolerant Mobile Agents. In Dony, C., Knudsen, J.L., Romanovsky, A., Tripathi, A., eds.: LNCS 4119. (2006) 181–199
12. Tripathi, A., Miller, R.: Exception Handling in Agent-oriented Systems. In: Proceedings of the 21st IEEE Symposium on Reliable Distributed Systems (SRDS'02), ACM Press (2002) 304–315
13. van Roy, P., Haridi, S., Brand, P., Smalka, G., Mehl, M., Scheidhauer, R.: Mobile Objects in Distributed Oz. ACM Transactions on Programming Languages and Systems **19**(5) (1997) 804–851
14. Iliasov, A.: Implementation of Cama Middleware. http://sourceforge.net/projects/cama (Last accessed: 3 Jan 2007)
15. Balzarotti, D., Costa, P.: LighTS: A Lightweight, Customizable Tuple Space Supporting Context-Aware Applications. In: Proceedings of the 20th Annual ACM Symposium on Applied Computing (SAC 2005), ACM Press (2005) http://lights.sourceforge.net/ (Last accessed: 3 Jan 2007).
16. IBM: TSpaces. http://www.almaden.ibm.com/cs/TSpaces/ (Last accessed: 3 Jan 2007)

17. GigaSpaces: Grid Computing - Distributed Computing Application Server. http://www.gigaspaces.com/ (Last accessed: 3 Jan 2007)
18. Troubitsyna, E., ed.: Rodin Deliverable D18: Intermediate Report on Case Study Development. Project IST-511599, School of Computing Science, University of Newcastle (2006)
19. Griswold, W.G., Shanahan, P., Brown, S.W., Boyer, R., Ratto, M., Shapiro, R.B., Truong, T.M.: ActiveCampus - Experiments in Community-Oriented Ubiquitous Computing. IEEE Computer **37**(10) (2004) 73–81, http://activecampus.ucsd.edu/ (Last accessed: 3 Jan 2007).
20. Ratto, M., Shapiro, R.B., Truong, T.M., Griswold, W.G.: The ActiveClass Project: Experiments in Encouraging Classroom Participation. In: Computer Support for Collaborative Learning 2003, Kluwer (2003) 477–486
21. Gay, G., Stefanone, M., Grace-Martin, M., Hembrooke, H.: The Effects of Wireless Computing in Collaborative Learning Environments. International Journal of Human-Computer Interaction **13**(2) (2001) 257–276
22. Dufresne, R.J., Gerace, W.J., Leonard, W.J., Mestre, J.P., Wenk, L.: Classtalk: A Classroom Communication System for Active Learning. Journal of Computing in Higher Education **7** (1996) 3–47
23. Arief, B., Coleman, J., Hall, A., Hilton, A., Iliasov, A., Johnson, I., Jones, C., Laibinis, L., Leppanen, S., Oliver, I., Romanovsky, A., Snook, C., Troubitsyna, E., Ziegler, J.: Rodin Deliverable D4: Traceable Requirements Document for Case Studies. Technical report, Project IST-511599, School of Computing Science, University of Newcastle (2005)
24. Abrial, J.R.: The B-Book: Assigning Programs to Meanings. Cambridge University Press (2005)
25. Iliasov, A., Laibinis, L., Romanovsky, A., Troubitsyna, E.: Towards Formal Development of Mobile Location-based Systems, Presented at REFT 2005 Workshop on Rigorous Engineering of Fault-Tolerant Systems, Newcastle Upon Tyne, UK (http://rodin.cs.ncl.ac.uk/events.htm) (June 2005)
26. Rodin: Rigorous Open Development Environment for Complex Systems. IST FP6 STREP project, http://rodin.cs.ncl.ac.uk/ (Last accessed: 3 Jan 2007)

Challenges for Exception Handling in Multi-Agent Systems

Eric Platon[1,2,*], Nicolas Sabouret[2], and Shinichi Honiden[1]

[1] National Institute of Informatics, Sokendai,
2-1-2 Hitotsubashi, Chiyoda, 101-8430 Tokyo
[2] Laboratoire d'Informatique de Paris 6,
104, Avenue du President Kennedy, 75016 Paris
{platon,honiden}@nii.ac.jp, nicolas.sabouret@lip6.fr

Abstract. Exception handling has a commonly agreed semantics in many programming languages. When an operation is called with inappropriate conditions, the control flow of the program is reversed back to the caller to trigger some handling mechanisms. In Multi-Agent Systems (MAS), this semantics applies to the code of agents, but it does not cover the kind of exceptions that occur at the agent level. For instance, the usual handling semantics does not address the cases where the plan of an agent fails and re-planning is required. In fact, the agent code does not necessarily encounter a programming fault or a 'catch' clause in such a case, but the agent has yet to deal with an exceptional situation.

In this paper, we survey the literature on exception handling with the aim to demonstrate that research needs to be conducted in the case of MAS due to their openness, heterogeneity, and the encapsulation of agents. We identify research directions from the survey, and we present a simulation scenario to illustrate the occurrence of agent-level exceptions in a simple case. The current result of the survey analysis is that agent exceptions mechanisms should rely on the proactivity of agents, on exploiting the agent environment, on collaborative handling mechanisms, and on the potential links between code-level and agent-level exceptions.

1 Introduction

Exception handling in Multi-Agent Systems (MAS) differs from exception handling in sequential and traditional distributed systems. Traditional exception models assume the collaboration of the software elements, either procedure, objects, or components. An exception is there handled in the local scope of its occurrence, or it can be propagated to a more appropriate scope encountered along the execution chain of the program. In MAS, this way of managing exceptions is appropriate for programming exceptions (e.g. a null pointer), but it does not address some characteristics of MAS such as openness, heterogeneity, and agent encapsulation. Openness implies that agents can be benevolent as well as

* This research is partially supported by the French Ministry of Foreign Affair under the reference BFE/2006-484446G, Lavoisier grant program.

R. Choren et al. (Eds.): SELMAS 2006, LNCS 4408, pp. 41–56, 2007.

malicious and exception handling should not flow the same way as in sequential or distributed objects systems to deal with this situation. Heterogeneity means the software elements of the system can be developed in different languages and architectures. The interoperability of elements is ensured by the use of common interaction means (remote procedure calls, agent communication language, etc.), so that exception handling must be appropriate to cope with the variety of designs. Agent encapsulation is related to the 'autonomy' that guarantees the agent is a 'black box' endowed with an independent behavior. The black box image refers to the impossibility to inspect the state of the agent (members, architecture) from external code. Independence means agents are loosely coupled to one another. Usual exception models assume code can be inspected in the scope of handling, and this is not wanted to preserve the encapsulation.

The need for studying agent-level exceptions therefore arises from the nature of MAS. Although the definition of agent-level exception handling has not been formally determined yet, typical examples are inconsistencies in agent reasoning mechanisms, flawed knowledge, opportunities, or unexpected exchanges in interaction protocols [1].

In this paper, we propose an explanation of what agent-level exception handling consists in to address the requirements of MAS. The explanation relies on a survey of the exception handling literature in the perspective of the agent paradigm. Although the survey is not exhaustive, it encompasses a significant range of relevant research and achievements. The survey is exploited to identify major issues in current exception handling techniques for MAS, and to present research directions.

The organization of the paper is as follows. Section 2 surveys the related literature for exception handling in MAS. Based on this survey, we identify in section 3 some relevant research directions. In section 4, we describe a series of experiments we conducted to illustrate agent-level exception handling. Finally, we summarize in section 5 the challenges for exception handling in MAS and present some future endeavors.

2   Related Work

The literature on exception handling for MAS remains scarce despite the challenges identified by Tripathi and Miller [2] and Klein et al. [3]. Related work in distributed systems and system architectures complete however the current achievements in MAS with further approaches and concepts. We discuss hereafter research work along two dimensions to emphasize the relative positions of the approaches.

- **Degree of distribution** of the exception handling approach: MAS are typically distributed (physically or logically), but both central and distributed handling frameworks were designed.
- A **scale that ranges from object, to reactive agents, to proactive agents**. Objects are passive units of an application. Reactive agents are autonomous units whose behavior is strongly coupled to the environment,

e.g. agents based on the subsumption architecture of Brooks [4]. Proactive agents are autonomous units weakly coupled to but depending on their environment, e.g. BDI agents of Rao and Georgeff [5]. This classification is inspired by the view on autonomy of Odell [6].

The two dimensions allow us to classify related work as shown in Fig. 1. The classification distributes the work that we consider representative. The star mark highlights work that focuses on benevolent agents (willing to cooperate and not malicious).

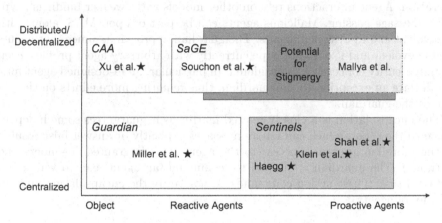

Fig. 1. Related work over two dimensions: (x-axis) object to agent scale, (y-axis) degree of distribution of the exception handling system. The star marks approaches for benevolent agents.

2.1 The Guardian

In the bottom left corner, Miller and Tripathi occupy the area of work dedicated to centralized exception handling in object-oriented and reactive agent systems. Their approach named 'the guardian' is a set of software constructs to handle exceptions in a distributed-object system, with applications in the mobile agent context [2]. The guardian is a dedicated object that encapsulates rules to handle 'global exceptions' involving several processes (here called agents). The approach is centralized as the guardian represents the exception handling service in case of problem. It is not totally centralized though, since a set of guardians could be allocated a subset of agents only (consequently the box on Fig. 1 is raised toward distributed approaches), but this model does not refer to any coordination mechanism among guardians.

The advantage of the guardian is to deal with exceptions in a similar way as for sequential systems. It focuses on the software aspect of the agent and it lets aside the reasoning parts. A detailed example of exception handling is presented by Miller and Tripathi where the direct relationship with Java facilities can be observed [7]. The guardian assists a client-server system that implements the 'primary-backup' approach to deal with server-side failures [8]. If the primary server fails, a 'global exception' is raised, so that the guardian handles the error by asking the backup to take the role of primary, and by starting a new backup. The specification of this example is related to reorganization of teams in MAS, and the server failure can be thought of as an agent-level exception.

The guardian does not capture however the characteristics of agent systems. The guardian initially targets distributed objects with (remote) procedure call, and the coupling is higher than an agent system architecture. Concretely, the interaction model of the guardian has a very similar semantics to usual object-oriented handling facilities (the `try/catch` approach) which 'binds' invoker and operation. Agent interactions rely on other models with 'weaker bindings', typically message passing. Malicious agents can be part of open MAS, along with benevolent and ill-designed agents. The guardian approach assumes that agents are benevolent and it does not cope currently with arbitrary agent profiles, even though security concerns are considered. In particular, an ill-designed agent may not declare an exception to the guardian, thus requiring more efforts on the design of the guardian.

The encapsulation is a closely related matter as it guarantees some independence to the agent, which can ignore messages explicitly or answer false results. In the guardian approach, access to the agent state is granted (members and methods). The guardian is allowed to 'command' an agent, e.g. to wait or to restart a task. These action commands do not verify the encapsulation and autonomy of agents.

2.2   The Sentinels

In the bottom right corner of Fig. 1, the sentinels approach from Hägg is applicable to agents with more proactive behaviors than the guardian [9]. Sentinels are agents introduced in a MAS application to provide a fault-tolerance service layer. The approach has been extended in the work of Klein et al. with an exception handler repository [10,3]. Another extension has been developed by Shah et al. to focus on an exception diagnosis mechanism for detecting when sentinels must react [11,12,13]. The sentinels appear as a centralized solution, as explained by Hägg in its original work, but the extensions take a more distributed stance owing to their architectures. In all cases, the sentinel approach adds communication capabilities among agents that extend the functionalities introduced in the guardian model. Also, the sentinels were developed in a MAS research and it features more agent-specific exception handling capabilities. For example, sentinels are able to deal with problems in the agent beliefs, whereas the guardian focuses on software and architecture aspects. A detailed application from Hägg is a system and its sentinels for a power distribution company. Application agents negotiate energy consumption credits for load-balancing on an electric grid. Sentinels can detect and remedy to erroneous behaviors in negotiation processes by inspecting 'checkpoints' in the agent code.

Nevertheless, sentinels also violate assumptions of the agent paradigm. Encapsulation is not respected since sentinels can access and execute code in the so-called 'agent-head' [9], which should be a black-box. Similarly to the Guardian, agents are supposed benevolent and this hypothesis does not always hold.

2.3 Stigmergic Systems

The upper central part of Fig. 1 refers to stigmergic systems [14]. Stigmergy is an interaction model where agents put marks in the environment (messages with no intended recipient) that other agents exploit to determine their next actions. Stigmergy models the behavior of social insects such as termites. One termite starts to build a nest by putting a piece of material on the ground (a mark in the environment). Other termites use this information to determine where to pile the piece they carry. Stigmergy is thus an indirect interaction model as there is no direct message passing. Stigmergic systems are shown to be particularly robust to exceptions such as the death or the failure of agents [15]. The robustness of these systems is mostly due to the high redundancy of agents, which reminds the choice for modularity of software architectures that could limit the impact of exceptions in sequential systems.

Little work on stigmergic systems discusses robustness issues, and no work on exception handling to our knowledge. Although the robustness inherent to such systems entails that no significant advance might be expected in exception handling, recent extensions of stigmergic systems to proactive agents are to be demanding for such techniques [16] (that is why the box on Fig. 1 stretches toward proactive agents).

2.4 Coordinated Exception Handling in Distributed Objects

The coordinated exception handling model from Xu et al. deals with exceptions in distributed object systems (upper-left part of Fig. 1). Coordinated exception handling relies on the concept of coordinated atomic actions and exception graphs to deal with concurrent issues that can occur in the system [17]. A coordinated atomic action is a group activity, where a group is a set of processes that can be isolated from others for this activity (there is no other interactions in the group than for the activity at that moment). For example, the execution of a protocol with a fixed number of actors defines a group for the duration of the protocol. Groups are thus the context of any exception signaled by its members. Coordinated atomic actions are the response of a group to the concurrent signaling of exceptions. Groups are recursively defined, so that the occurrence of exceptions can be propagated according to the group hierarchy. An exception graph serves to manage the execution of coordinated actions in groups. The graph allows to determine a common strategy for handling concurrent exceptions, so that each process can invoke an appropriate handler. This approach was validated on a production cell application, which is the theme of several MAS implementations [18,19].

Such approach explicitly deals with traditional exceptions, but the mechanisms based on distributed algorithms and programming seem also applicable to MAS, where some reorganization processes are necessary to deal with exceptional conditions. This approach cannot be exploited directly however, owing to the assumptions that agents are cooperative and inspected. In addition, some agent exceptions such as the agent death are not taken into account [3].

2.5 SaGE

The upper central part of Fig. 1 also refers to approaches that deal with objects and a model of agent exceptions in a distributed way. In the case of agents, Souchon et al. proposed the SaGE[1] framework for systems based on the Agent-Group-Role model of agency (AGR) [20,21,22]. SaGE extends the exception handling system of Java with facilities to handle agent-specific issues. In particular, SaGE provides a mechanism for 'concerted exception handling' to resolve exceptions depending on several agents [23]. Concert exceptions allow to coordinate the reaction of agents and recover when necessary. Souchon et al. describe an example of such exceptions in a travel reservation scenario where service providers encounter a failure. When few providers fail, some results can be generated in a degraded mode. A higher ratio of failures to the number of providers triggers a specific method in the agent code for concerted exception handling to terminate the transaction for the reservation properly.

Compared to the previous work presented in this section, SaGE complies further with the agent encapsulation hypothesis. However, SaGE does not scale to open system issues as it assumes benevolent agents only. Nevertheless, SaGE brings notable instances of mechanisms for exception handling, namely the exception propagation according to the AGR model, and the concerted exceptions.

2.6 Proactive Agent Exceptions

In the top-right corner of Fig. 1, the work of Mallya and Singh deals with exception handling for proactive agents in a fully distributed way [1]. The work of Shah et al. presented with the sentinel approach enters also this category, since this extension of the sentinels analyzes the performatives in agent messages to provide diagnosis and detect exceptions in a decentralized way [11].

As for the work of Mallya and Singh, the approach relies on commitment protocols to model agent interactions and guarantee the autonomy assumption. When such a protocol is not respected, an exception is signaled and two formal methods allow agents to handle expected and unexpected situations. Expected exceptions are foreseen by the designer who wrote a specific handler beforehand (here, another protocol), which is the most common case in software programs. Unexpected exceptions are not coded beforehand and some constructs allows to dynamically build a handler from a basic set of protocols.

This method has been illustrated for a hotel reservation protocol. An expected exception can be the case where there is no vacancy in the hotel. The designer usually foresees this issue and a specific handler is available in the system to

---

[1] Agent Exception Handling System, from French acronym.

deal with it. An unexpected exception can be the occurrence of a dramatic event (a fire declared in the hotel), so that the cancellation or delegation of some reservations to another hotel are necessary. At design time, the handling of such an exception might not have been fully prepared. Mallya and Singh propose to rely on an external repository to fetch specific handlers and merge them automatically for an adequate handling.

Although this approach is very attractive and verifies the agent paradigm (encapsulation and openness), it still remains theoretical and it lacks validated results concerning scalability, even in later work [24]. The current issues are indeed the computational complexity of the selection of handlers and the dynamic assembly of new handlers.

2.7 Survey Conclusion

Fig. 1 shows the spread of endeavors in dealing with exception handling in the MAS community, and the potential of some approaches. In the present paper, we rely on this body of work to identify research directions for MAS, toward a distributed approach for proactive agents that both respects the agent paradigm and remains practical, with the experience gained from the research referred to in this section.

3   Challenge and Research Directions

MAS call for specific exception handling to deal with their characteristics. In this section, we identify challenges and research directions in proposing an appropriate handling facility.

3.1 Full-Fledged MAS

In this paper, we consider full-fledged MAS as follows.

- Agent paradigm respect: The main characteristic of agents is encapsulation (the black-box image) and the consequent autonomy.
- Distributed systems: The general case refers to multi-process or multi-threaded systems that span over an arbitrary number of machines.
- Open & heterogeneous systems: Agents are not supposed to be collaborative or benevolent, the population can evolve, and the system infrastructure is reduced to a minimal set of services and their (standardized) interfaces.

Such characteristics define systems that would lie in the upper right corner of Fig. 1. From our survey of related work, it appears that no approach exists that can deal with such characteristics simultaneously and concretely. The survey refers to these three characteristics, but the current achievements are either abstract and difficult to engineer, or lack of generality as would be expected for a work similar to Goodenough [25]. In other words, the techniques exposed on Fig. 1 should be a foundation for the development of exception handling mechanisms that address full-fledged systems.

3.2   Properties of Exception Handling for MAS

Appropriate exception handling mechanisms should comply with the following properties, in order to verify the characteristics of MAS and their engineering.

- Non intrusive: Respect of the agent paradigm. Exception mechanisms external to agents should not be able to control or inspect freely agent internals. This property does not oppose however to external mechanisms that would support agents *on request* or for event notification.
- Distributed: Agents should handle exceptions by themselves or in groups. In other words, handling is distributed over the agents to match their individual context (agents have local range of perception and action) and their independence. Centralized handling can also be considered when necessary and compatible with the other properties.
- Redundant: The presence of non-collaborative agents in open systems entails a need for heuristics to find 'alternatives' when one cannot handle an exception. Standard replication of agents is insufficient since non-collaborative behaviors can be common to all replicates. Heuristics must then target redundancy of 'roles' or 'service providers' instead of agents to search for appropriate alternatives.

Non-intrusive mechanisms lead to exploit the *proactivity of agents* for handling agent-level exceptions. The guardian and sentinels exemplify intrusive approaches in the sense they determine the handling behavior of agents. A mechanism that relies on the agent capability to reason on exceptions (proactivity) seems appropriate to verify the non-intrusion property. For example, a multilateral business process built upon the collaboration of several companies could use a MAS architecture. Such system relies on a strong independence of the different parties (by extension the autonomy of agents), so that a non-intrusive exception handling mechanism is required as none of the agents can reasonably let others *decide* how to recover an exception instead of them. Each agent should be proactive to recover by themselves, or in collaboration with others in related situations.

Considering the properties of distribution and redundancy, history of exception handling shows that an important system feature is modularity, as the syntactic units of Goodenough or, later, the object-oriented design [25]. Modularity in MAS is due to agents having only partial knowledge about the whole system. Agents have only access to a 'local scope' of their environment that we call agent *context*. Existing work shows that the context can be efficiently exploited in distributed systems to determine appropriate exception handlers [9,17,7]. The context usually refers to the information available to executing processes (e.g. fields of an object). In the agent paradigm, the notion of context is related to information and resources available in the agent environment [26,27]. In other words, a MAS exception handling mechanisms should allow agents to leverage information and resources in their contexts. Agent proactivity then permits to reason with extended data and potentially be able to handle or try delegating an exception. In the business process example, the context of each agent can be the presence of all other agents. If an agent dies, others can rely on their shared context to detect the death and react accordingly. In addition, the context could contain some facilities, such as a shared repository of exception handlers [10], to let agents rely further on the context.

3.3   Research Directions and Issues

Exploitation of an Enriched Context in the Agent Environment. The result of our current analysis is that research on the environment and the context it provides to agents would benefit to exception handling techniques in MAS. The current agent context is in practice reduced to information received by message-passing, which is the usual way of interacting among agents. However, the types and number of messages passed to an agent is pre-determined, e.g. by the protocols or plans authorized for this agent. It means that a given agent only knows about its context through such a restricted set of messages. Although these messages are sufficient for activities under normal conditions, they contain little extra information that agents can exploit in case of exception (either reactively or pro-actively) to try to terminate or resume their execution.

For the above reasons, we think that a potential research direction is the design of mechanisms in the environment to enrich the agent context automatically at runtime with application-dependent information [28]. Enriching the context appropriately should yield timely information to treat some exception conditions or organize a concerted resolution [7,21]. A simple example of enriching the context is an agent-based supply chain system. An agent A of the chain receives orders from several agents and delegates some sub-tasks to some others. The basic context of A consists of these surrounding agents (concretely, the address of these agents). In case of failure of one acquaintance, A has two means to detect the failure from the context: It either polls the failed agent at some point (the poll itself should then fail), or it must be explicitly informed by another third-party agent. Both approaches might however come late and cause delays along the chain. The context could be enriched with agent state information and an appropriate notification service to inform agents about the death of a peer. For example, an explicit environment entity can request for a heart-beat signal to provide agents with such contextual information. Such an approach would verify the criteria we identified for full-fledge MAS as it is non-intrusive and relies on possibly decentralized mechanisms external to agents. The issues for such research direction is then how to build the right context dynamically, and how agents can exploit it in an efficient manner. We think that exception handling in MAS should continue this line of work.

Exploitation of Agent Internal Mechanisms. A second research direction is closely related to the first one. When the environment provides extra contextual information, agents must be able to exploit it, so that adapted reasoning mechanisms are necessary. Several architectures have been proposed for engineering proactive agents, but none integrates the perspective on an enriched context to our knowledge. Two notable cases are however the KGP model that treats 'unexpected messages' and could accept an enlarged context [29], and the agent architecture of Shah et al. specialized in exception diagnosis, which analyzes ACL messages for later reactions [12]. The place of the context and its modeling are nevertheless to be defined and integrated to these approaches.

Another area of work focuses on goal-driven agents that execute hierarchies of plans. When a plan fails in realizing a goal, alternative plans are deduced by exploring the hierarchy. This type of agent internal mechanisms is well-spread (see the work of Teamcore for example [30]), so that generic exception mechanisms should be adapted to this case. The relation to the agent context has been explicated by Kaminka with the development of algorithms for execution monitoring. Agents 'overhear' others in their vicinity to maintain their individual awareness of the team state and ensure the proper execution of the plans [31]. In other words, overhearing allows agents to enrich their context with information by observation. This direction of research is under further investigation in collaborative and competitive scenarios [32,33].

In relation to the initial meaning of exceptions in software programs [25], exceptions can be *faults* or *opportunities*, and the second case can be frequent in MAS [33]. The case of opportunities requires specific reasoning schemes to distinguish them from faults and errors. Agent proactivity is therefore a relevant research direction to explore advanced but efficient mechanisms for exploiting opportunities.

Concert Handling in Open Systems. The work on concert exception handling targets initially collaborative processes and agents [23,21]. In the case of MAS, the assumptions of previous work do not hold a priori. In open systems, agents should be assumed as non-collaborative in the first place. The research issue is then to define ways to have agents cooperate, perhaps temporarily, to handle common or related exceptions in concert.

The research direction that stems from this situation therefore addresses coordination problems in agent societies. Some potential approaches in this direction are the use of organizational models and reputation mechanisms. Typically, organizations define power or dependence relationships among agents, and a set of rules, such as in the normative electronic institutions [34]. Even with non-collaborative peers, it is expected that agents can use dependencies and rely on rules to organize concert exception handling. An example of such approach is when a supplier agent does not deliver the items it was paid for by a client agent. This situation is an exception in the corresponding sell protocol, and the client can exploit its relationship to a banking agent to pressure the supplier for sending or refunding the item, thus forming a handling method for this exception.

Reputation mechanisms serve usually to guide agents in choosing interaction partners in open settings. In case where concert exceptions are required, reputation of peers can serve to evaluate which agents are the most reliable to participate in the handling. For example, a predictive market could rely on a MAS architecture where trade agents would exchange stocks. The occurrence of exceptional important events (e.g. the election of X while Y was given winner) causes agents to react quickly in concert. In such case, some low-weight traders rely on the reputation of others and their financial strengths to react or form coalitions.

Agent-Level and Other Exceptions. The last research direction is an issue of integration of different exception techniques to form multi-level exceptions management approaches. The related work section shows several endeavors for extending the techniques for sequential and distributed systems with agent-specific ones. However, the requirements we presented in this section emphasize the shift between agents and traditional techniques. For example, the technique of Mallya and Singh [1] has not been related yet to traditional ones. Furthermore, an interesting research direction would be to study when exceptions at the programming-level imply agent-level exceptions. This research direction is suggested by current work where exceptions are raised and wrapped or transformed into more 'handy' exceptions. Multi-level exceptions might create intricate and powerful situations, and formal methods may be necessary to deal with such cases. Notice that agent-level exceptions can occur while the system is functioning normally at the language level, typically when agents need to reorganize a team or to re-plan their missions. In general, it is desired that agent-level exceptions do not cause a programming exception, whereas the contrary is likely, for example in the case of the agent death.

4   Preliminary Experiments

Our ongoing work follows the research directions identified in this paper. We developed an ad hoc agent-oriented event notification system that enriches the context of each agent with relevant information for their activities. Early results in preliminary experiments show that agents can leverage the enriched context to take advantage of some exceptional and fortuitous situations [33].

4.1   Experimental Settings

The experiments were conducted on an electronic market place developed for trading agents ('bazaar' type). The purpose of the system was to show that agents can often face exceptional events and that they can exploit these events for their own benefits. In the market, buyer and seller agents follow the Contract Net protocol (CNet) to trade some items [35]. This protocol has a strict order: Agents cannot join a running protocol and they must either create their own CNet or wait for being invited. The agent context is limited to the information received by the messages specified in the protocol. Our experiments first runs the system with this capability only.

In another series of runs, the agent context is enriched with two types of information. Overheard messages and 'agent public situation' notifications are introduced dynamically by an explicit environment entity [36]. The topology defines how agents are related, i.e. agents that trade the same type of items are in the same neighborhood of the topology. An agent can thus access in its context to relevant information from the agents in the CNet it has joined and to messages of other agents in the neighborhood (overhearing). The environment also notifies the agent about the public situation of others in its context. Overheard messages allow agents to be aware of opportunities. If a deal fails exceptionally, an agent is further aware of potential agents to contact. The public situation is the list of items an agent is interested in, e.g. a shopping list. In particular, seller agents can determine from the notifications which buyers are interested in their products. In these particular cases, agents are able to initiate a sub-protocol of the CNet, where the seller directly sends an offer and the buyer accepts or rejects.

In these experiments, agents process in order the messages they receive. The reasoning capabilities of agents are reaction rules adapted to the CNet and to the enriched context. For example, sellers react respectively to a message and an overheard message with the following rules.

Algorithm 1. Two example rules of seller agents

if message received & I am recipient then	if message received & I am *not* recipient then
send offer	store alternative
end if	end if

The left rule is a standard message in the CNet, whereas the right rule aims at storing supplementary and relevant information that can be exploited in case of exception. In this experiment, the capabilities are fixed by design. This work only simulates an open MAS, even though agents randomly exit the market, enter, and trade on the market (behaviors are specified as cyclic state machines). Agents have the rational behavior to try to maximize the number of successful deals with the lowest price they can negotiate.

4.2   Experiments and Analysis

In this series of experiments, agent-level exceptions are failures to settle a deal and opportunities of interactions. In fact, this scenario has been designed to show that agents can frequently encounter opportunities in some settings (statistically). The following Fig. 2 shows the number of failed deals in different market configurations, i.e. different number of buyers B and sellers S. Failures to deal items in the market can be of different kinds, including receiving better offers and canceling other negotiations, or lacking time to contract some clients.

The graph values rely on statistical averages over repeated runs in different configurations. In most cases, the system with event notification allows reducing significantly the number of failed deals by offering opportunities and initiative mechanisms to the agents. In these experiments, we did not allow agents to resume negotiations. In other words, agents recover from deal failures by immediately looking for other deals. Failed protocols are terminated and properly canceled, but the execution of the agent goes on normally with the next deal attempt. This situation is a typical example of agent-level exception that does not cause termination of the agent or a language-level fault.

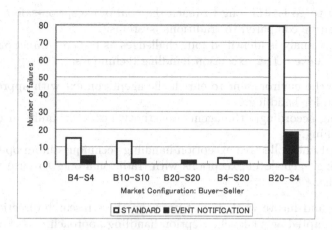

Fig. 2. Number of failed deals in different market configurations

The B20-S20 run differs from others as the event notification system does not perform better. Our interpretation is that in a balanced and 'crowded' market the number of agents is such that the probability of failure is lower than other settings. In addition, the agents are very resilient, according to the previous comment, and they take any opportunity to conclude deals.

4.3   Limitations of the Experiments

The experiments illustrate how enriching the agent context and exploiting adequate agent internal mechanisms allow building a MAS where agents can deal with failures and opportunities in their activities. The experiments restrict the demonstration to a simulation of concept, and it only focuses on the first two research directions proposed in this paper. We have not explored yet more general criteria for the selection of contextual information.

Agents in the simulation are selfish buyers and sellers and they do not implement any mechanism for concerted exception handling. In the present configuration of the market, such a case would require more complex agents and settings. The experiment does not refer as well to the relations between agent-level and lower-level exceptions. One interesting case that could be illustrated in the market is whenever an agent dies due to a code-level exception (or a voluntary termination by the administrator). The other agents would have to deal with the protocols shared with the dead agent.

5   Conclusion and Opening

This paper attempts to identify challenges and research directions of exception handling in MAS. We consider MAS as open, heterogeneous, distributed, and strongly abiding by the agent paradigm. As such, our survey in the field shows that the way to go is still long to reach the goal of exception-safe and reliable MAS that can be compared to traditional systems.

Our current analysis identified four challenges as research directions that are relevant to achieve better exception handling techniques.

- Leverage the environment to enrich the agent context with appropriate information for handling.
- Exploiting accordingly the agent proactivity, either for faults or opportunities handling.
- Individual and collective exception handling techniques in an open context.
- Integrating agent-level exceptions with traditional ones to form multi-level exceptions.

Our ongoing and future work aim at pursuing these research directions and to propose an adapted agent-level exception handling approach.

Acknowledgment

The authors would like to thank the anonymous reviewers of this paper who participated in improving significantly the initial version of this work.

References

1. Mallya, A.U., Singh, M.P.: Modeling exceptions via commitment protocols. In: Autonomous Agents and Multi–Agent Systems, New York, NY, USA, ACM Press (2005) 122–129
2. Tripathi, A., Miller, R.: Exception handling in agent-oriented systems. [37] 128–146
3. Klein, M., Rodríguez-Aguilar, J.A., Dellarocas, C.: Using domain-independent exception handling services to enable robust open multi-agent systems: The case of agent death. Autonomous Agents and Multi-Agent Systems 7(1-2) (2003) 179–189
4. Brooks, R.: Intelligence without representation. Artificial Intelligence 47(1–3) (1991) 139–159
5. Rao, A.S., Georgeff, M.P.: BDI Agents: From Theory to Practice. Technical report, Australian Artificial Intelligence Institute (1995)
6. Odell, J.: Objects and agents compared. Journal of Object Technology 1(1) (May-June 2002) 41–53
7. Miller, R., Tripathi, A.: The Guardian Model and Primitives for Exception Handling in Distributed Systems. IEEE Trans. Software Eng. 30(12) (2004) 1008–1022
8. Tanenbaum, A.S.: Distributed Operating Systems. Prentice Hall (1994)
9. Hägg, S.: A Sentinel Approach to Fault Handling in Multi-Agent Systems. In Zhang, C., Lukose, D., eds.: Distributed AI. Volume 1286 of Lecture Notes in Computer Science., Springer (1996) 181–195
10. Klein, M., Dellarocas, C.: Exception handling in agent systems. In: Agents. (1999) 62–68
11. Shah, N., Chao, K.M., Godwin, N., Younas, M., Laing, C.: Exception Diagnosis in Agent-Based Grid Computing. In: International Conference on Systems, Man and Cybernetics, IEEE (2004) 3213–3219

12. Shah, N., Chao, K.M., Godwin, N., James, A.E.: Exception diagnosis in open multi-agent systems. In Skowron, A., Barthès, J.P.A., Jain, L.C., Sun, R., Morizet-Mahoudeaux, P., Liu, J., Zhong, N., eds.: IAT, IEEE Computer Society (2005) 483–486

13. Shah, N., Chao, K.M., Godwin, N., James, A.E., Tasi, C.F.: An empirical evaluation of a sentinel based approach to exception diagnosis in multi-agent systems. In: AINA (1), IEEE Computer Society (2006) 379–386

14. Brueckner, S.: Return from the Ant — Synthetic Ecosystems for Manufacturing Control. PhD thesis, Humboldt University, Berlin, Germany (2000)

15. Parunak, H.V.D.: "Go to the Ant": Engineering Principles from Natural Multi-Agent Systems. Annals of Operation Research **75** (1997) 69–101

16. Parunak, H.V.D.: A survey of environments and mechanisms for human-human stigmergy. [39] 163–186

17. Xu, J., Romanovsky, A.B., Randell, B.: Coordinated Exception Handling in Distributed Object Systems: From Model to System Implementation. In: ICDCS. (1998) 12–21

18. Fischer, K., Müller, J.P., Pischel, M.: A pragmatic BDI architecture. In Wooldridge, M., Müller, J.P., Tambe, M., eds.: ATAL. Volume 1037 of Lecture Notes in Computer Science., Springer (1995) 203–218

19. Eymann, T., Padovan, B., Schoder, D.: Avalanche - An Agent Based Value Chain Coordination Experiment. In: Workshop on Artificial Societies and Computational Markets (ASCMA'98) at Autonomous Agents '98. (1998) 48–53

20. Ferber, J., Gutknecht, O.: A Meta-Model for the Analysis and Design of Organizations in Multi-Agent Systems. In: ICMAS, IEEE Computer Society (1998) 128–135

21. Souchon, F., Dony, C., Urtado, C., Vauttier, S.: Improving Exception Handling in Multi-agent Systems. In de Lucena, C.J.P., Garcia, A.F., Romanovsky, A.B., Castro, J., Alencar, P.S.C., eds.: SELMAS. Volume 2940 of Lecture Notes in Computer Science., Springer (2003) 167–188

22. Dony, C., Urtado, C., Vauttier, S.: Exception Handling and Asynchronous Active Objects: Issues and Proposal. In Dony, C., Knudsen, J.L., Romanovsky, A.B., Tripathi, A., eds.: Advanced Topics in Exception Handling Techniques. Volume 4119 of Lecture Notes in Computer Science., Springer (2006) 81–100

23. Issarny, V.: Concurrent Exception Handling. [37] 111–127

24. Mallya, A.U.: Modeling and Enacting Business Processes via Commitment Protocols among Agents. PhD thesis, North Carolina State University, Raleigh, United States (2005)

25. Goodenough, J.B.: Exception Handling: Issues and a Proposed Notation. Commun. ACM **18**(12) (1975) 683–696

26. Weyns, D., Parunak, H.V.D., Michel, F., Holvoet, T., Ferber, J.: Environments for Multiagent Systems, State-of-the-Art and Research Challenges. In Weyns, D., Parunak, H.V.D., Michel, F., eds.: Environment for Multi-Agent Systems'04. Volume 3374 of Lecture Notes in Artificial Intelligence., Springer (2005) 1–47

27. Weyns, D., Omicini, A., Odell, J.: Environment, First-Order Abstraction in Multiagent Systems. In *Autonomous Agents and Multi-Agent Systems* [38] 5–30

28. Platon, E., Mamei, M., Sabouret, N., Honiden, S., Parunak, H.: Mechanisms of the Environment for Mutli-Agent Systems, Survey and Opportunities. In *Autonomous Agents and Multi-Agent Systems* [38] 31–47

29. Stathis, K., Lu, W., Kakas, A.C., Demetriou, N., Endriss, U., Bracciali, A.: PROSOCS: A platform for programming software agents in computational logic. In: From Agent Theory to Agent Implementation. (2004)

30. Kaminka, G.A., Pynadath, D.V., Tambe, M.: Monitoring Teams by Overhearing: A Multi-Agent Plan-Recognition Approach. Journal of Artificial Intelligence Research **17** (2002) 83–135
31. Kaminka, G.A.: Execution Monitoring in Multi-Agent Environments. PhD thesis, Computer Science Department—University of Southern California (2000)
32. Legras, F., Tessier, C.: LOTTO: Group Formation by Overhearing in Large Teams. In: Autonomous Agents and Multi–Agent Systems, ACM Press (2003) 425–432
33. Platon, E.: Artificial intelligence in the environment: Smart environment for smarter agents in open e-markets. In: Proceedings of the Florida Artificial Intelligence Research Society, AAAI (2006)
34. Vázquez-Salceda, J.: The Role of Norms and Electronic Institutions in Multi-Agent Systems, The HARMONIA Framework. Whitestein Series in Software Agent Technologies. Springer (2004)
35. Smith, R.G.: The contract net protocol: High-level communication and control in a distributed problem solver. IEEE Trans. Computers **29**(12) (1980) 1104–1113
36. Platon, E., Sabouret, N., Honiden, S.: Overhearing and direct interactions: Point of view of an active environment. [39] 121–138
37. Romanovsky, A.B., Dony, C., Knudsen, J.L., Tripathi, A., eds.: Advances in Exception Handling Techniques (the book grow out of a ECOOP 2000 workshop). In Romanovsky, A.B., Dony, C., Knudsen, J.L., Tripathi, A., eds.: Advances in Exception Handling Techniques. Volume 2022 of Lecture Notes in Computer Science., Springer (2001)
38. Parunak, H.V.D., Weyns, D., eds.: Autonomous Agents and Multi-Agent Systems, Special Issue on Environment for Multi-Agent Systems. Volume 14, number 1. Springer Netherlands (February 2007)
39. Weyns, D., Parunak, H.V.D., Michel, F., eds.: Environments for Multi-Agent Systems II, Second International Workshop, E4MAS 2005, Utrecht, The Netherlands, July 25, 2005, Selected Revised and Invited Papers. In Weyns, D., Parunak, H.V.D., Michel, F., eds.: E4MAS. Volume 3830 of Lecture Notes in Computer Science., Springer (2006)

Exception Handling in
Context-Aware Agent Systems: A Case Study

Nelio Cacho[1], Karla Damasceno[2], Alessandro Garcia[1],
Alexander Romanovsky[3], and Carlos Lucena[2]

[1] Computing Department, Lancaster University, UK
[2] Computer Science Department, Pontifical Catholic University of Rio de Janeiro, Brazil
[3] Computer Science School, Newcastle University, UK
{n.cacho,a.garcia}@lancaster.ac.uk,
{karla,lucena}@inf.puc-rio.br,
alexander.romanovsky@newcastle.ac.uk

Abstract. Handling erroneous conditions in context-aware mobile agent systems is challenging due to their intrinsic characteristics: openness, lack of structuring, mobility, asynchrony and increased unpredictability. Even though several context-aware middleware systems now support the development of mobile agent-based applications, they rarely provide explicit and adequate features for context-aware exception handling. This paper reports our experience in implementing error handling strategies in some prototype context-aware collaborative applications built with the MoCA (Mobile Collaboration Architecture) system. MoCA is a publish-subscribe middleware supporting the development of collaborative mobile applications by providing explicit services that empower software agents with context-awareness. We propose a novel context-aware exception handling mechanism and discuss some lessons learned during its integration in the MoCA infrastructure.

Keywords: Exception handling, mobile agents, mobile computing, pervasive computing, context-awareness, middleware, ambient intelligence.

1 Introduction

There is a growing popularity of pervasive agent-based applications that allow mobile users to seamlessly exploit the computing resources and collaboration opportunities while moving across distinct physical regions. Typically mobile collaborative applications need to be made context aware in order to promote adaptation of the agent functionalities in the presence of contextual changes. In particular, they need to deal with frequent variations in the system execution contexts, such as fluctuating network bandwidth, temperature changes, decreasing battery power, changes in location or device capabilities, degree of proximity to other users, and so forth. However, the development of robust context-aware mobile systems is not a trivial task due to their intrinsic characteristics of openness, "unstructureness", asynchrony, and increased unpredictability [6, 22].

These system features seem to indicate that the handling of exceptional situations in mobile applications is more challenging, which in turn makes it impossible to

R. Choren et al. (Eds.): SELMAS 2006, LNCS 4408, pp. 57–76, 2007.

directly apply conventional exception handling mechanisms [20, 21]. First, error propagation needs to be context aware since it needs to take into consideration the dynamic system boundaries and changing collaborative agents. Second, both the execution of error recovery activities and determination of exception handling strategies often need to be selected according to user contexts. Third, the characterization of an exception itself may depend on the context, i.e. a system state may be considered an erroneous condition in a given context, but it may be not in others.

Several middleware systems [6,14,23] are nowadays available to support the construction of mobile agent-based applications. Their underlying architecture relies on different coordination techniques, such as tuplespaces [6], publish-subscribe mechanisms [14], and computational reflection [23]. However, such middleware systems rarely provide explicit support for *context-aware exception handling*. Often the existing solutions (e.g. [17,22,24]) are too general and not specific for the characteristics of the coordination technique used. Typically they are not scalable because they do not support clear system structuring using exception handling contexts, which are tightly integrated with their underlying middleware abstractions. Our analysis shows that understanding the interplay between context awareness and exception handling in mobile agent systems is still an open issue, since to deal with the complexity of context-aware exceptions, application programmers need to directly rely on existing middleware mechanisms, such as interest subscriptions or regular tuple propagation. The situation is complicated even further when they need to express exceptional control flows in the presence of mobility.

We have implemented error handling features in several prototype context-aware collaborative applications built with the MoCA (Mobile Collaboration Architecture) system [14]. MoCA is a publish-subscribe middleware that supports the development of collaborative mobile applications by incorporating explicit services empowering software agents with context-awareness. This paper presents the lessons learned while developing exception handling in MoCA applications. We have identified a number of exception handling issues that are neither satisfied by the regular use of the exception mechanisms of programming languages nor addressed by conventional mechanisms of the existing context-aware middleware systems, such as MoCA.

The main contributions of this paper are as follows. First, we present a case study helping us to identify the requirements for the context-aware exception handling mechanism. The system is a typical ambient intelligence (AmI) application developed with the MoCA middleware. Secondly, using these requirements we formulate a proposal for a context-aware exception handling model. Thirdly, we describe a prototype implementation of the model in the MoCA middleware; it consists of an extension of the client and server APIs and new middleware services, such as management of *exceptional contexts*, context-sensitive error propagation, proactive exception handling, concurrent exception resolution and execution of context-aware exception handlers. We also analyze the difficulties in using a typical publish-subscribe infrastructure for supporting context-aware exception handling.

The plan of the paper is as follows. Section 2 presents the basic concepts associated with context awareness, surveys context-aware middleware styles and introduces the fundamental exception handling terminology. Section 3 describes the case study in which we have identified challenging exception handling issues for the development of robust context-aware agent applications. Section 4 discusses an implementation of the proposed mechanism in MoCA. Section 5 overviews the related work. Section 6 concludes the paper by discussing directions of future work.

2 Background

Exception mechanisms are either built as an inherent part of the language with its own syntax, or as feature of middleware architectures coping with the intricacies of the different application domains and architecture styles. This paper focuses on the evaluation of context-aware middleware mechanisms to support proper exception handling in agent-based mobile applications. This section discusses the background of our work by describing candidate middleware architectures to support context-sensitive exception handling. Section 2.1 introduces the terminology and a categorization of context-aware middleware systems. Section 2.2 overviews the MoCA system. Section 2.3 introduces the exception handling concepts used in this paper.

2.1 Context and Context-Aware Middleware

The concepts of context and context-aware systems have been defined in a number of ways (e.g. [2, 3, 4]). According to Dey and Abowd [1], context is any information that can be used to characterize the situation or an entity. A system is context-aware if it uses context to provide relevant information and/or services to the user. Thus, one entity can be represented by an agent or a person with a mobile device, and the context-aware system can provide information about location, identity, time and activity for these entities. Before the context can be used, it is necessary to acquire data from sensors, conduct context recognition and some other tasks [5]. These tasks are usually implemented by context aware middleware, which hides the heterogeneity and distributed nature of devices processing the contextual information. In general, three types of architectural styles are used to implement context-aware middleware systems: (i) tuplespace-based architectures [9], (ii) reflective architectures [10,11] and (iii) publish/subscribe architectures [7].

A *tuplespace* is a form of distributed shared memory spread across all participant processes and/or hosts. Processes using this model communicate by generating *tuples* and *anti-tuples* which are submitted to the tuple space [9]. Tuples are typed data structures (e.g., objects in C++ and Java), and each tuple is formed from a collection of typed data fields and represents a cohesive piece of information. In a tuplespace-based system, all inter-process communications is conducted using the tuple space, and any process using a tuple space has the ability to access all the tuples it contains, insert new tuples, find matches for nondestructive anti-tuples and remove tuples by generating matching destructive anti-tuples [9]. CAMA (Context-Aware Mobile Agents) [6] is an example of tuplespace based middleware. The four basic CAMA abstractions are location, scope, agent, and role. A location is a container for scopes.

A scope provides a coordination space within which compatible agents can interact. This interaction is supported by restricting visibility of tuples contained in the scope only to compatible agents [6]. In this framework, agents can move from location to location. Each location runs a host computer supporting wireless connectivity. This computer keeps and controls the local tuple space to be accessed from the devices connected locally. This tuple space is the only media supporting communication between these devices.

Reflective middleware [10, 11] exploits mechanisms of computational reflection [12] to implement mobility and context-awareness services. Reflection is used to monitor the middleware's internal (re)configuration [13]. A reflective middleware system is divided in two levels: *base level* and *meta level*. The base level represents the middleware and the application core. The meta level contains the building blocks responsible for supporting reflection. These two levels are connected through a meta-object protocol (MOP) to ensure that modifications at the meta level are reflected into the corresponding modifications at the base level. Thus, modifications at the core should be reflected at the meta-level. The elements of the base level and of the meta level are respectively represented by base-level objects and meta-level objects. For example reflection is explored in CARISMA [23] to enhance the construction of adaptive and context-aware mobile applications. The middleware provides software engineers with primitives to describe how context changes should be handled using policies. The reflective middleware is in charge of maintaining a valid representation of the execution context by directly interacting with the underlying network operating system. Applications may require some services to be delivered in different ways (using different policies) when requested in a different context.

Publish/Subscribe (pub/sub) architectures rely on an asynchronous messaging paradigm that allows loose coupling between publishers and subscribers. Publishers are the agents that send information to a central component, while subscribers express their interest in receiving messages. A Broker [7] or Dispatcher [8] is the central component of a pub/sub system and is responsible for recording all subscriptions, matching publications against all subscriptions, and notifying the corresponding subscribers. The following section describes MoCA, a context-aware publish/subscribe middleware which has been used in our first experiment to incorporate exception handling strategies in context-aware mobile agent systems. Such an architecture was selected because of the growing number of context-aware middleware systems based on the publish-subscribe model [7,8,14].

2.2 MoCA: Mobile Collaboration Architecture

MoCA [14] is a middleware system supporting development and execution of context-aware collaborative applications which work with mobile users. Figure 1 shows the three elements that compose the MoCA application: a server, a proxy, and clients. The first two are executed on the nodes of the wired network, while the clients run on mobile devices. A proxy intermediates all communication between the application server and one or more of its clients on mobile hosts. The server and the client of a collaborative application are implemented using the MoCA APIs, which hide from the application developer most of the details concerning the use of the services provided by the architecture. The *ProxyFramework* white-box framework is used for developing and customizing the proxies according to the specific needs of the application [14]. It allows adaptation to be triggered by the context-change events.

The internal MoCA infrastructure is shown in Figure 2. To support context-aware applications, MoCA supplies three services: Context Information Service (CIS), Symbolic Region Manager (SRM) and Location Inference Service (LIS). The CIS component receives and processes state information sent by the clients. It also receives notification requests from the application Proxies and generates and delivers events to a proxy whenever a change in a client's state is of interest to this proxy. To provide transparency, CIS takes decisions on behalf of the publish/subscribe mechanism; which is implemented using built-in mechanisms that cater for the basic functionalities rather than deal with the high levels of heterogeneity and dynamicity intrinsic to mobile environments, such as the problem of late delivery [7].

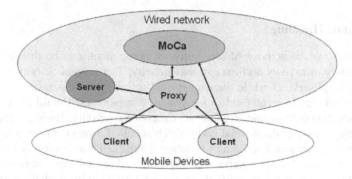

Fig. 1. MoCA application

SRM provides an interface to define and request information about hierarchies of symbolic regions, which are names assigned to well-defined physical regions (i.e. rooms, halls, buildings) that may be of interest to location-aware applications [14]. Based on SRM information, LIS infers the approximate location of a mobile device from the *raw* context information collected by CIS of this device. It does this by comparing the current pattern of radio frequency (RF) signals with the signal patterns previously measured at the pre-defined *Reference Points* of the physical region. Therefore, to make any inference, the LIS database has to be populated with RF signals at each reference point, and with the inference parameters that are chosen according to the specific characteristics of the region.

The communication infrastructure consists of the pub/sub mechanism and a communication protocol. The former supplies the basic functionality to the CIS, once the context recognition is done by the definition of subscriptions that specify a set of features to activate a specific user-defined context. The communication protocol currently works with an 802.11 wireless network based on the IP protocol stack, but the architecture could be extended to accommodate a cellular data network protocol, such as GPRS.

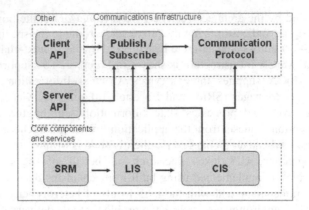

Fig. 2. MoCA internal infrastructure

2.3   Exception Handling

Agent activity, as the activity of any software component, can be divided into two parts [25]: *normal activity* and *exceptional activity*. The normal activity implements the agent normal services while the exceptional activity provides measures that cope with *exceptions*. Each agent (and other system components) should have *exception handlers*, which constitute and structure its exceptional activity. Handlers are attached to a particular region of the normal code which is called *protected region* or *handling scope*. If an agent cannot handle an exception it raises, the exception is signaled and *propagated* to other handling scopes defined in the higher-level components of the system. After the exception is handled, the system returns to its normal activity.

Developers of dependable systems often refer to errors as exceptions because they manifest themselves rarely during the agent normal activity. Exceptions can be classified into two types [21]: (i) *user-defined*, and (ii) *pre-defined*. The user-defined exceptions are defined and detected at the application level. The predefined exceptions are declared implicitly and are associated with the erroneous conditions detected by the run-time support, the middleware or hardware.

Exception handling mechanisms [20,21] developed for many high-level programming languages allow software developers to define exceptions and to structure the exceptional activity of software components. An exception handling mechanism introduces the specific way in which *exceptions are propagated* and the normal control flow is replaced with the *exceptional control flow* when an exception is raised. It is also responsible for supporting different exceptional flow strategies and searching for the appropriate handlers after an exception occurs.

3   Context-Aware Exception Handling in Mobile Agent Systems

This section describes a typical context-aware agent-based application, for which we have implemented a prototype system with the MoCA architecture and identified a number of difficulties in incorporating error handling. Section 3.1 describes the case study, while Sections 3.2-3.6 present the identified requirements for a mechanism smoothly supporting context-aware exception handling.

3.1 AmI: A Case Study

The case study is an ambient intelligence (AmI) [16] application, which is composed of numerous sensors, devices and control units interconnected to effectively form a machine [15]. A wide range of sensors and controllers (actuators) could be utilized, including the ones dealing with fire alarm, energy control, heating control, ventilation control, climate, surveillance, lighting, power, and automatic door and window. Figure 3 depicts an AmI scenario where each office contains sensors and output devices, which are monitored and controlled locally by software agents. All these agents are connected together via a network, forming a decentralized architecture that enables building-wide collaboration.

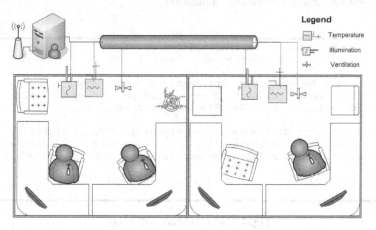

Fig. 3. Plant: A floor of a typical building structured into offices. All sensors are wired to a common field-bus network.

Each piece of equipment has an associated actuator controlling its activation. All users have a smartcard that operates as a mobile device supplying the current position and employee ID. Immediately after the user enters the office, the system needs to identify the user preferences and start the procedures for dealing with the temperature, ventilation, illumination, and climate adaptation for the specific user preferences. For instance, Figure 4 shows the code responsible for defining a user preference for a specific office. Due to the user movement, it is necessary to subscribe a listener in the LIS service to notify whenever a new device enters in the office. When this occurs, the agent gets user preferences and invokes all actuators which are responsible for switching the equipments on/off according to the user preference. Due to the unreliable wireless communication in context-aware applications, all actuators are asynchronously invoked to avoid blocking communication. This kind of invocation makes the management of exceptional control flow more difficult. The main reason is that connection instability impedes the utilization of synchronous communication protocols in order to deviate from the normal to the exceptional control flow in the presence of exceptional conditions. Thus, it is not possible to ensure that all asynchronous invocations are properly executed at the end of method *onDeviceEntered* since some exceptions can arrive after the control flow has had left the *try/catch* block.

To deal with this issue, two techniques [26, 27, 28] are commonly used to handle exceptions raised by asynchronous method calls: future objects and callback mechanisms. Asynchronous method calls can return a future object to hold a reference of the invocation and also to receive the returned result upon availability. The occurrence of an exception during the method execution implies in updating the result of the future object as a reference of the raised exception. Thus, all attempts to manipulate the future object will result in throwing the received exception [27, 28]. On the other hand, callback mechanisms are used to attach handlers with asynchronous method calls which will be executed in the circumstance of any exception during the asynchronous computation [26].

```
RegionListen listen = new RegionListen();
Lis_service.subscribe(UserDevice, listen);
...
private class RegionListen implements RegionListener {
 public void onDeviceEntered(String regionID, String deviceID)
   HashMap userpref = getUserPref(deviceId,regionID);
   try{
     heatActuator.defineNewCycle(userpref.get("Temperature"));
     lightActuator.defineNewIllumination(userpref.get("Light"));
     humidityActuator.defineNewLevel(userpref.get("Humidity"));
           . . .
   }catch(Exception e){// deal with all exceptions}
}}
```

Fig. 4. User preference definition

Despite these facilities to deal with exceptions in asynchronous scenarios, both approaches rely on the availability of the invoked actuator to detect the exception. However, context-aware applications are generally implemented [29] by ad-hoc networks which are unreliable in terms of response time and so an exception can indefinitely delay to return to its caller. This means that it is not possible to know which actuators are active or not. This is a real problem to context-aware applications since the actuators should work together to provide a comfortable environment. Whenever an actuator fails to provide its service, the whole system should adapt to avoid an uncomfortable environment. For instance, the heater should operate together with the humidifier since both complement each other to keep the environment warm and humid. If the heater does not produce the expected heat, the system should somehow detect this failure and handle it by adjusting down the humidifier operation cycle.

Hence, additional mechanisms should be used to detect the environmental exceptions of this type. Such exceptions also include fire alarms or an excessive number of users in a given building region, or the occurrence of problems in the diverse primary and/or secondary climate system distributed over the building. The handling of such exceptional conditions depends on the combination of changing contextual information, such as the location and type of the heating systems, the physical regions where the different system administrators are, and so on.

In the following, we discuss problems relative to the incorporation and implementation of error handling scenarios in such a context-aware mobile agent-based application. First, we explain the problems found in the context of our case study. Second, we explain why they cannot be addressed while using the underlying mechanisms of the MoCA architecture. The shortcomings here vary from exception declaration to exception handlers and error propagation issues.

3.2 Specification of "Exceptional Contexts"

During design of the AmI application we have identified a number of user-defined "exceptional contexts" that depend on a multitude of contextual information and also on user preferences, which in turn are typically application-specific. For us, exceptional contexts mean one or more conditions associated with the context types, which together denote an environmental, hardware, or software fault. For example, the exceptional contexts can be characterized by the situations when the temperature of an office or public room in the building occasionally exceeds the maximum limit according to user preferences, which can indicate a serious problem in the heating system (not detected by the associated controlling system). Handling of such situations requires an exceptional control flow different from the normal one, consisting of regular notification-based reactions. The seriousness of this context requires propagation of such exceptional context information to the proper administrators, which also may vary depending on their physical location. It may also require involvement of several people.

The specification of contextual conditions of interest in the publish-subscribe systems, such as MoCA, requires explicit subscriptions based on regular expressions. A subscription is usually carried out by the code in the devices or proxy servers, which will be receiving notifications when those contextual conditions are matched according to the changing circumstances. However, the specification of an exceptional context situation inherently has a different semantics and, as such, needs to encompass different elements, including the handling scope, alternative "default handlers", types of contextual information which *should* and *should not* be propagated together with the exception occurrence, and so on. This is why in MoCA normal contextual subscriptions need to be different from the exceptional subscriptions.

3.3 Lack of Exception Handling Scoping

There are several situations in the AmI case study (Section 3.1) when handling exceptions requires several software agents and users to be involved depending on the physical regions and other types of contextual information. For example, as discussed in Section 3.2, the proper handling of some exceptional conditions in the mobile heaters requires exceptions to be propagated to a set of devices belonging to the staff responsible for heater maintenance. However, the propagation needs to be context sensitive in the sense that it should take into account the suitable maintainers for the specific heater type that are closest to the region where the faulty heater is located. The contextual exception needs to be systematically propagated to broader scopes until the appropriate handlers are found. Moreover, if a fire exception is detected, it needs to be propagated to all the building regions and group of mobile users. Hence the physical regions or a group of devices (such as those with the maintenance people) are examples of contextual handling scopes that should be supported by the underlying middleware. In this way, the proper exception handlers could be activated in all the relevant devices according to different user preferences. However, the MoCA middleware does not support such scopes for context-aware error handling, which hinders the modularity of the system on the presence of exceptional contexts.

3.4 Need for Context-Aware Handlers

There are also some cases where the choice of proper exception handlers depends on the contextual conditions associated with devices involved in the coordinated error handling. For the same exception, we need to create handlers tailored to different contextual conditions, and make sure that they are correctly executed. For instance, we need to associate contextual information about the heater's physical location to the handlers dealing with the faulty heaters. Some handlers can be only selected if the mobile heater is in the context of a specific department. Again, we have to implement such a control of context-aware handlers as part of the application since there is no MoCA facility for that purpose.

3.5 Proactive Exception Handling

In an open mobile system, like the AmI study (Section 3.1), we can not expect that all the devices, in which software agents were developed by different designers, would be able to foresee all the exceptional contexts. In the AmI case, for example, the presence of fire in the building may not have been foreseen by all the designers of the software agents running in the mobile devices located in the different building regions. As a result, there is a need for exploiting the mobile collaboration infrastructure when an exceptional context is detected by one of the peers. Depending on the exception, it should be notified to other mobile devices even when they have not registered interest in that specific exceptional context. In other words, the contextual exception should be proactively raised in other mobile collaborative agents and/or mobile devices pertaining to the same region. Thus robust context-aware mobile systems require more intelligent, proactive exception handling due to their features of openness, asynchrony, and increased unpredictability. The problem is that conventional coordination models (Section 2.1) such as tuplespace-based and publish-subscribe architectures (e.g. MoCA), require the explicit subscription of interest from the collaborative agents.

3.6 Concurrent Exception Resolution

During the execution of the AmI application, we have also noticed that several concurrently thrown exceptions can occur, which actually mean the occurrence of a more serious abnormal situation. A common example is the simultaneous detection of a fire occurrence and high temperature exceptions. Thus, the exception mechanism should be able to collect all those concurrent exception occurrences and resolve them so that the proper action can be triggered. Note that the activation of several handlers associated with individual exceptional condition is no longer satisfactory. MoCA did not provide any support for such concurrent resolution of events.

4 Exception Handling in MoCA

This section presents our context-aware exception handling model and its MoCA implementation, which deal with the problems discussed in Sections 3.2 – 3.6. Our current approach basically supports the notion of *exceptional context* (Section 3.2) and *different levels of handling scopes* (Section 3.3) to treat the limitations of conventional (Section 2.1) APIs and mechanisms provided by existing context-aware middleware systems, such as proactive detection (Section 3.5) and concurrent resolution (Section 3.6).

Exceptional contexts. The goal of exceptional contexts is to facilitate the definition of exceptional situations in applications that have a great number of devices and sensors that collect information for a specific purpose. An exceptional context corresponds to an undesirable or dangerous set of conditions pertaining to different contexts. They can be associated with one specific user, application's agents, or mobile devices.

Scope nesting: protected device(s), regions, or groups. In order to support a modular context-aware approach for error propagation, exceptions can be caught by scopes at four different levels: a device, a group (of devices), a proxy server, and a region. In our MoCA implementation, the central MoCA server, where the CIS and LIS services (Section 2.2) are located, is also treated as an exception handling scope. To illustrate these types of handling scopes, Figure 5 depicts how scopes of different types cover different elements of our AmI case study (Section 3.1). Device and server scopes comprise basic operational units of the context-aware system, which allows the exception handler functionality to be encapsulated into the scope of its own unit (device or server).

Group-based scopes. Group scope encompasses a set of devices which are defined by the application to support mobile cooperative handling of an exception amongst the device's agents pertaining to that group. This kind of scope is not directly related to any spatial relationships, and it makes it possible to insert or remove elements from the scope according to application necessity. Thus software agents can autonomously join and leave a group. For example, the agents acting on behalf of heat maintainers (Section 3.1) can form a specific group, as when heating-related exceptions are raised all of them may be notified.

Region-based scopes. Differently from the three first ones, a region scope has a more dynamic behavior to identify the devices that are part of the scope. In our implementation, this scope is strongly related to the MoCA LIS service (Section 2.2) as it provides a reference mechanism that allows a device be aware of its neighbors.

Volatile exception interface. In the AmI application, devices can enter and leave a region scope. A device movement also characterizes a change in the exception handling scope. In other words, whenever a device moves from a physical region X to Y, it automatically moves from the region-based handling scope X to Y. Hence this movement encompasses the context-sensitive change of the exceptional conditions that the device can handle. The mobile devices encountered in the new region can also influence the list of possible exceptions being raised in collaborations. It implies that exception interfaces in mobile collaborative applications may vary according to new contexts and collaboration opportunities. Such volatile exception interfaces motivate the need for some source of proactive exception handling (Section 3.5). Note that this requirement cannot be easily met by the traditional distributed systems, where the exception interface associated with each collaborative component is well-known in advance.

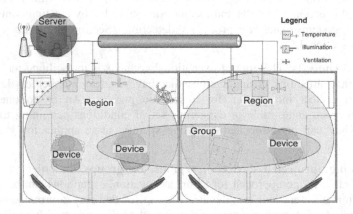

Fig. 5. Different scope levels: Device, Region, Group, Server

Region hierarchy. Moreover, region scope can be organized in a hierarchy fashion in which is possible to define that, for example, *Office 1* is part of *Offices*, and subsequently, *Offices* is part of *Computing Dep.* that is also part of *University* region. This hierarchy allows a specific handler or exception for a specific region or sub-region to be defined. To support hierarchy arrangement, users should define the relationship between LIS symbolic regions and SRM hierarchy tree (Section 2.2). This can be done by the MoCA API.

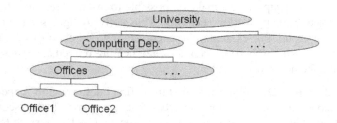

Fig. 6. Scope hierarchy definition

An exceptional context example. As discussed in Section 3, a device's agent suddenly detects that the temperature is exceeding the maximum limit, and then it infers that there is a fault in the mobile heating system. In this situation, the device should throw and propagate an exception to inform the other mobile users and the heater support about the problem. This step is done by the code shown in Figure 7. The *UnableToHeat* exception is created and thrown automatically when the constraint condition *"Temperature < 15"* is satisfied.

Context-aware error propagation. It also specifies that it needs to be propagated to a set of scopes. To define the sequence of exception propagation, the user must use the *propagateTo* method. This method receives as parameter the scope reference, the sequence number, and also the condition constant. The scope reference determines for which scope the exceptional context will be propagated, the sequence number, and in which order. Scope constant defines the propagation policy in which the error propagation will occur; it determines when the exception needs to propagated: whether when none (NONE value), one (ONE value) or all handlers (ALL value) were found and successfully executed to deal with this exception. For instance, in Figure 7, *UnableToHeat* will firstly propagate to the region and group. If none of them handles this exception, it is delivered to the server scope.

```
UnableToHeat unaheat = new UnableToHeat("Temperature < 15");
unaheat. propagateTo((RegionScope.getInstance(),1, Scope.NONE);
unaheat.propagateTo((RegionScope.getInstance("HeatMaintainer")
                    ,1,Scope.NONE);
unaheat.propagateTo((ServerScope.getInstance("MainServer"),2);
unaheat.getContext().setStringProperty("HeaterType","Electric");
unaheat.getContext().setStringProperty("Brand","HeaterCompanyA");
```

Fig. 7. Device code: throwing exception

Contextual information propagation and context-aware selection of handlers. In addition, the *UnableToHeat* exceptional context can carry information related to the exceptional occurrence. This may include the operation status of the thermostat, the heater type, and also the heater brand. This contextual information is carried with the propagated exception to allow the exception mechanism to select an appropriate context-aware handler for a specific exception.

Context-sensitive handlers. In order to handle the *UnableHeat* exception, four handlers are defined in different scopes. The first one deals with the university maintenance group; it is defined by each maintainer device and informs each one if the heaters related to the offices have a problem. Figure 8 describes (i) the *BrandSupport* handler definition and also (ii) its association with the maintainer group of users. To define a handler in our mechanism it is necessary to extend the *Handler* abstract class. This class requires the implementation of the *verifyContextCondition* and *execute* abstract methods defined in the API of our mechanism. The first method performs verification if the exceptional context is really appropriate for this handler and the second one executes the handler functionality. For instance, in our case study, each maintainer employee is responsible for a specific university region and also for a specific type of heating. For this reason, there is a handler for each employee with appropriate conditions. Therefore, when an exception is caught, the mechanism executes *verifyContextCondition* for each handler defined in that scope. If this method returns *true*, the mechanism invokes *execute*, but if not, the mechanism follows to the next defined handler. The purpose of this approach is to promote extra flexibility that supports the definition of context-aware handlers. After the handler definition, Figure 8 depicts the scope group definition and its association with the handler. To deal with *UnableHeat* exception, each maintainer device gets an instance of the *HeatMaintainer* scope group and adds itself to this scope. Thus, whenever *UnableToHeat* was propagated to *HeatMaintainer*, each device can carry out the exceptional context through its context-aware handlers (Ex.: *BrandSupport*).

```
//(i) BrandSupport handler definition
public class BrandSupport extends Handler {
   public boolean verifyContextCondition(){
      SimpleContext simple =getException().getContext().find(
                        "Computing Dep","HeaterType = 'Ceramic'");
      if (simple != null) return true;
      else return false;
   }
   public boolean execute(){
      makeAppointment();
   }
 }
}
            . . .
//(ii) association the handler with the maintainer group scope.
BrandSupport suppCeramic = BrandSupport(unaheat);
DeviceGroupScope groupScope = DeviceGroupScope.
         getInstance("HeatMaintainer");
groupScope.addDeviceList(this.getMyDevice());
groupScope.attachHandler(suppCeramic);
         . . .
```

Fig. 8. Group scope definition

The second approach to handling *UnableToHeat* is to inform the fire brigade about a more dangerous situation that is potentially going on (Figure 9). This is done by the mobile agents that have subscriptions in all maintainer groups. The agent defines the *DangerousHeaterFail* exception that deals with the *University* region, temperature and thermostat information which can ignite combustion.

```
DangerousHeaterFail dangerfail = new
      DangerousHeaterFail("(UnableToHeat.Thermostat='noanswer')and
                  (UnableToHeat.Region= Temperatura.Region")and
                  (Temperatura.value > 30)");
FireBrigade avoidfire = FireBrigade(dangerfail);
DeviceGroupScope groupScope = DeviceGroupScope.
         getInstance("HeatMaintainer");
groupScope.addDeviceList(getMyVirtualDevice());
groupScope.attachHandler(avoidfire);
```

Fig. 9. Group scope for mobile agent

There is a need for a mechanism ensuring that the temperature is really coming from the correct region when the environment contains a huge number of sensors that supply temperature information. For this reason, the user can define a combination of the constraints that compare the exception and temperature source region. This comparison does not use the LIS mechanism to support hierarchical regions; once we want the exact regions, not "super" regions, as for instance, *University* is equal to *Computing Dep.*

```
BeAwareException awarex = new BeAwareException ();
awarex.addContext(device.getRegion());
NotifyUsers ntusers = new NotifyUsers(awarex);
RegionScope regionScope = RegionScope.getInstance();
regionScope.attachHandler(ntusers);
```

Fig. 10. Region scope definition

To be aware of what is happening in the office, the user device needs to define the exception shown in Figure 10. This exception represents all exception occurrences that come from its own current region. It is associated with a handler that informs the user about the current problem.

```
UnableToHeat uncatch = new UnableToHeat();
MakExternal makexternal = new MakExternal(uncatch);
ServerScope serverScope = ServerScope.getInstance("MainServer");
serverScope.attachHandler(makexternal);
```

Fig. 11. Server scope definition

As we can see in Figure 7, if none of the devices that are part of the group scope handle the UnableToHeat exception, it will be propagated to the server scope. To deal with this exception, Figure 11 illustrates the exception and server scope definition. The MakExternal handler creates an external request to fix the problem that no internal maintainer is able to satisfy.

Proactive Handling and Propagation. However, if the system propagates the exception as proactive in order to handle the unforeseen exception, one of the officemates could receive it and start a collaborative activity to search for an adequate handler for this exception. In this situation, the receiver is going to collaborate with other users devices to deal with exception and, for instance, perform the first measures while the maintainer does not arrive. Figure 12 depicts a proactive exception definition.

```
UnableToHeat unaheat = new UnableToHeat();
Unaheat.propagateAsProactive(RegionScope.getInstance("neighborhood"),
                             2, Scope.NONE);
                            . . . .
```

Fig. 12. Proactive exception definition

The main difference from Figure 7 is the *propagateAsProactive* method. This method propagates (using *throw*) the *PulseOximetryError* exception to all devices available in the neighborhood region whether any agent has dealt with this exception before. This propagation allows an expansion into a new collaboration group and also supports a dynamic mechanism to discover new handlers. For instance, the next destination of the exception - the neighborhood group - does not know how to handle it. In order to deal with it, the neighborhood group starts a collaborative activity to discover and to execute possible handlers.

Due to the possibility of many devices start proactive propagation of exceptions, this functionality can be activated or not, according to the context conditions. For instance, an user can active proactive treatment of exceptions for a specific room or fire alarm conditions. This measure can avoid the over-treatment of exceptions that are not related to the device interest.

```
FireException firexe = new
FireException("Exception('HighTemperature')
    |(1)|Exception('SmokeDetection')");
firexe.propagateTo(ServerScope.getInstance("MainServer"),1,null);
```

Fig. 13. Concurrent exception definition

Concurrent exception resolution. Context-Aware applications can concurrently throw many different exceptions that may or may not be related, but in many cases these exceptions mean the occurrence of a more serious abnormal situation. In this way, Figure 13 depicts a slice of code which allows the programmer to define all concurrently raised exceptions and to subsequently propagate a concerted exception which best captures the particular exceptional situation. Thus two exceptions *HighTemperature* and *SmokeDetection* are caught and resolved into the composite

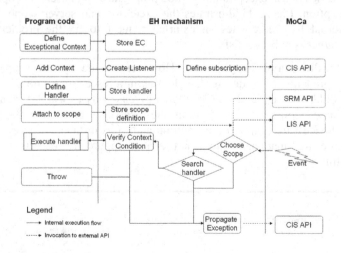

Fig. 14. Different views of the exception mechanism

exception *FireException* that represents the simultaneous occurrence of both exceptions. To define such concurrent exceptions, our approach supports the following operators: *simultaneous* - ‖ (two exceptions occurring exactly at the same time); *simultaneous with a time frame* – |(X)| (where, for example, X = 1 means one minute time frame); *follow* to define a sequential occurrence within a time frame – FOLLOWED(X) (where, X = 5 means the occurrence of the second event happened 5 minutes after the first event); *interaction* occurrences like HighTemperature FOLLOWED (INTERACTION(FireAlert,3)).

Finally, Figure 14 shows three dimensions in which our exception handling mechanism is applied: the application elements, the internal mechanism components, and the MoCA components. For example, the application programmer needs to define application-specific exceptional contexts, add contextual information, define context-aware handlers, and attach them to the scopes. In MoCA exceptional contexts are defined in the CIS as a set of subscriptions and listeners supplied by the MoCA API.

5 Discussion and Related Work

Although our current implementation (Section 4) supports a heterogeneous set of handling scopes, their granularity may not be always appropriate. To this end we are planning to adopt role-like abstractions, as supported by the CAMA tuplespace-based middleware [6], in order to allow handlers to be attached the specific agent actions or plans. Furthermore we plan to extend our mechanism to support code mobility in addition to physical mobility. In our previous work [18, 19], we have combined reflective and tuple-space middleware features (Section 2.1) in order to smoothly support code migration.

Developing advanced exception handling mechanisms suitable for multi agent systems is an area that needs serious efforts from the research community even though there have been a number of interesting results. A scheme in [17] supports exception handling in systems consisting of agents that cooperate by sending asynchronous messages. This scheme allows handlers to be associated with services, agents and roles, and supports concurrent exception resolution. Paper [22] identifies several typical failure cases in building context-based collaborative applications and proposes an exception handling mechanism for dealing with them.

An approach in [24] is based on defining a specialized service fully responsible for coordinating all exception handling activities in multi agent systems. Although this approach does not scale well, it supports separation of the normal system behavior from the abnormal one as the service curries all fault tolerance activities: it detects errors, finds the most appropriate recovery actions using a set of heuristics and executes them. As opposed to the last three schemes above which do not explicitly introduce the concept of the exception handling context (scope), the CAMA framework [6] (introduced in Section 2.1) supports the concept of (nested) scopes, which confine the errors and to which exception handlers are attached. However, CAMA and the other mechanisms mentioned above do not support a fully context-aware exception handling, as supported by our approach (Section 4). In particular, they do not implement context-aware selection of handlers, proactive exception handling, and the definition of exceptional contexts.

6 Conclusion

Error handling in mobile agent-based applications needs to be context sensitive. This paper discussed our experience in incorporating exception handling in several prototype MoCA applications. This allowed us to elicit a set of requirements and define a novel context-aware exception handling model, which consists of: (i) explicit support for specifying "exceptional contexts", (ii) context-sensitive search for exception handlers, (iii) multi-level handling scopes that meet new abstractions (such as groups), and abstractions in the underlying context-aware middleware, such as devices, regions, and proxy servers, (iv) context-aware error propagation, (v) contextual exception handlers, (vi) proactive exception handling , and (vii) concurrent resolution of exceptions. We have also presented an implementation of this mechanism in the MoCA architecture, and illustrated its use in an AmI agent-based application.

Acknowledgments. This work is partially supported by European Commission as part of the grant IST-2-004349: European Network of Excellence on Aspect-Oriented Software Development (AOSD-Europe), 2004-2008, for Nelio Cacho and Alessandro Garcia. Alexander Romanovsky is supported by the IST RODIN project.

References

[1] Abowd, G. D., Dey, A. K., Brown, P. J., Davies, N., Smith, M., and Steggles, P. 1999. Towards a Better Understanding of Context and Context-Awareness. In *Proceedings of the 1st international Symposium on Handheld and Ubiquitous Computing* (Karlsruhe, Germany, September 27 - 29, 1999). H. Gellersen, Ed. Lecture Notes In Computer Science, vol. 1707. Springer-Verlag, London, 304-307.

[2] Abowd, G. et al. 1999. Towards a Better Understanding of Context and Context-Awareness. In *Proc. of the 1st Intl. Symp. on Handheld and Ubiquitous Computing* (Karlsruhe, September 1999, LNCS 1707. Springer, 304-307.

[3] Dey, A. 2001. Understanding and Using Context. *Personal Ubiquitous Comput.* 5, 1 (Jan. 2001), 4-7.

[4] Schilit, B. N, Adams, R. and Want, R. Context-aware computing applications. In *Proc. Workshop on Mobile Computing Systems and Applications.* IEEE, December 1994.

[5] Davidyuk, O. et al. Context-aware middleware for mobile multimedia applications. In *Proc. of the 3rd international Conference on Mobile and Ubiquitous Multimedia* (College Park, Maryland, October 27 - 29, 2004). vol. 83. ACM Press, New York, NY, 213-220.

[6] Iliasov, A. and Romanovsky, A. CAMA: Structured Communication Space and Exception Propagation Mechanism for Mobile Agents. In *ECOOP-EHWS 2005*, 19 July 2005, Glasgow.

[7] Muthusamy, V. et al. Publisher Mobility in Distributed Publish/Subscribe Systems. In *Fourth International Workshop on Distributed Event-Based Systems* (DEBS) (ICDCSW'05), 2005.

[8] Cugola, G. and Cote, J. E. M. On Introducing Location Awareness in Publish-Subscribe Middleware. In *Fourth International Workshop on Distributed Event-Based Systems* (DEBS) (ICDCSW'05), 2005.

[9] Gelernter, D. Generative communication in Linda. *ACM Trans. Program. Lang. Syst.* 7, 1 (Jan. 1985), 80-112.

[10] Blair, G. et al. An architecture for next generation middleware. In Proceedings of the IFIP International Conference on Distributed Systems Platforms and Open Distributed Processing. London: Springer-Verlag, (1998).

[11] Tripathi, A. Challenges designing next-generation middleware systems. *Commun. ACM,*ACM Press, v. 45, n. 6, (2002), p. 39–42.

[12] Smith, B. C. Procedural Reflection in Programming Languages. These (Phd) — Massachusetts Institute of Technology, (1982).

[13] Roman, M., Kon, F. and Campbell, R.H. Reflective Middleware: From Your Desk to Your Hand. In *IEEE Distributed Systems Online Journal*, 2(5), (2001).

[14] Sacramento, V. et al. MoCA: A Middleware for Developing Collaborative Applications for Mobile Users. In *IEEE Distributed Systems Online*, vol. 5, no. 10, 2004.

[15] Sharples, S., Callaghan, V. and Clarke, G. A Multi-Agent Architecture for Intelligent Building Sensing and Control. In *International Sensor Review Journal*, May 1999.

[16] Shadbolt, N. Ambient intelligence. In *IEEE Trans. Intell. Transp. Syst.*, vol. 18, no. 4, pp. 2-3, Jul. – Aug. 2003.

[17] Souchon, F. et al. Improving exception handling in multi-agent systems. In C. Lucena et al (Eds), *Software Engineering for Multi-Agent Systems II*, number 2940. Feb. 2004.

[18] Silva, O., Garcia, A. and Lucena, C. The Reflective Blackboard Pattern: Architecting Large-Scale Multi-Agent Systems. In: *Software Engineering for Large-Scale Multi-Agent Systems*. Springer, LNCS 2603, April 2003, pp. 76-97.

[19] Silva, O., Garcia, A. and Lucena, C. T-Rex: A Reflective Tuple Space Environment for Dependable Mobile Agent Systems. In *Proc. IEEE Workshop on Wireless Communication and Mobile Computation* (WCSF'01), Recife, Brazil, Aug 2001.

[20] Garcia, A. F., Rubira, C. M. F., Romanovsky, A. and Xu, J. A Comparative Study of Exception Handling Mechanisms for Building Dependable Object Oriented Software: *Journal of Systems and Software. 59(2001), 197-222.*

[21] Goodenough, J. B. 1975. Exception handling: issues and a proposed notation. Commun. ACM 18, 12 (Dec. 1975), 683-696.

[22] Tripathi, A. Kulkarni, D. and Ahmed, T. Exception Handling Issues in Context Aware Collaboration Systems for Pervasive Computing. In Romanovsky, A., Dony, C., Knudsen, J. L., Tripathi, A. (Eds.) Developing Systems that Handle Exceptions. Proc. ECOOP 2005 Workshop on Exception Handling in Object Oriented Systems. TR 05-050. LIRMM. Montpellier-II University. 2005. July. France.

[23] Capra, L. Emmerich, W. and Mascolo, C. CARISMA: Context-Aware Reflective Middleware System for Mobile Applications. *IEEE Transactions on Software Engineering* 29(10): pp. 929--944, Oct 2003.

[24] Klein, M. and Dellarocas, C. Exception Handling in Agent Systems. In *Proc. of the 3rd Int. Conference on Autonomous Agents*, Seattle, WA, May 1-5, 1999. Pp. 62-6

[25] Anderson, T. and Lee, P. A. *Fault Tolerance: Principles and Practice.* Prentice-Hall, 2nd edition, 1990.

[26] Keen, A. W. and Olsson, R. A. Exception Handling during Asynchronous Method Invocation. In *Proc. 8th international Euro-Par Conference on Parallel Processing* (August 27 - 30, 2002). B. Monien and R. Feldmann, Eds. Lecture Notes in Computer Science, vol. 2400. Springer-Verlag, London, 656-660.

[27] Raje, R. R., William, H. I. William and Boyles, B. An Asynchronous Remote Method Invocation (ARMI) Mechanism for Java. In *Concurrency: Practice and Experience*, vol. 9. John Wiley & Sons, 1207-1211, 1997.

[28] Caromel, D. and Chazarain, G. Robust exception handling in an asynchronous environment. In Romanovsky, A., Dony, C., Knudsen, J. L., Tripathi, A. (Eds.) Developing Systems that Handle Exceptions. Proc. ECOOP 2005 Workshop on Exception Handling in Object Oriented Systems. TR 05-050. LIRMM. Montpellier-II University. 2005. July. France.

[29] Roman, G., Julien, C., and Huang, Q. 2002. Network abstractions for context-aware mobile computing. In Proceedings of the 24th international Conference on Software Engineering (Orlando, Florida, May 19 - 25, 2002). ICSE '02. ACM Press, New York, NY, 363-373.

Exception Diagnosis Architecture for Open Multi-Agent Systems

Nazaraf Shah[1], Kuo-Ming Chao[2], and Nick Godwin[2]

[1] Software Engineering Research Group,
Sheffield Hallam University,
Sheffield, UK
n.shah@shu.ac.uk
[2] DSM Research Group,
Department of Computer and Network Systems
Coventry University, Coventry UK
{k.chao, a.n.godwin}@coventry.ac.uk

Abstract. Multi-Agent Systems (MAS) are collection of loosely coupled intelligent agents. These systems operate in a distributed, highly dynamic, unpredictable and unreliable environment in order to meet their overall goals. Agents in such an environment are vulnerable to different types of run time exceptions. It is necessary to have an effective exception diagnosis and resolution mechanism in place in order to ensure reliable interactions between agents. In this paper, we propose novel exception diagnosis architecture for open MAS. The proposed architecture classifies the runtime exceptions and diagnoses the underlying causes of exceptions using a heuristic classification technique. The proposed architecture is realised in terms of specialised exception diagnosing agents known as sentinel agents. The sentinel agents act as delegates of problem solving agents and mediate interactions between them.

1 Introduction

Open multi-agent systems (MAS) are decentralised and highly distributed systems that consist of a large number of loosely coupled autonomous agents. It is difficult to manage such systems in a highly dynamic environment where agents enter and leave the system at their own will. Open MAS's are vulnerable to different kinds of exceptions. An exception in an MAS is regarded as an unexpected behaviour encountered by an agent during its execution. Exceptions may occur for a number of reasons such as: program bugs; operating system resources not being available; I/O errors; unexpected conditions within a participating element; a message lost; protocol violations; malicious interference with normal operation; deadline failure; deadlock; conflicting attitudes exhibited by agents; service errors, and so on. Diagnosing the underlying causes of these exceptions is of paramount importance in dealing with them effectively at runtime. Diagnosing exceptions in such systems is a complex task due to the distributed nature of their data and their control. This complexity is exacerbated in open environments where independently developed autonomous agents interact with each other in order to achieve their goals. Inevitably, exceptions will occur in such

R. Choren et al. (Eds.): SELMAS 2006, LNCS 4408, pp. 77–98, 2007.

MAS and these exceptions can arise at one of three levels, namely environmental, knowledge or social levels.

Exception detection, diagnosis and resolution is not a well addressed area in open MAS research, much of the work has been done in closed and reliable environments without taking into account the challenges of an open environment. In this paper, we address the monitoring and diagnostic aspects of the exception handling process.

A few well known approaches have been proposed by MAS researchers in order to address this issue [4, 5, 8]. These approaches generally fall into two categories, those using external agents called sentinel agents that monitor problem solving agents' interactions and those that are based on introspection and provide an agent with the ability to monitor its own runtime behaviour and detect failures. Each of these approaches uses some form of redundancy. Proposals can also be categorised as either domain dependent or domain independent approaches. A brief overview of these approaches is given in section 2.

Our proposed architecture takes the sentinel agent approach using specialised exception diagnosis agents to diagnose exceptions in open MAS. A sentinel agent is assumed to be infallible. The sentinel agents are equipped with knowledge of observable abnormal situations, their underlying causes, and resolution strategies associated with these causes. The sentinel agents apply a Heuristic Classification (HC) [1] approach and collect related data from affected agents in order to uncover the underlying causes of the observed symptoms. As far as we know no approach exists in the literature that deals with exceptions at these three levels nor does any existing approach deal with a plan's action failure using plan abstract knowledge [2]. The proposed architecture is FIPA [3] compliant and can be integrated into any FIPA compliant MAS.

The rest of the paper is organized as follows: In Section 2 we describe existing mechanisms for exception diagnosis and resolution. In section 3 we provide a brief discussion of our proposed architecture. In section 4 we describe case study and performance analysis. Finally section 5 provides discussion and concludes the paper.

2 Related Work

Exception handling (detection, diagnosis and resolution) is not a well addressed area in open MAS research. A few well known approaches have been proposed by MAS researchers in order to address the issue of exception handling.

Hägg [4] proposes the use of sentinel agents that build the models of interacting agents by monitoring their interaction and intervene on the detection of an exception according to given guidelines. The sentinel agents copy the world model of the problem solving agents, thus giving sentinel agents access to the problem solving agent's mind. Such mind reading has serious consequences for the autonomy of an agent.

Kaminka and Tambe [5] propose an approach called 'social attentive monitoring' to diagnose and resolve exceptions in a team of problem solving agents. This approach involves the monitoring of peers, during execution of their team and their individual plans and the detection, and diagnosis of failures by comparing their own state with the state of their monitored team-mates. The monitoring of agents is external to them, but there is no sentinel agent involved in this monitoring, the responsibility of monitoring is delegated to one or more of the team-mate agents.

Kumar and Cohen [6] propose the use of redundant agents in order to deal with broker agent failure. This approach only deals with failure detection of agents in a team of agents.

Horling et al. [7] suggest the use of a domain independent technique to diagnose and resolve inter-agent dependencies. Their work is concerned with the issue of performance using situation specific coordination strategies. In contrast our approach deals with abstract action failure diagnosis in plans.

Klein et al's effort [8, 9] is the first step towards open MAS exception detection, diagnosis and resolution. They argue that domain independent sentinel agents can be used to monitor the interactions among problem solving agents in an open MAS. Their sentinel agents deal with protocol related exceptions only, without any regard to the application domain. Although this approach is a step towards domain independent exception handling in open MAS's, it has its own limitations. It is inclined towards reactive agent systems without any regard to the mental attitudes (Belief, Desire, and Intention) of the agent.

Schroeder et al. [10, 11] introduce a model based multi-agent system approach to the diagnosis of faults in distributed systems. They used what they call a vivid agent [12] for diagnostic purposes. The diagnostic agents continue to monitor the behaviour of their associated subsystems. When exceptional behaviour is detected the agents run tests to diagnose the underlying cause of the exceptional behaviour and may communicate their findings to other agents. Diagnostic agents must be capable of running diagnostic tests on receipt of requests from their peers and then communicate their findings back to the requesting agents. This approach is suitable for the diagnosis of faults in technical systems such as telecommunication networks, computer networks and manufacturing systems, where mathematical models of devices are easier to construct.

Fröhlich et al. [13] introduce a multi-agent based framework for the diagnosis of spatial distributed technical systems. This agent based approach decomposes the system to be diagnosed into a set of subsystems. Each subsystem is allocated to a diagnostic agent. The diagnostic agents have detailed knowledge of their associated subsystems and abstract knowledge of their neighbouring subsystems. A diagnostic agent uses its declarative knowledge of the system description to diagnose its subsystem independently. In situations where a diagnostic agent is unable to diagnose the cause of the observed fault, it triggers a cooperation process.

Guiagoussou et al. [14] applied a multi-agent diagnostic approach to diagnose faults in cellular switching systems. Fault diagnosis is provided by a group of agents. A *Correlation Agent* reduces the number of relevant data related to some parameters thus providing a simplified global view of the problem. A *Diagnostic Tests Agent* selects the test to be performed and requests a capable monitoring agent to perform the tests. A *Known Faults Recognition Agent* is a case based reasoning agent. It is responsible for the recognition of fault cases from its knowledge of previous experience. This approach uses a set of agents that cooperatively makes fault diagnosis from alarms and event flows. The ARCHON project [15] involves the diagnosis of several real world distributed applications. It is an application driven approach and focuses on problems of global coordination and coherence. Exception diagnosis is treated as a part of managing global coordination not as a problem in its own right.

Roos et al. [16, 17] presented an approach and distributed protocol to diagnose faults using spatially distributed knowledge of the system. This approach is realised by an MAS of diagnostic agents, where each agent has a model of its associated subsystem.

Letia et al. [18] present an approach to diagnosing faults in distributed systems. They developed a diagnosis ontology to represent and reason about system elements. The diagnosis agents work by using the ontology both for monitoring and for cooperation. Diagnosis agent plans are logically divided into two groups of plans; one that diagnoses the fault at a local level; the second deals with cooperation with neighbours if the fault is not verified locally. This approach uses BDI agents instead of extended logic programming agents [10, 11].

Thottan et al. [19] introduce an agent based approach to detect and diagnose potential network problems and initiate recovery. The agents reside on network nodes, and monitor a set of the management information base (MIB) variables that are pertinent for anomaly detection. The agents use a statistical approach to generate alarms at variable levels.

Venkatraman et al. [20] present a generic approach to detecting the non-compliance of agents to coordination protocols in an open MAS. It uses model checking to determine whether the present execution satisfies the specifications of the underlying coordination protocol. This approach is limited to one class of exceptions and its does not include its diagnosis and resolution methods.

Fedoruk et al. [21] introduce a technique for fault tolerance in MAS's by replicating individual agents within the system. This approaches uses proxy-like structure to manage agents in a replicate group. A group proxy acts as an interface between replicates in a group and the rest of the MAS. This arrangement makes the replicate group appear as a single entity. When an active agent fails, its proxy will detect the failure, activate a new replicate and transfer the current state to the new replicate.

Mishra et al. [22] present fault-tolerant protocols for detecting communication or node failure and for recovery of lost mobile agents. Every mobile agent is associated with an agent watchdog, which monitors the functioning of the agent and manages the agent migration. The watchdog agent uses checkpointing and rollback recovery [23] for recovering the lost agent's state. The approach targets the mobile agent's mobility failure related issues only.

Xu et al. [24] introduce a fault management technique for MAS's. This is an event based approach requiring agents to report on changes regarding their own state and the environment state by emitting event messages to an event manager. The event manager is equipped with the knowledge of the patterns for correct and faulty sequences of events. When an event is detected which deviates from a standard pattern, diagnostic and corrective actions are initiated. This approach requires all agents in a given MAS to report their activities to a central event manager. The event manager can be a non agent component.

Rutogi et al. [25] introduce an approach to detect, diagnose and handle semantic exceptions in MAS's. This approach is based on high-level abstractions such as commitments, process meta-models, agents' behaviour models, and a persistent execution architecture. Semantic exceptions are handled by formulating a number of commitment patterns in an MAS. The commitment patterns are translated into rules and executed by agents based on their roles. The general structure includes a way of deciding how to react to other agents when a commitment is revoked or modified by an agent. On detecting an exception, a single agent decides about the modification/cancellation of an associated commitment and then informs the concerned agents about the result. This approach does not consider the coordination related issues and is mainly focused on the issue of task result dissatisfaction.

Sundresh [26] introduces the concept of semantic reliability in intelligent agents. He focuses on semantic related issues of information exchange between agents since an agent's behaviour is influenced by the information it receives and its interpretation. The underlying idea is to facilitate a uniform interpretation of information among agents in order to facilitate their correct function. The concept is realised by a common ontology. This approach ensures the uniform interpretation of information among agents without any consideration of exceptions that may occur within agents.

Chia et al. [27] address the issues related to agents' coordination in distributed scheduling. They call the agents' undesired behaviours in such an environment 'distractions' and 'poaching'. Their mechanism requires the scheduling agents to model the likely future actions of other agents in addition to states of the resources. This closed system approach focuses on enhancing the quality of the schedule produced by the agents.

Youssefimir et al. [28] address the issue of resource contention in MAS's by allowing agents to follow different strategies consistent with equilibrium. This approach is concerned with dealing with the problem of suboptimal resource usage, which is a performance related issue rather than an exception on the part of the agents.

Tripathi et al. [29] propose an exception handling model for mobile agent systems. This model is based on the idea of separating and encapsulating the exception handling knowledge into a special agent called a guardian agent. The guardian agent acts as a global exception handler for a set of agents. The guardian agent deals with the unhandled exceptions of the agents. It comes into action on receipt of an exceptional event. It then executes precompiled exception handling strategies in response to the exceptional event. This approach typically deals with exceptional issues associated with agent mobility.

Platon et al. [30] provide a literature survey on exception handling in MAS. They propose that exploitation of agent's proactivity and context can provide better exception handling in MAS. They also identified that an effective exception handling mechanism should take into account agent paradigm characteristics such as autonomy, distribution, openness and proactiveness. Their proposed approach uses an event based notification system that enriches the agents' context with relevant information. Our approach takes into account autonomy, proactivity and openness characteristics of MAS. We use sentinel agents to diagnose a wider classes of exceptions, instead of enriching agents' contexts to take advantages of some favourable situations. Currently our research focuses on diagnosing the underlying causes of runtime exceptions to enable selection and execution of effective resolution strategies.

None of this work deals with classification of exceptions, plan failure action diagnosis in open MAS's, neither does it consider the cognitive properties of the agents while making diagnosis.

3 Proposed Approach

In this section we discuss our proposed architecture and examine its key capabilities in relation to exception diagnosis in an open MAS. We will also give a detailed description of the architectural components and their functionalities. The proposed architecture is realised in terms of agents known as sentinel agents. Sentinel agents are based on belief desire and intention (BDI) model. The belief component represents the information the agent has about its environment and its capabilities, desire represents the state of affair the agent want to achieve and intention corresponds to the desires the agent is committed to achieve.

Our proposed architecture enables the real time exception detection and diagnosis in an MAS operating in a complex and dynamic environment, by monitoring the agents' interactions. A sentinel agent can also start a diagnostic process on receiving a complaint from its associated problem-solving agent or from another sentinel agent regarding a disputed contract.

3.1 Open MAS Exception Diagnosis Architecture Requirements

In order to detect and identify exceptions at various levels in an open MAS, the diagnosis system should meet the following three requirements.

- Firstly, the system should be able to identify the causes of the exceptions at three levels, namely environment, knowledge and social levels, as well as being able to identify the originating cause of the exception. Thus, the system should have a diagnosis mechanism that can reason about the set of observable symptoms resulting from potential underlying causes.
- Secondly, the system should not violate the property of autonomy associated with agents. Agents must retain control over their individual states. The diagnosis mechanism should be conducted in non-invasive manner to ensure the autonomy of affected agents. However, agents should provide state information cooperatively on receiving requests from the diagnosis mechanism.
- Finally, the system should minimise the agent's workload in the process of identifying exceptions. The ability to identify exceptions represents additional functionality to an agent, and it should be separated from the normal functions that the agent provides, in order to facilitate system maintenance.

The above requirements are not intended to represent an exhaustive list of desirable characteristics for an agent oriented exception handling mechanism, but rather they represent the minimal requirements for such a system, which the architecture proposed in this paper achieves.

In next sections we discuss our proposed exception diagnosis architecture that meets the above requirements and attempts to address the issues of exception diagnosis in an open MAS.

3.2 Architecture

The proposed architecture [31, 32] is shown in Figure 1, and its key components are described below. The purpose of the architecture is to provide a structure for the detection and diagnosis of runtime exceptions in an open MAS. The proposed architecture is realised as a sentinel agent and each problem solving agent is assigned a sentinel agent. This arrangement offloads from agents the burden of implementing the complex exception diagnosis capabilities. It results in an MAS composed of problem solving agents and sentinel agents.

The sentinel agents are provided by the MAS infrastructure owner and treated as trusted agents, which are assumed to be truthful. The sentinel agents require the problem solving agents to provide information cooperatively regarding their mental attitudes, whenever requested to during the exception detection and diagnosis process. This enables the sentinel agents to diagnose exceptions interactively and heuristically by asking questions from effected agents through ACL messages [33]. This means that the sentinels do not have direct access to the mental states of problem solving agents. The sentinels also reason using the knowledge of the role played by its associated agent in a given interaction. In this way sentinel agent knows the way an agent can possibly violate its role's responsibilities in a given coordination protocol. The sentinel agent is implemented as a heuristic classifier system for making exception diagnosis by applying a HC method. Exceptions that may have occurred in an agent

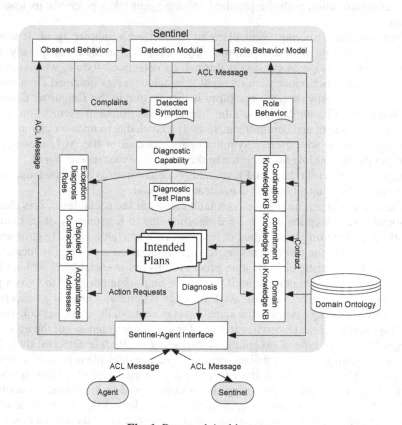

Fig. 1. Proposed Architecture

system are likely to manifest themselves at the social level if not dealt at their originating level (environment or knowledge). This requires specific knowledge about the
abstract domain, the coordination protocol and commitment strategy as well as
knowledge of faults and symptoms.

It is proposed that exceptions in MAS's are characterised at three levels, known as:
environmental level; knowledge level; and social level. Environmental exceptions are
those exceptions that occur within the internal environment of an agent and its associated software components. In procedural and object oriented programming models
invalid inputs are considered as environmental exceptions. The knowledge level exceptions are those exceptions that result from a wrong selection of action due to the
agent's outdated environment knowledge, or to a misunderstanding of a domain concept. Exceptions related to the malfunctioning of: an interaction channel; agent dependencies, and, organisational relationship, are classified as social exceptions.

When an agent joins an MAS, a sentinel agent with default functions is created and
assigned to it. Agent developers need to provide their agents with the ability to inform
the sentinel agent about their goals, plans, and also the ability to report on their mental
state. The sentinel agent is used as a delegate of the problem solving agent, and all
further communication with the problem solving agent takes place via its associated
sentinel.

When a problem solving agent plans to interact with another agent, it sends an
ACL message via its associated sentinel. The sentinel agent then detects any abnor-
malities in the message by passing it through its detection module, which compares
the agent's actual behaviour with its ideal role behaviour as obtained from the *Role
Behaviour Model*. Any detected symptom is then passed to the *Diagnosis Capability*.
The *Diagnostic Capability* applies the heuristic classification method on domain,
coordination protocol and commitment strategy knowledge to uncover any underlying
symptoms. If there are no error symptoms are detected in the ACL message, it is
passed via the *Sentinel-Agent Interface* to the sentinel of the receiver agent.

Diagnosis starts from the social level and proceeds towards the knowledge and environment levels using a heuristic classification method.

If the cause of a given symptom is a fault caused at the social level, it is classified
as a social level exception (e.g. missed deadline due to low priority of task) and the
heuristic classification process then determines its underlying cause (e.g. absence of
intention for doing the task) by asking the agent questions regarding its mental state.
In this case the heuristic classification process stops at the social level without investigating other levels. On other hand if the underlying assumptions of the given protocol are not violated, instead a "fail" ACL message is communicated. If an exception is
not classified as being caused at the social level exception, the classifier considers the
knowledge level and the environment level, for a possible diagnosis of the exception.

Regardless of the type of exception, if the *Detection Module* detects it then the *Diagnostic Capability* produces a diagnostic test, and executes plans from a set of applicable plans. The symptoms of the exception are heuristically classified as one of a
predefined set of abstract faults using: knowledge stored in its abstract domain, and,
the coordination protocol and commitment strategy knowledge bases. The abstract
fault is mapped to a diagnostic plan that contains a list of analysis actions to refine the
possible causes of an exception. The diagnostic plan may perform communication

with the effected agent or sentinels in order to reach a conclusion regarding the symptom presented by the *Detection Module*. Due to different levels of abstraction a diagnostic plan can represent, it may not be able to identify the cause by itself. It may trigger other diagnostic plans by posting exceptional events. This method takes advantage of heuristic classification, ACL, and commitment strategies to form an effective exception diagnostic system. If a sentinel agent is unable to find the cause of an exception then the sentinel agent alerts the system operator regarding this matter.

The following briefly describes the required knowledge bases and components of our proposed exception diagnosis architecture.

3.2.1 Observed Behaviour Module

This module contains the plans for checking the agent's current observed behaviour during each stage of an interaction. The observed behaviour consists of an ACL message. A sentinel agent may receive an ACL message from its associated agent or from another sentinel agent.

This module contains a plan to determine which messages need to go through the *Detection Module*. All messages that come from or go to problem solving agents are passed through the *Detection Module* for detection of possible abnormality in the message. On the other hand messages that are related to complaints are not passed to the *Detection Module*, because complaint events are taken as abnormal events and they do not need to be classified again by the sentinel agent. Such an exceptional event could be a complaint from an associated agent, when that agent finds that what it received was not what it expected.

3.2.2 Role Behaviour Model

This module provides a model of the role played by a problem solving agent and the behaviour associated with this role. The role that an agent can play in any FIPA compliant coordination protocol [34] can be classified as either an initiator or as a responder. This module provides the *Detection Module* with its information related to the expected behaviour of a role. It contains the implementation of FIPA standard interaction protocols. It also provides the *Detection Module* with relevant information and resources for creating a commitment instance and a state machine instance for the given interaction. This will be provided at the initiation of the interaction. It then assumes the responsibility for providing an expected behaviour for the role in the context of the given interaction. This enables the *Detection Module* to compare the expected behaviour of a role with the actual behaviour of the role.

3.2.3 Detection Module

This module is responsible for the detection of abnormal situations during an interaction. It provides a monitoring capability to a sentinel agent. It uses the *Observed Behaviour* and the *Role Behaviour Model* of the agent in order to discover the exceptional situations. It activates the *Diagnostic Capability* only after a symptom is detected in a problem solving agent's behaviour. In other words it acts as a monitor of message traffic coming toward or departing from a problem solving agent.

Figure 2 provides a detailed view of the operational semantics of this module. It shows lower level information flow and the interactions of this module with other components. It is not only monitoring the message traffic and deciding on correct or abnormal behaviour, but also manages the states of the state machines and the commitments. When an incoming message event is posted to the *Detection Module* by a plan within in the *Observed Behaviour*, the sentinel agent initialises and executes plans from a protocol monitoring plan library. The selected plan uses the knowledge of: coordination; the role of the problem solving agent, and, the current state of the commitment associated with this message.

If the message is valid in a current context, then it is passed to the *Sentinel-Agent* interface for delivery to the associated problem solving agent or to another sentinel agent. Otherwise an exceptional event containing information about the current message is posted to activate the *Diagnostic Capability*. The *Role's Intended Plan* is a plan to be executed in a give context. A new plan is initialised and executed each time a new message event is handled by the *Detection Module*.

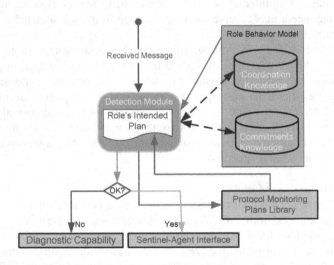

Fig. 2. Detection Module Information Flow and Interaction

3.2.4 Coordination Knowledge Base

In our implementation we use FIPA standard interaction protocols for managing interactions among independently developed autonomous agents. Any other mutually agreed upon coordination policies and protocols in a given domain may be implemented in the knowledge base structure to monitor the interactions governed by such additional protocols and policies. Sentinel agents do not learn and adopt themselves to new interaction protocols. The implementation of a new protocol is provided by the MAS infrastructure owner. Currently the coordination knowledge base contains the implementation of FIPA Request, FIPA Query-Ref and FIPA Contract Net protocols [34]. Other protocols can be added in this KB without disturbing the other components. The *Coordination Knowledge Base* also contains the information about the roles an agent may play in a given MAS. In our implementation we use a peer to peer organisational relationship among interacting agents; any other organisational relationships that may exist in an MAS can also be represented in a similar fashion.

The coordination knowledge base consists of state machines representing ongoing interactions. A state machine of each interaction based on an interaction protocol is maintained in the *BeliefSet* of a sentinel agent. The advantage of maintaining a state machine for an interaction in the *BeliefSet* is that the state machine is available during the life time of an interaction. Keeping a state machine in a plan results in a loss of state information after the plan exits. The state machine of each protocol is implemented by a Java class. A sentinel loads an object representing a given protocol's state machine at the start of each interaction. A sentinel agent uses a state machine according to the roles of its associated problem solving agent in an interaction.

3.2.5 Commitments Knowledge Base

This knowledge base contains the records of currently active commitments. Once an "agree" or "accept" proposal message is sent/received from a problem solving agent a commitment is created and added to this knowledge base. Each entry in this KB contains a data structure that represents the attributes of a give commitment, such as contract-id, initiator, responder, deadline and so on. The maintenance of the *Contracts KB* is carried out by the *Detection Module* and the *Diagnostic Capability*. Commitments are formed explicitly by exchanging information regarding an agreement being formed between agents and the conditions upon this agreement. Such commitments are known as social commitments. The commitments that an agent makes to itself are known as local commitments.

Every social commitment is formed based on a protocol known to the agents involved in the commitment. The chosen protocol provides the guidance for the creation, satisfaction and cancellation of a commitment. Agents are implicitly committed to interaction protocols they are employing when forming social commitments and explicitly committed to the performance of a task once an agreement is mutually made by the agents. Social commitments are also influenced by the social policies of

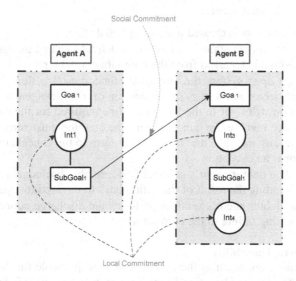

Fig. 3. Social and Local Commitments

an MAS and an agent's local policies. A social commitment between "Agent A" and "Agent B" and local commitments are depicted in Figure 3. Social commitment is shown by an arrow emanating from "Agent A" to "Agent B". Local commitments are shown by agents' internal selected intentions. Only social commitments are visible to sentinel agents, local commitments are know to individual agents only. The sentinel agents monitor social commitment only, monitoring of individual commitments is the responsibility of problem solving agents.

In the following we provide the description of roles involved in a social commitment and the operations allowed on it. These operations provide us a tool for maintaining social commitments in a dynamic and complex MAS environment.

a. Roles in Commitments
Each social commitment has two roles know as debtor and creditor roles [34].

Creditor: The initiator agent who seeks some action to be performed by a responder agent. A creditor is responsible for satisfying any condition that is placed by a responder, in order to finalise a deal.

Debtor: The agent who makes a commitment by making a promise to perform a requested action.

In our implementation we use initiator and responder in order to refer to creditor and debtor roles.

b. Commitment Operations
Singh [35] treats a commitment as a first class object and defines six different operations on a commitment object known as; *Create, Discharge, Cancel, Release, Delegate*, and *Assign*. We use the *Create, Cancel, Discharge* operations of a commitment as defined by Singh [34] and two of our proposed operations known as *Activate* and *Violate*.

These operations are performed on a commitment by a sentinel agent according to the role of its associated agent.

- *Create:* Commitment is created and put in initial state.
- *Activate:* Commitment status is changed to activated when an agree or an accept-proposal message is received from the commitment debtor.
- *Cancel:* In an open system the conditions for a cancel action must be explicitly stated by the debtor agent, e.g. in the domain of a travel agent a flight ticket cancellation action will refer to the minimum time required for the cancellation action and the penalty involved in cancellation. The creditor must send a valid cancellation message; any message that does not conform to the cancellation conditions set by the debtor is an exception.
- *Discharge:* The debtor agent's sentinel performs the discharge action on the commitment by sending the result of the action back to the creditor agent.
- *Violate:* The debtor agent's sentinel performs the discharge action on the commitment by reporting failure to the creditor agent.

3.2.6 Diagnostic Capability
This is a primary component of the system, and is responsible for the diagnosis process. It is activated by the *Detection Module* by presenting it with a detected symptom.

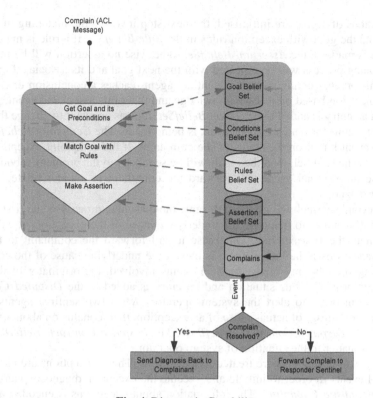

Fig. 4. Diagnostic Capability

It applies the Heuristic Classification approach to uncover the underlying cause of a given symptom. It formulates a diagnostic set to test the conditions that confirm or contradict the presence of underlying causes of the given symptom.

The presence and confirmation of such a condition is ascertained by using plans in the *Diagnostic Plan Library*. The diagnosis plans are activated by posting exceptional events. The invocation of plans simulates the backward chaining reasoning process. Figure 4 shows the HC process involved when a sentinel agent receives a complaint from its associated problem solving agent. Four *BeliefSets* are used to simulate the HC method for diagnosing all types of exception, the fifth *BeliefSet* is different, it is for complaint related exceptions and other exceptions detected by the *Detection Module*.

For example when an ACL message containing a complaint is received by a sentinel agent, the complaint information is retrieved from the ACL message and a complaint exceptional event is posted to the *Diagnostic Capability*. A chain of plans in the *Diagnostic Capability* is invoked in order to diagnose the cause of the complaint.

The reasoning process starts by retrieving goals[1] and their associated preconditions from the *Goal BeliefSet* and the *Conditions BeliefSet*. All preconditions of a goal are initialised by asking questions of the associated problem solving agent. After all

---

[1] Goals in Goal BeliefSet represent exceptions, and their preconditions represent the causes of those exceptions.

preconditions of a goal are initialised, the next step involves the matching of preconditions and the goal with exception rules in the *Rule BeliefSet*. If a rule is matched, an
assertion is made in the *Assertion BeliefSet*, otherwise no assertion will be made and
the reasoning process will be repeated with the next goal and its associated preconditions. This process continues until a sentinel agent reaches a conclusion or could not
make conclusion based on its own knowledge and that of its associated agent.

When an entry is added to *Assertion BeliefSet*, it posts an event to change the status
of the complaint for which the diagnosis is being made. The *Complaint BeliefSet* then
posts an event based on the status of the complaint. If the complaint exception is diagnosed by the sentinel, then the result will be sent back to the problem solving agent,
otherwise the sentinel agent will forward the complaint to another related sentinel
agent for diagnosis.

The second sentinel will go through same the reasoning process as the first sentinel
agent. If it manages to diagnose the underlying cause of the exception, it will return
the result to the first sentinel. Otherwise it will forward the complaint to the next
sentinel agent down the line, if there is one. If the underlying cause of the complaint
is not diagnosed by any of the sentinel agents involved, the originator of the complaint is informed of this situation and an entry is added to the *Disputed Contracts
BeliefBase* in order to alert the system operator. When two sentinel agents do not
agree on the findings of actual cause of an exception, their conclusion about exception
is added into *Disputed Contracts BeliefBase*. The *Disputed Contracts BeliefBase* then
brings this matter to the attention of system operator.

All types of complaints are treated as exceptions. These exceptions are used as exceptional events in order to initiate and execute the exception diagnosis plans present
in the *Diagnostic Capability*. The information about exceptions is encoded as a data
member of an exceptional event.

The following subsections describe the HC method used in diagnosis process and a
fault tree on which HC rules are based.

3.2.6.1   Heuristic Classification.

Heuristic classification is one of the widely used
problem solving methods in expert systems [41]. This method is suitable for domain
such as medical where there is no mathematical model of the system exists and problems are solved by using experiential knowledge.

Traditionally HC is employed in standalone diagnosis expert systems. The diagnosis of an entity provides the cause of malfunction without considering other interacting entities. The diagnostic knowledge is under the control of a single expert system,
whereas our proposed approach deals with the causes of symptoms distributed among
multiple agents. Exception diagnosis involves the cooperation among multiple sentinels agent and problem solving agents.

In an MAS, exceptions such as lost messages or failure to receive a reply can be
viewed as symptoms of failures. There are a variety of potential causes of such failures ranging from I/O errors to agents rescinding their commitments to cooperate. The
nature of the diagnosis of exceptions in an MAS is similar to the way a medical doc-
tor might diagnose a patient by applying knowledge in reasoning about the symptoms
to identify the cause.

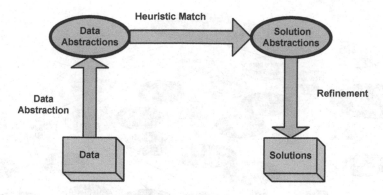

Fig. 5. Inference Structure of Heuristic Classification

Heuristic classification approaches [1] with a knowledge base and rules that map observable symptoms to causes have been widely used in the medical domain.

The MYCIN [41] system is a classical example of medical domain diagnosis system, based upon the heuristic classification approach. In the heuristic classification approach, programs employ an inference structure that systematically relates data to a pre-enumerated set of solutions by abstraction, heuristic association and refinement [1]. Figure 5 shows the inference structure of the heuristic classification problem solving method. A heuristic classification approach includes four main components in its knowledge base: data, data abstractions, solution abstractions and solutions. When symptoms are observed, the system populates symptoms to the data abstraction; the data abstraction then matches the solution abstraction; and refines the solution. For example, if an agent expects to receive a message from another, the agent can compare the actual time of receiving the message with the expected time. This is the used to obtain a qualitative statement such as late message (a data abstraction). This qualitative statement can be heuristically mapped to the possible cause categories (solution abstraction). The agent may heuristically ask the replying agent questions to refine and decide the real cause of the delay (solution refinement). From the above example, the solution and solution abstraction in the heuristic classification can be interpreted in wider sense according to the application areas.

The heuristic classification approach could support agents in detecting the root cause of observed faults and in determining the level of such faults. However, traditional heuristic based diagnostic tools are typically standalone systems having access to a single broad knowledge base. Such a single system approach is inappropriate for an MAS due to the physical distribution of the system's knowledge among different agents. Therefore, the design of a distributed heuristic-based diagnostic system is required to uncover the underlying cause of observed symptoms in an MAS by relating data received from affected agents to pre-enumerated causes.

3.2.6.2 Fault Tree. We have arranged exceptions and their underlying causes hierarchically into a taxonomy. The resultant fault tree is shown in Figure 6. The fault tree represents the relationship among different exceptions and their causes. The root

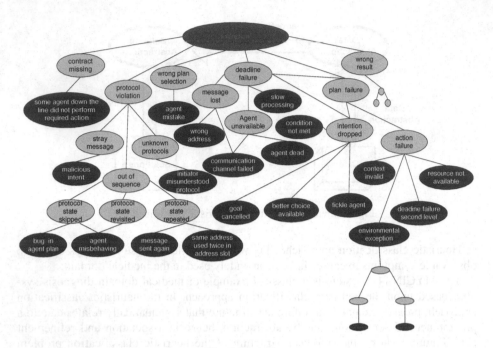

Fig. 6. Fault Tree

represent the underlying cause of the exception and the non root elements represent the exceptions at different levels.

The main advantage of arranging exceptions in a hierarchy is that such an arrangement facilitates the search of the exceptions and their cause in a systematic way. When an exceptions occurs the sentinel agent could follow one of the six paths emanating from the root of the fault tree. This reduces the search space and increases efficiency of the diagnosis process. All causes have their associated tests which are encoded in terms of the sentinel agent's diagnostic plans. These plans are executed by the sentinel in order to confirm or refute a hypothesis.

All exceptions in the hierarchy apart from action failure and wrong result exceptions are domain independent; they can occur in any FIPA compliant MAS regardless of the problem domain. The proposed sentinel agent has capability of diagnosing these exceptions in a domain independent way. In our implementation we treat a plan's action failure exceptions in form of abstract representations rather than using the stack trace of the exceptions. These abstract exceptions are defined as predicates in the Ontology of exceptions object. A low level exception representation may be used by the individual agents when dealing with their environmental exceptions.

As shown in Figure 6 the environmental exceptions can have deep hierarchy depending upon the types of exception. We are not concerned with this level of information; such information is not of any uses outside the plan where they occurred. Similarly a domain related exception can be represented in an hierarchy of exceptions, based on the structure of the domain and the possible exceptions in that domain. We do not have such domain related hierarchy to deal with wrong result exception automatically. The implementation of such a hierarchy requires a knowledge acquisition process in order to accumulate exception knowledge from domain experts. The current implementation classifies such exceptions as disputed contracts and brings them to the attention of system operator.

It is not possible for a sentinel agent to always pinpoint exact cause of exception. During accuracy evaluation of the proposed approach we injected deadline failures by making an agent's plan: sleep for a specified period of time to simulate slow processing; by disconnecting the agent from platform; by inserting wrong address in message, and, by making the agent drop its intention. The sentinel agent was unable to distinguish between agent communication link failure and agent death. This case is treated by the sentinel agent as agent unavailable. The only way a sentinel can distinguish between the two cases is if the sentinel agent and its associated agent are on same machine. In all other cases the sentinel agents diagnose the deadline failure causes correctly.

3.2.7 Diagnostic Plan Library

This is a plan library that belongs to the *Diagnostic Capability*. All diagnostic plans belong to this library. There are three types of plan in this library. Type 1 uses abstract domain knowledge in order to diagnose and identify domain level exceptions. Type 2 is concerned with the protocol; it uses the underlying semantic models of protocols to uncover exceptional situations and their underlying causes. Type 3 is concerned with how to investigate the commitment violations that result from environmental faults and the agent's commitment strategy. The final diagnosis is sent to the *Sentinel-Agent Interface* that manages the communication between the sentinel and other agents in the system.

3.2.8 Intended Plans

This component is a set of plans that is initialised and is applicable in the context of a given exception. These intended plans are also known as the agent's current intentions. These plans use the knowledge from different knowledge bases and also acquire knowledge from the effected agents by asking questions during plan execution. This plan set is a subset of the diagnostic plan library that is applicable to the current context.

3.2.9 Detected Symptoms

This component represents events that are posted to indicate abnormal situations. These events are generated by the *Detection Module*, and the *Diagnostic Capability* when an abnormal situation is encountered. The abnormal events can also be posted automatically by the *BeliefSet,* since the events are the only way to generate a task within an agent.

3.2.10 Disputed Contracts Knowledge Base

This knowledge base contains all commitments that have not been diagnosed as "failed" by a sentinel agent. There could be two possible reasons for a sentinel's inability to diagnose the underlying cause of an exception; first the problem solving agent is not capable of providing necessary information required by a sentinel agent for making a diagnosis, second the sentinel encounters a new type of exception.

When a disputed contract is added to this knowledge base an event is generated that alerts the system's operator using a pop up or an email. The diagnosis and resolution of disputed contracts requires detailed domain knowledge and the involvement of a human. Situations where the low quality of the task's performance is an issue, are frequent source of exceptions that result in disputed contracts.

3.2.11 Acquaintances Knowledge Base

This component contains the addresses of a sentinel's acquaintance agents. The acquaintances include the Directory Facilitator (DF) the Agent Management System (AMS) [36], and the problem solving agent associated with the sentinel. It may contain the addresses of other agent such as a system reliability agent or other agents, which provide the support to the system. A sentinel agent also keeps the capability related information of its associated agent in this component.

3.2.12 Exception Diagnosis Rules

This knowledge base is defined in as a set of rules required to diagnose exceptions. Each rule set is stored in a separate text file. The format of these rules is similar to production rule format used in HC based expert systems. These rules encode experiential knowledge. Initially a sentinel agent loads its rules files into its *BeliefSets* after parsing them. The *BeliefSets* populated by the sentinel agent using the rules files are known as *Goals BeliefSet, Conditions BeliefSet,* and *Rules BeliefSet.*

When an exceptional event is detected, relevant plans are invoked from the *Diagnostic Capability*. These plans have access to the exceptions diagnosis rules present in a sentinel agent's belief. A sentinel agent uses these rules to guide the diagnosis process as shown in Figure 4.

The idea of providing exception related rules in separate text files makes it easy to modify a new rule in a given rule set without disturbing the sentinel agent's plans. An addition of a new rules set requires a new implementation of a set of plans and events without requiring any modification to existing plans.

4   Case Study and Evaluation

In this section we will evaluate the effectiveness of our proposed exception diagnosis agents, when used in an open environment. To evaluate the capability of our proposed exception diagnosis agents, we have applied them to a Personal Travel Assistant (PTA) System [37]. The PTA system is a case study provided by FIPA as an example to show the benefits of applying agent technology in an open, dynamic and diverse electronic travel domain.

There are two scenarios for each task completion. In scenario one, agents are used without their associated sentinel agents and they interact directly to perform their tasks. In scenario two each agent is associated with a sentinel agent and all interactions in a system take place via agents' associated sentinel agents. In both cases the time taken by agents to complete a specific task is measured.

In the next subsection we provide a comparison between the performance of a system using sentinel agents and the performance of a system without sentinel agents. A more detailed performance analysis can be seen in [40].

4.1 FIPA Request Interaction Protocol

In our case study, the PTA agent employs the FIPA Request protocol [34] in order to book a trip. The Flight and Hotel agents are service provider agents that have the ability to provide their service using FIPA Request and FIPA Contract Net [34] protocols. We have chosen a request protocol in order to determine the cost of using sentinel agents in Request protocol based interactions. The task involved in this interaction is the booking of a flight ticket. We have recorded the task completion time for thirty runs in both scenarios.

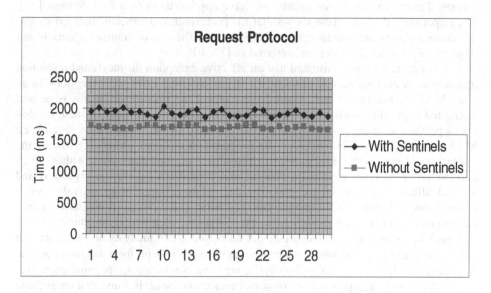

Fig. 7. Performance of MAS with and without Sentinel Agents

In scenario one the average time taken by the agents to complete the task of booking a flight ticket is 1706 milliseconds. It took an average of 1934 milliseconds to complete the same task after the introduction of sentinel agents into the system.

Figure 7 shows the performance comparison of the task employing FIPA Request interaction protocol in the presence and in the absence of sentinel agents in the MAS. As indicated by the graph the MAS took more time to complete the same task in all thirty runs when employing sentinel agents. In this case the overhead of using sentinels is 13%.

This diagram shows that the addition of the sentinels does add a performance overhead. It also shows that the magnitude of overhead at 13% is not purely due to chance. The above measurements of overhead depend on a particular choice of problem solving load. Smaller problems have been shown to give higher percentage but for larger problem loads the overhead will be a smaller percentage of the processing time. The results are not exhaustive performance measurements but they do make the case that in performance terms the sentinels are not impractical.

5 Discussion and Conclusions

We have designed and implemented all components of the proposed architecture according to their specifications discussed above. The implementation uses the JACK™ [38] agent framework and the Java programming language and combines these implementations into a sentinel agent (called the *Diagnosis* agent). JACK™ exceptions are considered as environmental exceptions and handled using the fail method of the plan. We have evaluated the effectiveness of our proposed exception diagnosis agents, when used in an open environment. To evaluate the capability of our proposed exception diagnosis agents, we have applied them to a PTA System [37]. The experimental results have shown that the performance overheads incurred by use of sentinel agents are within reasonable limits and the use of sentinel agents is not impractical. For detail, readers are referred to [39, 40].

In this paper, we have illustrated that an effective exception diagnosis and resolution mechanism is an important instrument for diagnosing and resolving exceptions in an open MAS. A number of researchers have realised the importance of this issue and attempted to provide mechanisms based on various assumptions. None of these mechanisms provide adequate answers to the questions raised by the requirements for an open MAS exception diagnosis method. Our proposed mechanism addresses some of the limitations of the current approaches and provides a detailed framework within which knowledge of different kinds of exception and their diagnosis can be organised and utilised effectively. None of the previous sentinel based approaches provide such a comprehensive framework for representing and utilising the exception diagnosis knowledge to facilitate reasoning about runtime exceptions and their underlying causes.

Interestingly to our knowledge there is no performance analysis or standards that exist in literature against which we can make our system's performance comparison. In absence of these standards and analysis, we have conducted an informal users survey to find out an acceptable level of performance overhead; it found that on average an overhead of 20% is acceptable. In our case study we analyzed the performance overhead of using our proposed exception diagnosis approach and have shown that the overhead of using our proposed sentinel based approach is within reasonable limits: 13% for a FIPA Query Protocol based task and 15% for a FIPA Request Protocol based tasks. For our purpose a performance overhead of less then 20% is acceptable in an e-commerce domain like travel agency.

References

1. Clancy W. J., Heuristic Classification. Artificial Intelligence 27 Elsevier Science Publishers, (1985) 289-350.
2. Shah, N., Chao, K-M., N. Godwin, James, A., , Diagnosing Plan Failures in Multi-Agent Systems Using Abstract Knowledge, In proceedings of the 9th International Conference on Computer Supported Cooperative Work in Design, IEEE, (2005) 46-451.
3. Foundation for Intelligent Physical Agents (FIPA), www.fipa.org.
4. Hägg, S., A Sentinel Approach to Fault Handling in Multi-Agent Systems. In proceedings of Second Australian Workshop on Distributed AI, Carnis Australia, Verlog-Springer, (1997) 181-195.

5. Kaminka, G. A., Tambe, M., What is Wrong with Us? Improving Robustness Through Social Diagnosis. In proceedings of the 15th National conference on Artificial Intelligence, (1998) 97-104

6. Kumar, S., Cohen P. R., Levesque H. J., The Adoptive Agent Architecture: Achieving Fault Tolerance Using Persistent Broker Teams. In proceedings of the Fourth International Conference on MultiAgent Systems (ICMAS-2000), USA, (2000)159-166.

7. Horling, B., Lesser, V., Vincent, R., Bazzan, A., Xuan, P., Diagnosis as an Integral Part of Multi-Agent Adaptability, In Proceedings of DARPA Information Survivability Conference and Exposition, (2000) 211-219.

8. Klein, M., Dellarocas C., Exception Handling in Agent Systems. In proceedings of the Third Annual Conference on Autonomous Agents, (1999) 62-68.

9. Dellarocas, C., Klein, M., Juan, A. R., An Exception-Handling Architecture for Open Electronic Marketplaces of Contract Net Software Agents, In Proceedings of the Second ACM Conference on Electronic Commerce, Minneapolis Minnesota USA, (2000) 225-232.

10. Schroeder, M., Wagner, G., Distributed Diagnosis by Vivid Agents. In proceedings of the First International Conference on Autonomous Agents, California, United States, (1997) 268-275.

11. Schroeder, M. Autonomous, Model-Based Diagnosis Agents, Kluwer Academic Publishers Norwell, MA, USA, ISBN:0-7923-8142-4, (1998)

12. Wagner, G., A Logical and Operational Model of Scalable Knowledge-and Perception-Based Agents. In Proc. of MAAMAW96, LNAI 1038 Springer-Verlag (1996) 26-41.

13. Fröhlich, P., Móra I. A., Nejdl W., Schroeder M., Diagnostic Agents for Distributed Systems. Formal Models of Agents ESPRIT Project ModelAge Final Report Selected Papers, Lecture Notes In Computer Science, Vol. 1760, (1999) 173-186.

14. Guiagoussou, M., Soulhi S., Implementation of a Diagnostic and Troubleshooting Multi-agent System for Cellular Network. International Journal of Network Management", (1999)221-237.

15. Jennings N. R., Cora J. M., Laresgoiti I., Mandani, E. H., Perriollat F., Skarek P., Varga L. Z., Using Archon to Develop Real-World DAI Applications, Part 1. IEEE Expert: Intelligent Systems and Their Applications, (1996)64-70.

16. Roos, N., Teiji, A., Bos A., Multi-Agent Diagnosis with Spatially Distributed Knowledge. 14th Belgian-Dutch Conference on Artificial Intelligence (BNAIC'02), (2002) 275-282.

17. Roos N., Teije A., Witteveen C., A Protocol for Multi-Agent Diagnosis with Spatially Distributed Knowledge. AAMAS'03, Melbourne, Australia, (2003) 655-661.

18. Letia I. A., Craciun F., Kope Z., Netin A., Distributed Diagnosis by BDI Agents, IASTED International Conference Applied Informatics, Innsbruck, Austria, (2000) 862-867.

19. Thottan, M., Ji C., Proactive Anomaly Detection Using Distributed Intelligent Agent. IEEE Network, Special Issue on Network Management, (1998) 21-27.

20. Venkatraman, M., and Singh M. P., Verifying Compliance with Commitment Protocol: Enabling Open Web-Based Multiagent Systems Protocols, Autonomous Agents and Multi-Agent Systems. Vol.3, (1999) 217-236.

21. Fedoruk, A., Deters, R., Improving Fault Tolerance by Replicating Agents., In proceedings of the first International Joint Conference on Autonomous Agents and Multiagent Systems, Bologna, Italy, (2002)737-744.

22. Mishra, S., Huang Y., Fault Tolerance in Agent-Based Computing., In proceedings of the 13th ISCA International Conference on Parallel and Distributed Computing Systems, Las Vegas, NV, (2000).

23. Elnozahy E. N., Zwaenepoel W., Manetho: Transparent Rollback Recovery with Low Overhead, Limited Rollback and fast Output Commit., IEEE Transactions on Computers, Special Issue on Fault Tolerance Computing, (1992)526-531.
24. Xu P., Deters, R., MAS and Fault-Management., International Symposium on Applications and the Internet (SAINT'04), Tokyo, Japan, (2004). 283-286.
25. Rustogi S. K., Wan F., Xing J., Singh M. P. Handling Semantic Exceptions in the Large: A Multiagent Approach., North Carolina State University at Raleigh Raleigh, NC, USA, Technical Report, TR-99-02, (1999
26. Sundresh T. S., Semantic Reliability in Distributed AI Systems., IEEE International Conference on Systems, Man and Cybernetics, Tokyo, JAPAN, (1999) 798-803.
27. Chia M. H., Neiman D. E., Lesser V. R., Poaching and Distraction in Asynchronous Agent Activities., Proceedings of the Third International Conference on Multi-Agent Systems, (1998)99-95.
28. Youssefmir, M., Huberman, B., Resource Contention in Multiagent Systems., First International Conference on Multi-Agent Systems (ICMAS-95), San Francisco, CA, USA, (1995)398-403.
29. Tripathi, A., Miller, R., "Exception Handling in Agent-Oriented Systems. Advances in Exception Handling Techniques, A. Romanovsky et al. (Eds.), Springer-Verlag, New York ,USA, (2001) 129-146.
30. Platon, E., Honiden, S., Sabouret, N., Challenges in Exception Handling in Multi-Agent Systems, International Workshop on Software Engineering for Large-Scale Multi-Agent Systems, ACM Press (2006) 45-50.
31. Shah, N., Chao, K-M., Godwin, N., Younas, M., Laing C., Exception Diagnosis in Agent Based Grid Computing. Proceedings of 2004 IEEE International Conference on System, Man, and Cybernetic, The Hague, The Netherlands, (2004) 3213-3219.
32. Shah, N., Chao, K-M., Godwin, N., James, A., Exception Diagnosis in Multi-Agent Systems. The IEEE/WIC/ACM International Conference on Intelligent Agent Technology, (2005)483-486.
33. FIPA Communicative Act Library Specification, http://www.fipa.org/specs/fipa00037/SC00037J.pdf, (2000).
34. FIPA Interaction Protocols Specification Protocols. http://www.fipa.org/repository/ips.php3
35. Singh M. P., An Ontology for Commitments in Multiagent Systems: Toward a Unification of Normative Concepts., Artificial Intelligence and Law, volume 7, (1999) 97-113.
36. FIPA Agent Management Specification, http://www.fipa.org/specs/fipa00023/SC00023K.pdf.
37. FIPA Travel Assistance Specifications, http://www.fipa.org/specs/fipa00080/XC00080B.htm, 2001.
38. JACK™ Intelligent Agents, Agent Oriented Software, http://www.agent-software.com/shared/home/
39. Shah, N., Chao, K-M., Godwin, N., James, A., A Sentinel Based Exception Diagnosis in Market Based Multi-Agent Systems. The 2nd International Workshop on Data Engineering Issues in E-Commerce and Services, J. Lee et al. (Eds.): DEECS 2006, LNCS 4055, (2006) 258 – 267.
40. Shah, N., Chao, K-M., Godwin, N., James, A., Tsai C-F, An Empirical Evaluation of a Sentinel Based Approach to Exception Diagnosis in Multi-Agent Systems., 20th IEEE International Conference on Advanced Information Networking and Applications, IEEE CS, Volume.1 (AINA'06), (2006) 379-386.
41. Shortliffe E. H., Computer Based Medical Consultations: MYCIN, New York, Elsevier, 1976

SMASH: Modular Security for Mobile Agents

Adam Pridgen and Christine Julien

The Center for Excellence in Distributed Global Environments
The Department of Electrical and Computer Engineering
The University of Texas at Austin
{atpridgen, c.julien}@mail.utexas.edu

Mobile agent systems of the future will be used for secure information delivery and retrieval, off-line searching and purchasing, and even system software updates. As part of such applications, agent and platform integrity must be maintained, confidentiality between agents and the intended platform parties must be preserved, and accountability of agents and their platform counterparts must be stringent. SMASH, Secure Modular Mobile Agent System.H, is an agent system designed using modular components that allow agents to be easily constructed and the system to be easily extended. To facilitate security functionality, the SMASH platform incorporates existing hardware and software security solutions to provide access control, accountability, and integrity. Agents are further protected using a series of standard cryptographic functions. While SMASH promotes high assurance applications, the system also promotes an open network environment, permitting agents to move freely among the platforms and execute unprivileged actions without authenticating. In this paper, we elaborate on the components and capabilities of SMASH and present an application that benefits from each of these elements.

1 Introduction

Mobile agent systems and applications are poised to become highly prominent for tasks such as information sharing, analysis, evaluation, and response, but before these systems can be fully utilized security mechanisms in these services must be improved [1]. In general, software *agents* are regarded as highly autonomous processes which can perform tasks ranging from simple queries to complex computations. The counterpart to the agent is the platform, which loads and executes the agent. A mobile agent augments the traditional agent's autonomy with the ability to move from platform to platform to accomplish its tasks.

To demonstrate the realm of possibilities regarding mobile agents and their respective systems, consider the following motivating applications. In [2], a mobile agent system was developed to monitor and respond to machining equipment in real time if abnormal equipment behavior is detected. The system developed by Aye, et al. focuses on managing workflow, scheduling, and resources in an office environment [3]. A mobile agent based collaborative learning system is described in [4], and a mobile agent online auction system is described in [5]. Mobile agents have also been applied to a distributed network intrusion detection [6], where

R. Choren et al. (Eds.): SELMAS 2006, LNCS 4408, pp. 99–116, 2007.

the agents help reduce the network load and response latency. Furthermore, can be used in network management systems to promote collaboration between network monitoring devices by sharing interesting events or filters. Mobile agents have a high degree utility because they can be used to solve distributed problems in an asynchronous fashion. One of the greatest challenges to a variety of agent systems is security because agents may not be adequately authenticated, intractable privilege management, or the systems assume external sources will provide the needed security.

We introduce the Secure Modular Mobile Agent System.H (SMASH), which provides modularity for agent and platform components, information assurances, and mechanisms to assist mobile agents as they move between platforms. SMASH is also designed to enable coordination among agents and platforms, address context-based agent execution and security that enables adaptive services, and, overall, improve programmability, security, and extensibility for highly versatile mobile agent applications. SMASH utilizes asymmetric and symmetric cryptographic functions from existing encryption libraries, permitting more flexible authentication for both the agent and the platform, rather than restricting agent authentication to code signing as employed in Java-based approaches. To support unpredictable travel patterns, SMASH supports strict authorization and resource control measures yet eliminates the burden of excessive authentication for transient agents as they move to their destinations.

The rest of this paper is organized as follows. Section 2 will discuss the agent's components and functionality, and Section 3 will elaborate on the supporting platform's architecture and capability. In Section 4, properties of a secure system are discussed, and these qualities are related to SMASH's capabilities and design. Section 5 provides some example applications that can benefit from SMASH's architecture. Section 6 will discuss past work related to SMASH, while Section 7 concludes the paper.

2   Agent Components and Security Measures

This section will describe the SMASH agent architecture and then discuss how these components supply adequate security functionality. We start with an overview of the SMASH agent model and conclude with system and implementation details that provide a close inspection of a SMASH agent's inner workings.

2.1   The SMASH Agent Model

To adhere to an open architecture, SMASH supports two types of agents, *anonymous* and *authenticated* agents, in a manner similar to [7]. An anonymous agent is simply one that has not authenticated with the platform on which it is currently located. Such an agent may access designated read-only data, read and write to a Blackboard, perform simple unprivileged actions, or leave. This anonymous classification allows agents to move through intermediate platforms without having to authenticate with each of them, which can improve performance and reduce the latency caused by unnecessary authentication.

An authenticated agent, on the other hand, is one that has sufficiently proven its identity to the platform. An agent's identity refers to with whom the agent is associated and may represent a user, group, platform, application, etc. Once a platform verifies an agent's identity, the platform awards the agent rights based on its identity and/or the context of its task(s).

Fig. 1 shows a pictorial representation of the components found in any SMASH agent. All agents are composed of modules, which are simply defined architectural types, methods, and functions of the mobile agent. By taking this design approach, SMASH can take advantage of this component model and protect *pieces* of the agent in different ways, rather than protecting an entire agent in a single manner. In addition, this design supports modular development and evolution of agents, which reduces the development burden and may even enhance the ability to spawn new agents in an automated and consistent manner. SMASH agents contain an immutable *main* module shown at the top of the figure (with the darkened rectangular border). This main module comprises the following submodules: code, application data, agenda, itinerary, credentials, and a time-to-live. The main module is signed by the agent's creator, and this signature helps protect the agent's main module from unauthorized modification.

Fig. 1. A Mobile Agent in SMASH

The *code* shown in Fig. 1 is the executable portion of the SMASH agent, and the *application data* ("app data" in the figure) contains static data the agent carries during its travels. The application data is simply constant data that does not change throughout the execution lifetime of the agent. If the agent does need to modify this data, this modified data is placed in a secondary module ("data" in the figure), described in more detail below. The *TTL*, or time-to-live, is a time metric for specifying the lifetime of an agent. Since agents may get lost or the lifetime of data may expire, it is necessary to protect against agents that may loop through a network or possibly corrupt data caches with expired data.

The *agenda* contains the agent's application-level goals, including information about the agent's intended task(s), the resources required to perform those tasks (e.g., file or network access), and the expected cost of performing the tasks. (e.g., in terms of communication bandwidth or CPU time). An agent provides descriptions of its intended task and resource requirements, and these specifications are used as part of the authentication process between the agent and the platform. In addition, agenda information can aid the platform in determining the appropriate privileges to award an authenticated agent. To protect in transit information, the agent may encrypt portions or all of the agenda to ensure the secrecy of its tasks. In such cases, the target platforms for the agent must already be in possession of the proper key to use in decrypting the agent's agenda.

The *itinerary* submodule contains the agent's travel plan, designates the platforms the agent intends to visit, and also grants permissions to clone the agent. For each target host platform, the itinerary contains the host's unique identifier, the host's public key, material for authenticating the host, and, finally, a checksum of the software expected to be running on the host. The platform's unique identifier and public key are used by the agent to authenticate the platform, but other authentication materials, such as session tokens, may also be available to augment these more standard materials. The checksum is used by the agent to verify that the platform has not been modified from the expected execution environment, which could indicate a recent update or a compromise in the system. In addition to the above components, the itinerary is also used to designate whether an agent will permit platforms to refer it to another *trusted* platform. A referral occurs if a platform does not have a resource, but knows of another platform with the agent's required resources. If the agent accepts referrals, then the agent will go to the referred platform and honor the trust relationship between the platforms. Finally, the agent's true destinations can be obscured to hide an agent's association with a platform or prevent observers from understanding the purpose of the agent. This protection can be applied to individual entries of the itinerary without impacting an intended recipient's ability to receive the agent. The mechanisms behind this encryption are discussed in Section 2.2.

The final submodule in the agent's main module contains the agent's *credentials*, which define a *tamper detector* comprising a public key, a signature, and the agent's prescribed authentication methods, *authentication submodules*, which describe which algorithms an agent can use to authenticate with platforms. The platform must support at least one of an agent's prescribed methods, or the two will not be able to authenticate. Credentials are used to capture the identity of the agent, and the entries in this component allow the agent to be authenticated across domains with dissimilar authentication mechanisms.

The *creator key* shown in Fig. 1 is used to help protect all sub-modules within the main module. When the agent is completely assembled and prepared for dispatch, the creating entity will create an asymmetric key pair. The public key will be added to a list of keys used to sign the agent, and the private key will be used to sign the agent. In order to allow for agent cloning, the agent carries a *signing keys list*, and as the name suggests, the list will contain a list of all platforms that have cloned and signed an instance of the agent. This method of cloning is used for two reasons. First, the agent's main module must remain intact, so future platforms the agent reaches can validate the integrity of the agent. The second reason is more of a trust issue. Since the itinerary contains platform identifiers and public keys as well as permission to clone the agent, future target platforms can easily verify the validity of a cloned agent. If an agent is cloned but the platform did not have the proper permissions, the agent is considered illegitimate and can be destroyed and reported once it is discovered.

In addition to its main module, an agent may contain a dynamic module, the lower rectangle in Fig. 1. This module stores vital state and process data with a high degree of confidence as the agent moves from platform to platform. Its explicit separation from the main module also protects the crucial information described above from modifications that can occur in the dynamic module. Within the dynamic module, the *execution state* includes information about the variables in memory and the instruction where the agent left off on the previous platform. The *data* refers to any computation results, accumulation of logs, etc., that the agent generates throughout its tasks and wishes to maintain. A *digest* provides a mechanism of verification for this data. Before departing a platform, the agent creates a hash of the execution state and application data (using a function like SHA-512) and passes this hash to the platform. The platform signs the combination of the hash and the platform's public key. The agent receives the signed hash and the public key from the platform, which it stores as a digest and the digest public key. When the agent initializes on a new platform, it verifies the data and state information using the reverse process. The public key is also matched against the public key of the previous platform in the agent's itinerary. If the key does not match or the digest is wrong, the agent will self-destruct.

2.2 Implementing Secure Modular Agents

SMASH agents are designed to be resilient against many of the security attacks found in modern day systems yet remain flexible through platform interaction. Our framework builds on past work in agent systems, but integrates multi-directional security into the design from the ground up. SMASH is a multi-agent system built on top of the *Security Enhanced Linux* and uses Python as the execution environment for the agents.

General Agent Implementation. Agents are written in the Python scripting language to provide an easy-to-use interface to the application developer. Python is a powerful object-oriented language whose features make it attractive for rapid application development. In addition, the separation of the agent implementation (written in Python) from the platform implementation (described in the next section and written in C++) provides a layer of abstraction between the agent's security policies and the platform's implementation of those policies.

The Python interface for defining a SMASH agent provides an agent base class (`agent`) that any application agent must derive. This base class contains an __init__ method to which the deriving agent can provide the aspects of the main module. Each of these submodules *except the agent's code* (i.e., the agenda, the itinerary, the credentials, the TTL, and the application data) are represented by additional Python classes provided in the SMASH middleware implementation. When a SMASH agent is first created, its __init__ method is invoked, and, within this method, the submodule components are either received as parameters or created. When a SMASH agent arrives on a new platform, the Python interpreter uses boot-strapping methods within the agent to load essential environment variables and to prepare the agent for the platform's admission process. This entire process is described in more detail in Section 3.

One final aspect worth noting about this programming interface is the ease with which the developer can specify initialization of the submodules. For example, as described next, an agent's agenda is represented using an XML-like definition. To initialize the agenda submodule, the agent needs only to pass the XML file(s) defining the agenda to the Python `agenda` class, and the mechanics for parsing and properly storing the agenda's details are implemented within the middleware. The agent's itinerary (which includes various information about each of the agent's target platforms) is also defined via a standard XML format and can also be automatically processed. Similar standard approaches for representing the other submodules are used; details are omitted here for brevity.

SMASH is engineered to provide both strong and weak mobility. As such, the `agent` base class in the middleware contains two methods; an agent overrides one or the other depending on whether it desires strong or weak mobility. In addition, the deriving agent sets a flag in the base class indicating its selection. When using the `strong_run` method, when the derived agent decides it is time to move to a new platform, the exact execution state is saved and later restored on the new platform. The agent records how much processing has occurred and restarts itself on the new platform in exactly that location. In the case of weak mobility, when the agent moves, its `weak_run` method simply restarts from the beginning. To move, a derived agent calls the `move` method in the `agent` base class, which first determines which mobility method is being used and (if necessary) saves the agent's execution state. Then the `move` method hooks into the remainder of the middleware to find the next platform in the itinerary and move there.

Defining Expressive Agent Agendas. An example agent agenda is depicted in Figure 2, which shows the goal definition for a network event monitoring agent. The agent collects *any* of the *high* severity events that occur on network sensors. After identifying an event, it is hashed by the destination port and event name, so similar events on various sensors can be correlated. During the correlation, the agent counts similar events, and if any of the counts surpass the threshold, then the agent will retain these events. In this case (with a threshold of one), the agent will carry all events that are identified from the past 24 hours.

In cases where the agent would like to protect the goals, tasks, or resources from observers, the agenda entries can be encrypted for particular platforms using either symmetric or asymmetric cryptography. While other methods can be incorporated into our framework, we have defined the Secure Agent Container Transport Method (SACTM). SACTM is a single-use cryptographic container that allows both the agent and platform to validate the contents. The container is embedded in the agent before the agent is deployed, and the container is created with a symmetric key created during a secure key agreement between the agent's creator and the target platform. The creator also creates a random nonce and an asymmetric key pair, which are used to create a *seal* that is used by both the agent and platform to validate the SACTM. Essentially, the private key is used to sign the nonce and data, and the resulting seal is appended to

```
<GoalType = NetworkStatusReport>
  <Task>
    <NIDSQuery>
      <attribute> Description = "NIDS Event Query"</attribute>
      <type=HashedQuery>
        <attribute> EventType= "ANY,HIGH" </attribute>
        <attribute> HashBy = "DstPort,EventName" </attribute>
        <attribute> TimePeriod="Last Day" </attribute>
      </HashedQuery>
      <type=EventCorrelation>
        <attribute> GetCount  = "TRUE" </attribute>
        <attribute> TrackTime = "FALSE" </attribute>
        <attribute> KeepHostId= "FALSE" </attribute>
      </EventCorrelation>
      <type=EventFilter>
        <attribute> EventThreshold  = 1 </attribute>
        <attribute>  = "FALSE" </attribute>
        <attribute> KeepHostId= "FALSE" </attribute>
      </EventFilter>
    </NIDSQuery>
  </Task>
  <Resources>
    <Internal>
      <attribute> ProcessingTime = "300s" </attribute>
      <attribute> SensorDBAccess = "TRUE" </attribute>
    </Internal>
  </Resources>
</NetworkStatusReport>

<GoalType = SACTM>
  <attribute> PublicKey= AKey </attribute>
  <attribute> Nonce = 8686868 </attribute>
  <attribute> Data =    ...DATA... </attribute>
</SACTM>
```

Fig. 2. Model of an Network Event Monitor and Encrypted Goal

the data and encrypted with the key. The agent creator then appends the public key and nonce to finish the SACTM, and after the container is created, the creator destroys the container key, leaving the only copy in the possession of the platform. The SACTM is verified after the agent and platform mutually authenticate. The platform will decrypt the SACTM data with the stored key and use the nonce, the public key, and the decrypted data to check the *seal*. If the check succeeds, the platform can ensure the SACTM retains its integrity. Next, the agent performs the same check. The novel feature of this container is that if either element tries to lie, the other will be able to detect the lie through the integrity check, so the platform cannot pass-off data not in the SACTM to the agent, and the platform will be able to detect a masquerading agent.

Finally, the agenda can also be used as a dossier or condition upon which the agent is admitted to the platform, and, if the agent violates the agenda constraints, the agent can be removed from platform.

An agent's itinerary is also implemented as XML-like specifications, and portions of it (e.g., single destinations) can also be partially secured in much the same manner. The details of these approaches are omitted for brevity.

3   Platform Components and Security Measures

Like SMASH agents, the host platform is engineered to provide support for an open architecture with high levels of security. This section describes the details of the platform that support the mobile SMASH agents, starting with a description of the model, including the flow of agents and information through the model, and concluding with a brief description of some implementation details.

3.1   The SMASH Platform Model

As shown in Fig. 3, we use a layered approach to compartmentalize our architecture and to prevent an outbreak of malicious activity. At the lowest level, the operating system handles issues like communication, system level access controls, etc. When an agent arrives at the platform, an integrity check is administered, and, upon successful completion, the agent is moved to the Untrusted Layer. At this point the agent is considered to be an admitted *anonymous agent*. The agent then moves through the Authentication and Authorization Layer, where the

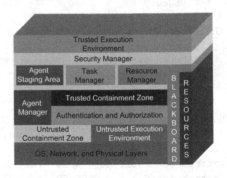

Fig. 3. SMASH Platform Architecture

agent and platform mutually authenticate to become a trusted entity. After successful authentication and authorization, the agent is placed into the Trusted Containment Zone (TCZ) and is considered an *authenticated agent*. From here up, the agent will interact directly with the Security Manager to obtain the required resources and be executed. Within the Security Manager, the Task Manager determines if the platform can provide useful services to the agent (based on the agent's goals), and the Resource Manager sets-up proxies so the agent can access resources external to the execution environment. The Agent Manager tracks all agents on the platform. The remainder of this section describes these layers and an agent's movement through them in more detail.

SMASH's final components, shown to the right in Fig. 3, represent publicly accessible platform resources. The Blackboard is a memory-constrained FIFO queue available to any agent (authenticated or anonymous) for read-write access.

Agents can use this space to coordinate tasks. Since agents are kept completely isolated, this is one way that they may interact with each other. This data space also allows agents to mark a platform as visited. The platform also has the ability to make other parts of memory public and read-only (similar to a glass-enclosed bulletin board).

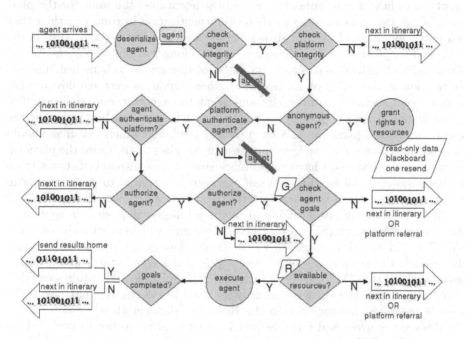

Fig. 4. Decision Tree Used by the SMASH Platform

Fig. 4 shows the entire process of admitting an agent to a platform. When an agent first arrives at the platform, the agent and platform perform initial integrity checks. The platform will use the *tamper detector* located in the agent's credentials to check the list of signatures and ensure the agent's integrity. The agent verifies the integrity of a platform by querying the TPM, which provides a signed hash of the platform's software, and the agent will compare this value with the one in its itinerary. If they match, the platform's check has passed and the agent will register with the Agent Manager (AM) as an *anonymous agent* and proceed to the Untrusted Containment Zone (UCZ).

The agent receives few privileges in the UCZ. Here the agent has limited processing power, may read and write to the platform's Blackboard, may access the platform's lesser privileged services, or may leave the platform. The agent may also piggyback on the platform to get to some physical location. When the agent is registered with the Agent Manager (AM), it is scheduled to receive minimal processing time in a low-priority queue. The AM also monitors agents, and, if they die unexpectedly, removes them from the UCZ. If an agent simply needs to obtain some public data from the platform, it can use its processing time to query and then leave. On the other hand an agent may also use this processing time to inform the AM that it wishes to authenticate with the platform.

After the agent signals the AM that it wishes to authenticate, the AM moves the agent into the Authentication and Authorization Layer (AAL). In the AAL, the agent and the platform mutually authenticate. The platform queries the agent about how it can authenticate, and the agent does the same for the platform. If the two possess some method of authentication in common, then they can mutually authenticate. If this is not the case the agent is removed from the AAL and flagged in the AM, meaning it can no longer attempt to authenticate. If mutual authentication succeeds, an authorization service is launched. The authorization service will look locally, to a remote server, or even employ another mobile agent service [8] to identify and grant the agent access privileges. The authorization source is platform-dependent, but it must establish whether the agent can use the platform, at what privilege level, and which resources should be accessible. The agent can leverage the same services to authorize the platform to ensure no revocations have taken place since it was dispatched. Once these authorizations complete, the status of the agent is updated to *authenticated* in the AM, and the agent is moved into the Trusted Containment Zone (TCZ).

After the agent is given an initial set of privileges, it passes its agenda to the Security Manager (SM). From here, the agent will interact only with the SM. The SM passes the agenda to the Task Manager (TM), which analyzes the agenda, the agent's privileges, and which of the agent's tasks are currently permissible. If the TM identifies a task that is permissible and requires equal or lesser access than the agent's currently assigned privileges, the TM passes the agent's requested resource list to the Resource Manager (RM), which locates the desired resources and initiates proxies for the agent to use to access those resources. The RM adheres to the order in which resources are required, if the agent provides such information. This expedites agent execution, reduces idle time, and helps release resources in a timely manner.

When the necessary resources become available, the agent is moved into the Agent Staging Area (ASA), and its status is updated in the AM. In the ASA, the agent's Bootstrap Code (BC) is identified and loaded. The BC first goes through all of the agent's modules to ensure no tampering or corruption has occurred in the agent's immutable sections. The BC then loads the agent into memory. The agent checks all execution environment parameters such as handles and variables and initializes them appropriately for this platform. If any failure occurs, the BC aborts, and the agent self-destructs or returns home. Finally, the BC updates the agent's status within the AM to *executing*.

While the agent executes, the SM monitors the agent for any deviant behavior like excessive bandwidth usage or attempts to access restricted resources. Depending on the severity of the violation, the SM can restrict or kill the agent, or force the agent to leave. When the agent's execution ends, the BC moves the agent back to the agent staging area. Here, the BC checks the agent's integrity and inventories the modules. The BC will obtain a digital signature for the data and execution state (the digest). After the BC completes the clean-up, it will signal to the AM its intention to leave, and the AM will provide a means to leave the platform.

3.2   Implementing a Secure Agent Platform

To enable several aspects of tamper detection in SMASH, our implementation utilizes Security Enhanced Linux (SE Linux [9]), which is a Linux kernel modified and partly maintained by the National Security Agency. SE Linux enables granular access controls and provides a powerful but securable multi-user environment. In addition, we require each platform to incorporate a Trusted Platform Module (TPM), a hardware chip specified by the Trusted Computing Group [10]. In combination, this hardware and operating system enable our implementation of the security and trust mechanisms outlined above.

As described in Section 2.2, we use the Python programming language to provide a programming interface for defining agents. For the platform, we use C++, on top of which the Python agents run. C++ is more amenable to interaction with the SE Linux operating system services, has better performance, and makes many of the subtle aspects described above possible. Finally, SMASH assumes network communication to be handled by the operating system, and the middleware simply handles agent movement between platforms at the application level.

4   Meeting a Wide-Range of Security Requirements

Multi-agent systems are very difficult to secure, simply because they invite foreign pieces of code to execute and fulfill a goal or objective. Even under the most ideal situations, security becomes highly complicated and requires applying not only cryptographic but also procedural measures to overcome threats and vulnerabilities in a system. A secure system typically satisfies properties of accountability, authentication, availability, confidentiality, and integrity [11]. The system must be able to authenticate users of the system, and in doing so ensure the user is who they say they are, commonly using any of the following factors: "what you know," "what you have," and "who you are." The next issue is availability, which implies that required services and resources will be available at least when they are needed. Confidentiality refers to the fact that information must remain secret through out the security cycle, and no information is leaked by processes acting on the data. The final property is integrity, and this implies two elements, data integrity and source integrity. Data integrity means that any data being processed via a security system should not be modified by unauthorized users whether intentional or unintentional. The second element is Source Integrity, and this item implies that the source of the given data or message is untainted and represents their true identity.

The underlying goals of *accountability* are to disallow deniability both on the part of the agent and the part of the platform and to be able to reconstruct events. SMASH ensures accountability by requiring mutual authentication, tracking an agent's states and resources on a platform, and governing an agent's access throughout its stay on a platform. If the platform detects abnormal behavior (e.g., an agent operating outside of its stated goals or resource requirements), the platform can intervene. Accountability of platforms may not be as exact, in part because, as the agent moves from platform to platform, it becomes difficult to determine exactly by which platform an agent was modified. Our use of the digest and its sequential keys helps in this process, but the approach may still suffer from a risk of rogue platforms attempting to modify agents en route to other platforms.

Authentication is the process of identifying an entity and asserting with a high probability that this is the entity it claims to be and not an impersonator. In a dynamic environment, authentication is complicated due to the lack of persistent connectivity to a central authority. Common approaches to authentication require a central host or certificate authority to provide information about the identity bound to the key in question. Currently, SMASH relies on a model in which platforms and agents alike have *a priori* information about other entities that enable authentication. Such an approach incurs a good deal of initialization or setup costs that may be unreasonable in a mobile environment. Other approaches in dynamic environments handle this authentication requirement in a different manner, for example through quorum-based authentication [12]. Future work will investigate the feasibility of incorporating similar approaches into the SMASH architecture. To implement the actual authentication process, SMASH uses Pluggable Authentication Modules (PAM), which interface with the Pluggable Authentication Service, to perform the authentication on the platform.

Availability emphasizes how components and the system as a whole address incidental and intentional failures. Incidental failures may occur when an agent loses a network connection, and the agent does not handle the resulting exception created by the incident. An intentional failure is due to a malicious entity actively engaging the system in an attempt to disrupt or compromise services and resources in the system, resulting in instability. SMASH focuses on ensuring stability from within and accomplishes this feat by applying a layered security approach. The first line of defense begins with the agent and its creator. In this layer, agents are coded in a defensive manner such that exceptions are caught and, to some extent, data and code are validated before being executed. The next line of defense falls within the platform. First of all, to prevent collateral damage, agents are executed in their own execution contexts using SE Linux [13]. Under this condition along with the *principle of least privilege* and SE Linux's access controls, agents are contained and unable to escalate their privileges, and once the platform detects the abnormal behavior, the agent is killed and system checks are performed to ensure everything is in order. If the platform becomes unstable, SE Linux is also used to contain this system, so it can actually be halted, reinitialized, and restarted into the last known good state.

In SMASH, *confidentiality* and *integrity* focus on keeping messages secret and intact. Confidentiality is typically accomplished through cryptographic measures, but methods like obfuscation can also be utilized to embed secret meanings into the existing messages, without changing the cover message. SMASH embraces current cryptographic techniques to accomplish secrecy, since these methods are proven secure and practical in real world environments, using algorithms like RSA, ECC, AES, etc. SACTM makes use of secure algorithms and protocols to help reinforce its security. Integrity is accomplished by using digest functions in conjunction with asymmetric cryptography. Digest functions are are non-invertible functions, meaning outputs can not be used to derive the inputs. This property allows information to be given a *probabilistically* unique value, where collisions (e.g., another input with the same output) are highly unlikely. To ensure information pertaining to the digest and the digest itself cannot be modified en route to a platform, asymmetric cryptography is applied to the digest, thus retaining the originality of the message.

5   Modeling Agent Interactions

The previous sections introduced SMASH's components, their respective functionalities, and their security guarantees. This section presents a real world example in which SMASH can be used to securely transmit mobile agents among platforms, providing an improved implementation of a common application. Specifically, we present the use of SMASH to support *epidemic updates* on, for example, commercial automobiles. As discussed in Section 1, epidemic updates can be used to intelligently propagate software updates to distributed platforms.

The implementation of this application begins on the factory floor, when the automobiles are originally manufactured. When the manufacturer creates a new automobile, it loads the vehicle with specific cryptographic keys, and the keys for the device are saved in the manufacturer's database as well. This initial "centralization" removes the need for a third party to be involved in verification processes at a later date. At some later time, the manufacturer may identify a (non-critical) software update that it would like to distribute to certain automobiles. While a dealership is servicing one of these automobiles, the vehicle can be given a mobile agent (or set of mobile agents) that can clone itself and move through vehicles, supplying the necessary software update. In this process, the maintenance personnel at the dealership loads a *carrier agent* onto the vehicle under service. As their name indicates, carrier agents carry the software updates to platforms targeted by the update. Carrier agents are given a specified TTL after which the carrier agents will self-destruct. If a carrier agent reaches an automobile that requires the update but has not yet received it, the carrier agent loads the new software (when the car is parked), and sends a *verification agent* back to the manufacturer. When the TTL for the initial carrier agents has expired, the manufacturer sends traditional recall slips to all un-verified automobiles requiring the software update. When a vehicle supporting a carrier agent reaches an idle state (e.g., is parked in a parking lot), it attempts to clone itself and send its clone to nearby SMASH platforms. Upon arriving at a SMASH platform, if the vehicle supporting the platform is not of the type impacted by the recall, or the vehicle has already been updated, the agent self-destructs. If it is, the carrier agent deposits the update and sits on the platform, proceeding to pass the new software to un-updated vehicles.

The first carrier agent is composed of the following material. The agenda describes the type of update being applied and the intended firmware version to update. The itinerary contains a list of (the platforms of) all vehicles impacted by the recall. When an agent clones itself to send to a new platform, it decreases the itinerary by the platform(s) it has already visited. Rather than specifically identifying the other platforms by unique id (in this case, likely the Vehicle Identification Number, or VIN), a carrier agent could identify properties of the vehicles it needs to visit. Adding such expressiveness to an agent's itinerary is left for future work. The admission process for a carrier agent from the anonymous status to the authenticated status uses the pre-loaded manufacturer's keys, and appropriate counterparts are carried by the carrier agent. The *code* and *app data* for the carrier agent contain the code for uploading the update, the update itself, and diagnostic scripts to test and ensure that the update was correctly installed. To indicate that a platform has successfully been updated, the installation also causes a marker to be written to the platform's blackboard that indicates success. Upon arriving at a new platform, any carrier agent first checks this blackboard, and, if the marker is apparent, the carrier agent self-destructs.

After an attempt to update the platform is made, a *verification agent* is sent back to the closest dealership or manufacturer. This verification agent carries information like log files and the diagnostic test results back to the manufacturer for records keeping and assurance that the update was successful. The files and logs sent back to the sender are encrypted with the their public key, which is already loaded on the platform or embedded in the carrier agent. The verification agent's agenda describes the agent as a courier, but the more revealing details about the agent are protected with encryption. While the use of an agent in this case at first seems unreasonable, the use of an agent will enhance the probability that the agent will reach its destination because the agent can travel in an ad-hoc and intelligent fashion. A message sent in a traditional manner may not reach its destination due to the network dynamics.

6   Related Work

Information assurance for mobile agents is a daunting task because security threats arise from agents attacking other agents or platforms and from platforms attacking agents. The ultimate challenge is to manage trust between components of the agent system. Providing middleware for such systems is non-trivial because it must forecast and abstract implications which may arise in the various roles and actions of remote agents and platforms. Issues such as software exceptions, resource availability, etc., can open subtle holes for exploitation or even cause a system to fail.

In the area of software assurance, a number of projects have increased the probability of dynamically detecting data or code tampering. One such framework [14] re-arranges code at compile time to obtain a unique binary and then embeds a unique watermark created from standard encryption algorithms. This dramatically suppresses the ability of an adversary to manipulate any portion of the code and can also be useful in maintaining a light-weight agent.

Page et. al. [15], explore a method in which each agent performs a randomly periodic self-examination to ensure no modifications have been made while the agent was executing. Other methods use reference states [16], state appraisals [17], and even agent execution traces [18]. These methods can add weight to the agent code and payload, require *a priori* knowledge or consistent connectedness of platforms for verification, and, under some circumstances, data appended to the agent can be forged.

Most mobile agent systems have been built on Java or varying scripting languages. Projects using Java utilize the JVM's Security Manager, but this management system can be intractable due to an excessive number of security policies and unscalable as mobile agent systems become more complex. On the flip side, Java offers more robust, object-oriented programming, an elaborate API library, and portable code. Mobile agent systems implemented in scripting languages are also portable and have stronger mobility, but they do not provide extensive security management and they tend not to be as object-oriented.

There are a number of middleware projects for secure mobile agents, and we sample only a small fraction of them here. MARS [19] explicitly separates the data an agent can access from the host's file system through a novel coordination approach, but this reduces flexibility and requires significant *a priori* knowledge to populate the agent accessible data space. In addition, MARS is dramatically limited in the granularity of access control it can provide. Nomads [20] implements many promising features such as fine-grained access control, strong mobility, and flexible execution profiles based on application and context; however, Nomad agents run in a custom execution environment that dramatically reduces the code portability of the agents. D'Agents [7] supports multiple agent implementation languages and also differentiates anonymous and authenticated agents. Aglets [21] are applet agents based on Javascript. They provide conditional access rights and moderate access control based on aglet "identity."

Ajanta [22] is another mobile agent system built on Java that implements extensive access control measures rather than relying entirely on Java's Security Manager. Ajanta suffers due to Java's constrained policy system. Ajanta introduces containers for appending read-only data and a stronger security manager that controls access to resources by requiring agents to set-up resource proxies that access resources through the manager as established by the platform's policies. In an effort to make agents lightweight, each agent carries an address for a trusted code server from which it can dynamically load supplemental Java classes.

Java has been a very important tool in the mobile agent community. Java's portability, type safety, automated memory management, serialization, and built-in security management have made it the language of choice for many developers. However, for the purposes of strict information assurance, Java has fundamental inadequacies. For example, the JVM is not intended as a multi-user execution environment, so a Java-based mobile agent system has limited ability to govern all resources of agents and threads [23]. A second issue with Java-based systems is that they were meant typically for on-platform management in which an agent derives its platform access rights from those established locally on the platform. There is no method for the platform to dynamically check access policies within a local domain. Also, because access controls are issued per domain, either each visiting agent must have its own domain or agents must share domain privileges. The former is unscalable and unfriendly to open systems. The latter neglects *The Principle of Least Privilege* allowing dissimilar agents to have the same permissions even when those privileges are unnecessary. Additionally, Java cannot authorize access based on a particular task or goal, dramatically restricting the potential for context-based authorization and privileges.

SMASH strives to enhance the software engineering of mobile agents by introducing a modular and adaptable system, so application developers can quickly customize mobile agents and platforms to their needed specifications and security requirements. SMASH emphasizes *security by design* but provides modularity so future application designers do not need to design around the architecture, but rather design for their application.

7   Conclusion

In creating and implementing this SMASH concept framework, we have created a flexible and expressive approach to defining secure mobile agent systems. This process has also elucidated several research issues for future work within the scope of improving the SMASH framework. As described earlier, a replacement language for the XML-like specifications of agendas and itineraries would help agents more flexibly define their plans and travel schedules. In addition, we plan to revamp the models of agent interactions within SMASH platforms to understand whether any relaxation of behaviors can be allowed without sacrificing the stringent security guarantees we have provided. The current restrictions placed on interactions among agents restricts the degree to which emergent behavior can be codified, possibly limiting the applicability of the current SMASH framework.

Another major undertaking is the formalization of the SMASH security guarantees and an evaluation of these guarantees against formalized security requirements. Section 4 provided an informal discussions of such issues, but a more rigorous evaluation will aid in arguing the system's robustness to common threats. Such a model will also help us assess the impact of future changes to the framework both in terms of expressiveness and security. Within this formalization, we will represent not only the secure architectural components but also the agents, their structure, and their interactions. This will help us more clearly explicate the manner in which we obfuscate agents' agendas and itineraries.

In this paper, we have defined SMASH, a mobile agent system with a unique combination of openness and security. SMASH affords agents confidence about the platforms with which they interact and platforms confidence about the agents they choose to support. In addition, SMASH makes it possible for an agent to move among platforms in a limited fashion without having to authenticate with platforms where the agent does not require access to privileged services. When an agent does authenticate with a platform, the two-directions of security help the platform ensure the agent is safe and helps the agent ensure that the platform is legitimate and that it can provide services required by the agent. As a final innovation, to support robust but simplified agent creation, SMASH agents are created using the Python scripting language. These agents are then supported by a middleware implemented in C++ and supported by a Trusted Platform Module (TPM) to provide the underlying stringent security guarantees.

In summary, multi-agent systems have the potential to improve current applications and open the door for new applications. Over the course of this paper, we have discussed how to improve the security in multi-agent systems, while allowing for an open architecture. SMASH is a new multi-agent system model that builds on past system innovations and incorporates new and existing security technologies. The paper discussed not only what SMASH can do, but it also showed that a multi-agent system can provide and implement an infrastructure based on information assurance. The paper also illustrated an application for *epidemic updates* build on the SMASH middleware. Overall, SMASH has the potential to improve the programmability of highly secure mobile agent systems.

Acknowledgments

The authors would like to thank the Center for Excellence in Distributed Global Environments for providing research facilities and the collaborative environment. This research was funded, in part, by the NSF, Grant # CNS-0620245. The views and conclusions herein are those of the authors and do not necessarily reflect the views of the sponsoring agencies.

References

1. Roth, V.: Obstacles to the Adoption of Mobile Agents. In: Proc. of the IEEE Int'l. Conf. on Mobile Data Management. (2004) 296–297
2. Ong, S., Sun, W.: Application of mobile agents in a web-based real-time monitoring system. The International Journal of Advanced Manufacturing Technology (2003) 33–40
3. Aye, T., Tun, K.M.L.: A collaborative mobile agent-based workflow system. In: Proc. 6th Asia-Pacific Symposium on Information and Telecommunication Technologies, APSITT. (2005) 59–65
4. San, K.M., Thant, H., Aung, S., Tun, K.M.L., Naing, T., Thein, N.L.: Mobile agent based collaborative learning system. In: Proc. 6th Asia-Pacific Symposium on Information and Telecommunication Technologies, APSITT. (2005) 83–88

5. Huang, J., Liu, D.Y., Yang, B.: Online autonomous auction model based on agent. In: Proc. of 2004 International Conference on Machine Learning and Cybernetics. Volume 1. (2004) 89–94
6. Jansen, W.: Intrusion detection with mobile agents. Computer Communications **25** (2002)
7. Gray, R.S., Kotz, D., Cybenko, G., Rus, D.: D'Agents: Security in a Multiple-Language, Mobile-Agent System. In: Mobile Agents and Security, London, UK, Springer-Verlag (1998) 154–187
8. Seleznyov, A., Ahmed, M.O., Hailes, S.: Agent-based Middleware Architecture for Distributed Access Control. In: Proc. of the 22nd Int'l. Multi-Conf. on Applied Informatics: Artificial Intelligence and Applications. (2004) 200–205
9. The National Security Agency: The SELinux Project. http://selinux.sourceforge.net/ (2005)
10. Trusted Computing Group: Trusted Computing Group Hompage. https://www.trustedcomputinggroup.org/home (2005)
11. Stallings, W.: Cryptography and Network Security: Principles and Practices. 4 edn. Prentice Hall, Englewood Cliffs, NJ, USA (2006)
12. V. Pathak and L. Iftode: Byzantine fault tolerant public key authentication in peer-to-peer systems. Computer Networks, Special issue on Management in Peer-to-Peer Systems: Trust, Reputation and Security **50**(4) (2006)
13. McCarty, B.: SELinux NSA's Open Source Security Enhanced Linux. 1 edn. OReilly Media, Inc., Sebastobol, CA, USA (2004)
14. Jochen, M., Marvel, L., Pollock, L.: A Framework for Tamper Detection Marking of Mobile Applications. In: Proc. of the 14th Int'l. Symp. on Software Reliability Engineering. (2003) 143–152
15. Page, J., Zaslavsky, A., Indrawan, M.: Countering Security Vulnerabilities in Agent Execution Using a Self Executing Security Examination. Proc. of the 3rd Int'l Joint Conf. on Autonomous Agents and Multiagent Systems (2004) 1486–1487
16. Hohl, F.: A Framework to Protect Mobile Agents by Using Reference States. Proc. of the 20th IEEE Int'l. Conf. on Distributed Computing Systems (2000) 410–419
17. Farmer, W., Guttman, J., Swarup, V.: Security for Mobile Agents: Authentication and State Appraisal. In: Proc. of the 4th European Symp. on Research in Computer Security, Springer-Verlag (1996) 118–130
18. Vigna, G.: Cryptographic Traces for Mobile Agents. In: Mobile Agents and Security. Volume 1419 of LNCS. Springer-Verlag (1998) 137–153
19. Cabri, G., Leonardi, L., Zambonelli, F.: MARS: A Programmable Coordination Architecture for Mobile Agents. IEEE Internet Computing **4**(4) (2000) 26–35
20. Suri, N., Bradshaw, J.M., Breedy, M.R., Groth, P.T., Hill, G.A., Jeffers, R., Mitrovich, T.S., Pouliot, B.R., Smith, D.S.: NOMADS: Toward a Strong and Safe Mobile Agent System. In: Proc. of the 4th Int'l. Conf. on Autonomous Agents. (2000) 163–164
21. Karjoth, G., Lange, D.B., Oshima, M.: A Security Model for Aglets. IEEE Internet Computing **1**(4) (1997) 68–77
22. Karnik, N.M., Tripathi, A.R.: Security in the Ajanta mobile agent system. Software—Practice and Experience **31**(4) (2001) 301–329
23. Marques, P., Santos, N., Silva, L., Silva, J.G.: The Security Architecture of the M&M Mobile Agent Framework. In: Proc. of the SPIE's Int'l. Symp. on The Convergence of Information Technologies and Communications. (2001)

Reasoning About Willingness in Networks of Agents

S. Dehousse[1], S. Faulkner[1], H. Mouratidis[2], M. Kolp[3], and P. Giorgini[4]

[1] Information Management Research Unit, University of Namur, Belgium
{stephane.dehousse, stephane.faulkner}@fundp.ac.be
[2] Innovative Informatics, School of Computing, Univ. of East London, England
h.mouratidis@uel.ac.uk
[3] Information System Unit - University of Louvain, Belgium
kolp@isys.ucl.ac.be
[4] Department of Information and Communication Technology, University of Trento
giorgini@dit.unitn.it

Abstract. The i* Strategic Dependency model has been successfully employed to analyze trust relationships of networks of agents during the early stages of multiagent systems development. However, the model only supports limited trust reasoning due to its limitation to deal with the vulnerability of the depender regarding the failure of the dependency. In this paper, we introduce the concept of willingness, which provides a solution to the above problem and therefore allows a more complete analysis and reasoning of trust relationships in networks of agents.

1 Introduction

An interesting challenge for the agent research community is the development of large-scale dependable Multiagent Systems. As stated in the Call for Papers (CFP) for the SELMAS'06 workshop, "the dependability of a computing system is its ability to deliver service that can be justifiably trusted". In multiagent systems, which consist of network of agents, this means that the developer needs to analyze explicitly the trust relationships between the different agents of the network/system.

The i* Strategic Dependency (SD) model has been employed to model trust relationships between agents and in many cases has been stated for its appropriateness to explore trust relationships during the early stages of a multiagent system development. Firstly, due to its rich modelling concepts, the model provides a better basis to explore the broader implications of trust relationships than conventional non-intentional models, such as data flow diagrams and/or object-oriented analysis languages (e.g. UML). Secondly, trust is not treated as an isolated concept with special semantics but it is considered simultaneously with other system goals. Moreover, the model facilitates the analysis of trust-related issues within the full operations and social context of the system-to-be and it also supports trade-off analysis of trust and other competing quality requirements such as performance.

The SD model [9] is used to construct a network of social dependencies amongst actors, where an actor represents an entity such as an agent that has intentionality and strategic goals within the information system or within its organisational setting. It is a graph, where each node represents an actor, and each link between two actors

R. Choren et al. (Eds.): SELMAS 2006, LNCS 4408, pp. 117–131, 2007.
© Springer-Verlag Berlin Heidelberg 2007

indicates that one actor depends on another for something in order that the former may attain some goal. A dependency describes an "agreement" (called dependum) between two actors: the depender and the dependee. The depender is the depending actor, and the dependee, the actor who is depended upon. The SD supports different types of dependencies describing the nature of the agreement. *Goal dependencies* are used to represent the transfer of responsibility for fulfilling a goal. *Softgoal* dependencies are similar to goal dependencies, but their fulfilments cannot be precisely defined (for instance, the appreciation is subjective, or the fulfilments can occur only to a given extent); *task dependencies* are used in situations where the dependee is required to perform a given action; and *resource dependencies* require the dependee to provide a resource for the depender.

However, the SD model demonstrates a limitation related to the vulnerability of the depender regarding the failure of the dependency[1]. Such limitation restricts developers in performing a full reasoning about the trust relationships of the system-to-be. In this paper we present an approach based on the concept of willingness to overcome this limitation.

It is worth mentioning that due to lack of space, we have decided to adopt a simplified notation for the purpose of this paper. In particular, agents are denoted by the set Ag noted as a, b,... $\in Ag$. We note the set of services S and a particular service as s_x where $s_x \subseteq S$.

- *depender(a, s_x)* means that a is depender for the service s_x.
- *dependee(a, s_x)* means that a is dependee about the service s_x.
- *depends(a, b, s_x)* means that a is depender, b is dependee about the service s_x

The rest of the paper is organized as follows. Section 2 discusses the vulnerability limitation inherent to $i*$. Section 3 introduces the concept of willingness and defines its different constituent elements, whereas Section 4 illustrates the concepts and limitations with the aid of scenarios. Section 5 discusses how willingness can be positively influenced to strengthen a dependency and Section 6 proposes the introduction of the delegation relationship. Finally, Section 7 presents related work while Section 8 concludes the paper and briefly presents future works.

2 The Down-Side of a Dependency

Although the Strategic Dependency model has been successfully employed to model trust relationships of networks of agents during the early stages of multiagent systems development, it supports limited trust reasoning due to its limitation to deal with the vulnerability of the depender regarding the failure of the dependency [9] (we call this the down-side of a dependency). This is an important issue since potential failure of dependencies may not only hurt the depender, but it may set off a perilous chain reaction that would endanger the whole system. This results that trust relationships cannot completely analyzed since developers cannot fully reason about the trust between the agents of the network.

---

[1] We define failure of a dependency as the situation in which a dependee fails to satisfy the dependency.

The above mentioned limitation is influenced by two elements. The first element is the vulnerability of the depender which is an intrinsic property of the dependency for the depender. The second element, that we call "failure of the dependency" is directly related to the dependee(s).

The next sections discuss these two components of the "down-side" of a dependency and present some definitions of the related concepts.

2.1 The Depender's Side

To sustain our analysis of the first constituent of the "down-side" of a dependency, we (re-)define the concept of vulnerability as follows:

Vulnerability is a characteristic of an agent, the depender that causes him to suffer of some incapability to achieve its goals as a result of the dependee failure to achieve the dependum.

This definition emphasizes that the vulnerability is an internal quality of the depender in a dependency. In other words, how vulnerable an agent is, regarding a dependum is only related to the importance of the dependum for the agent himself.

The i* SD model [9, 10] distinguishes three degrees of strength (importance) for a dependency applying independently on each side: Open ("O"), Committed (unmarked) and Critical ("X"). The degree of strength for the depender corresponds to its level of vulnerability about the dependum. In an *Open Dependency*, failure of the dependum would have no serious consequences on the depender: depender's vulnerability is low. In a *Committed Dependency*, failure of the dependum would significantly affect depender's goals: depender's vulnerability is average. In a *Critical Dependency* failure, of the dependum would seriously affect depender's goals: depender's vulnerability is high.

As a response to the "down-side" of a dependency, Yu [9] suggests three mechanisms: enforcement, assurance and insurance. An Enforcement mechanism consists of finding some way for the depender to cause some goal of the dependee to fail, e.g. if there is a reciprocal dependency. Assurance refers to a situation where there is some evidence that the dependee will deliver the dependum, apart from the dependee's claim, e.g. if the fulfilling of the commitment is in the dependee's own interest. These two measures would only have impact on the dependee's behaviour about the dependum, internally the depender's vulnerability would never be mitigated. Finally, insurance mechanisms are supposed to reduce vulnerability of a depender by reducing the degree of dependence on a particular dependee. The consequence of such measure is not a mitigation of the depender's vulnerability, but rather a potential increasing of the probability that the dependum will be achieved. Conversely to Yu's claim, all these mechanisms only contribute to fortifying a dependency, and do not help to mitigate vulnerability. Effective measures to mitigate vulnerability should rather try to influence importance of the dependum for the depender, e.g. by creating alternatives to the dependum or its parent goal(s) internally at the depender's side.

2.2 The Dependee's Side

This second element catches the dependee's influence on the "down-side" of the dependency. Especially, we study, at the dependee's side, the factors that contribute to the success or the failure of the dependency. To enable the success of a dependency, the dependee must have at least three qualities regarding the dependum: ability, authorization and willingness. The ability and authorization qualities of a dependee have been previously discussed by Giorgini et al. [6]. However, the dependee's willingness about the dependum remains an open question. The next section presents a detailed discussion of the dependee's willingness and its different constituents.

3 Dependee's Willingness

The *willingness (W°)* of an agent about a dependum expresses its intrinsic readiness to actually fulfil the dependum. It is based on the combination of three elements: the criticality (C°) of the dependum for the dependee, the pressure (P°) on the dependee about the dependum, the reciprocity (R°) with the depender(s). The willingness of an agent involved in the system can be derived for a specific goal, task or resource. The impact of the different constituent elements is weighted by weight parameters (α, β, γ) according to the domain application. These parameters enable the designer to adjust influence of the different factors to better suit the context of the implementation, i.e. greater β or γ than α corresponds to reputation-based systems or systems with a high degree of cooperation. Moreover, in order to be able to compare values computed for different agents, we constraint the willingness to be between 0 and 1 by imposing that the different factor's values range from 0 to 1 and that the sum of the weight parameters is equal to 1.

$$W°(a, s_x) = \alpha * C°(a, s_x) + \beta * P°(a, s_x) + \gamma * R°(a, s_x) \qquad \text{where } dependee(a, s_x)$$

The presentation of these elements will be illustrated through a running example. This example is a view of a substantial case study. For readability, we introduce here dramatis personae: **Bob** is purchasing manager, **Alice** and **Jos** are accountants and **Bert** is stock manager. Additionally, for sake of simplicity, in this approach, the notion of service is used to refer to a goal, a task, or a resource.

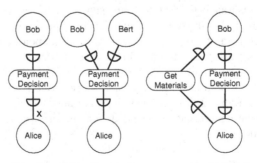

Fig. 1. a. Criticality - b. Pressure - c. Reciprocity

3.1 Criticality

The criticality ($C°$) factor catches information on the degree of importance a service has for an agent. This importance is based on the value of the service for the agent intrinsically, i.e. apart from any claim of other agent(s). This achievement of a dependum may be critical for a dependee, for different reasons like when the dependee has some goals related to the achievement of the dependum.

Example 1. *According to the company procedures, Alice is responsible for the accounting of the managers. She needs achievement of "payment decision" for each manager to do the accounting. Bob must have the payment decision about its order given by an accountant of the company. So Bob seek for Alice payment decision (Fig.1.a).*

In example 1, the goal of Alice, "do the accounting" is linked to the achievement of "payment decision" service. As a consequence, this service turns to be critical for Alice. These circumstances increase her willingness about its achievement. Through criticality analysis we have quantified some evidence that the dependee, Alice, has some interest to fulfill, apart from any claim of the depender, Bob.

Decision about the level of criticality of a service for an agent is taken by the designer.

$C°(a, s_x)$ in $[0,1]$ where dependee(a, s_x)

3.2 Pressure

The *pressure ($P°$)* catches information on the degree of influence that a group of dependers (targeting the same dependum) has on the dependee's behaviour. It is an external factor that impacts dependee's willingness about achievement of the dependum.

Example 2. *According to the company procedures, Bob needs a payment decision on its order and Bert needs payment decision to decide on the entry of an item in the stock. Yet, this decision can only be given by a company's accountant. So Bob and Bert seek for Alice payment decision. (Fig.1b)*

The dependency in example 2 has two dependers (Bob and Bert) about a dependum "payment decision" depending on Alice. Alice is therefore under pressure from Bob and Bert about this service. This pressure increases her willingness to fulfil the dependum.

To refine our analysis, the level of pressure can be different according to the relative position occupied by a depender. For example, the pressure imposes by Bob, purchasing manager, can be considered as greater than the pressure coming from Bert, stock manager. Consequently, the global pressure becomes the sum of the weighted individual pressure of the dependers involved. The weight (p) given to a position is determined by the designer or according to the application domain.

$P°(a, s_x) = 1 - 1/\exp(\sum p_{ag_i})$

where *dependee(a, s_x) and ag_i in {Ag | depends(ag_i, a, sx)}*

3.3 Reciprocity

The *reciprocity (R°)* factor catches information on the influence of relations of mutual dependence between the dependee and some depender(s).

Such reciprocal relationship makes the dependee, at her turn, vulnerable to the behaviour of the depender. Considering that agents basically follow rules of tit-for-tat, a situation of reciprocal relationship should positively influence the behaviour of the dependee agent about the fulfilment of the dependum.

Example 3. *According to the company procedures, the purchase manager is responsible for office materials order for all employees of the company. Therefore, Alice needs Bob to get her office material. Bob needs accountant payment decision on its order. So Bob seeks for Alice payment decision. (Fig.1c)*

In example 3, there is a relation of mutual dependence between Bob and Alice. As Alice is depending upon Bob, she would rather adopt behaviour in favour of Bob to positively influence Bob behaviour concerning her request. As agents adopt a tit-for-tat strategy, a reciprocal relationship increases the willingness of the dependee about the fulfilment of the dependum.

Moreover, we may reasonably argue that the more critical the dependum of the reciprocal dependency is for the dependee, the more this reciprocity increased its willingness. Therefore, the reciprocity factor is not only based on the number of mutual dependencies but also on their respective criticality for the dependee. In the example, if the criticality of "get material" service increases for Alice, her willingness about "payment decision" will be greater.

The formulae below can be used to determine the pressure that some depender(s) impose on a dependee.

$$R°(a, s_x) = 1 - \frac{1}{\exp\{\sum C°(a, s_y)\}}$$

where $s_x, s_y \in S, a, b \in Ag \mid depends(b, a, s_x) \wedge$
$depends(a, b, s_y)$

The reciprocity factor is directly related to the depender's claim; it turns into figures the ability of the depender to cause some goal of the dependee to fail.

4 Scenarios

When an agent needs to be involved in a dependency, he should trust the dependee. This trust reflects its estimation of the willingness of the dependee to actually personally fulfil the dependum. The previous section has presented the different elements that could help to determine this value. At the end of the estimation of a dependee's willingness about a service, the depender may have two conclusions either the value is greater enough to let unchanged the dependency either it is not. In the second case, the depender should try to improve willingness value. One solution consists in positively influencing, through specific measures, the determinants of this value: criticality, pressure or reciprocity. To sustain the presentation of such measures, we present three scenarios that emphasized different dependency's settings with variations on dependees' side.

Scenario 4 is the simplest dependency's configuration scenario which involves one depender and one dependee about a unique dependum.

Example 4. *According to the company procedures, Bob must have the payment decision about its order given by an accountant of the company. So Bob seek for Alice payment decision (Fig.2a).*

Scenarios 5 and 6 illustrate situation of one depender with several dependees.

Example 5. *According to the company procedures, Bob needs a decision on its payment order. Yet, this decision can only be given by one of the company's accountants. So Bob seeks for Alice **or** Jos payment decision. (Fig.2b)*

Example 6. *According to the company procedures, Bob needs a decision on its payment order. Yet, this decision must be given by two company's accountants. So Bob seeks for payment decision of Alice **and** Jos. (Fig.2c)*

While these scenarios are very similar, they present a difference of relationship between Bob, Alice and Jos. In example 5, Bob can have the payment decision from either Alice or Jos. Conversely, in example 6, Bob must have the payment decision fulfil by the intervention of both Alice and Jos. In the i* SD model, it is not possible to emphasize such distinction with concepts available. As a consequence, we propose to slightly extend the SD model of i* with concepts that enables the modelling of such situations.

A dependency with substitute dependees means that each dependee is able to fulfil alone the dependum.

A dependency with complementary dependees means that contribution of all dependees is required to fulfil the dependum.

The Bob, Alice and Jos relationship derived from scenario 5 corresponds to a dependency with substitute dependees. Indeed, Alice and Jos are both able to fulfil alone the payment decision service.

Conversely in scenario 6, neither Alice nor Jos can achieve alone fulfilment of payment decision service. Example 6 is a good illustration of a dependency with complementary dependees.

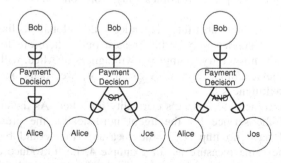

Fig. 2. a. One Dependee - b. Substitute Dependees - c. Complementary Dependees

5 Willingness Measures

5.1 One Depender-One Dependee

In Example 4, the willingness of Alice about "payment decision" dependum is clearly poor. The service is not critical at all for her, the pressure comes only from one depender and there is no reciprocal relationship. To improve her willingness, we can firstly try to influence the criticality of the service for her.

According to the definition of the criticality, a solution consists in creating a relation (precondition) between a goal of Alice with the dependum. It can be done through the introduction of a new procedure which could state that in order to achieve her goal "do accouting", Alice must have "payment decision" fulfilled (Fig.1a).

If it is not possible to increase criticality or not enough, then we could try to increase pressure on the dependee. Following example 1, Alice has only one depender. Adding a new depender will contribute to increase her willingness. In his position of stock manager, now, Bert has to have "payment decision" achieved in order to authorize or not the entry of ordered item in the stock. This procedure implies that Bert becomes an additional depender of the Bob-Alice dependency (Fig.1b).

Finally, if previous measures are not possible or enough, we could act on the reciprocity factor. The measure consists in adding a reciprocal dependency from Alice to Bob. For example, According to the company procedures, the purchase manager is responsible for office materials order for all employees of the company. As a consequence, to get her office material Alice must rely on Bob. This procedure implies the creation of a reciprocal dependency Alice-Bob about the dependum "get office material" (Fig.1c).

5.2 One Depender-Substitute Dependees

In the example 5, Bob seek for Alice or Jos consent about "payment decision". In the i* SD model, the situation leads to a dependency Bob-AliceorJos where Alice and Jos are substitute dependees. As Bob may rely either on Alice or Jos for its dependum, we should evaluate both the willingness of Alice and Jos.

The analysis of the willingness of Alice and Bob are quite similar and lead to the conclusion of a poor willingness about the service. For both Alice and Jos, the service is not critical at all, the pressure comes only from one depender and there is no reciprocal relationship.

As Alice and Jos are substitute dependees, the global willingness about the dependum for the depender Bob is the greatest one. Therefore to improve global willingness, we can chose to try to improve willingness of Alice, willingness of Jos or even both. To enable comparison with example 4, we focus on the solutions to increase Alice's willingness.

First option is to increase service's criticality for Alice. As the criticality is based on the value of the service for the agent intrinsically, the presence of another dependee should have no impact on the measures that could be taken. We can therefore used the same measure as for example 4, i.e. introduce a new procedure which state that in order to achieve her goal "do accouting", Alice must have "payment decision" fulfilled (Fig.3a). Thanks to the new procedure, the "payment decision" service becomes critical for Alice. In example 4, conclusion of this measure was an increasing of the criticality factor of Alice about the dependum.

But, due to the introduction of a new dependee, this measure appears to have another consequence on the relationships between Bob, Alice and Jos. As Jos is also able to fulfil Alice's critical service, she could initiate a dependency on Jos about it, in order for her to easily or better achieve her related goal, "do accounting". We can consider that Alice is becoming an additional depender on the dependency Bob-AliceorJos (Fig.3b). It increases the pressure factor of the other dependee(s), i.e. Jos, about the dependum. As a consequence, by making the dependum critical for a dependee, in a situation of substitute dependees, we not only have increased this dependee willingness but also the other dependee(s) willingness through an increasing of the pressure they face.

In a situation with substitute dependees another measure may be used to increase criticality of the dependum for a dependee. It consists in creating incentives for the dependee about personnaly achieving the dependum.

Example 7. *Alice receives a bonus for each payment decision. Alice wants to increase her personal payoff. So she has interest in achieving herself "payment decision". Bob can seek for Alice or Jos about payment decision.*

In example 7, Alice has now great interests in being the one that actually achieve "payment decision" while the situation of Jos is unchanged. It results in a situation of partial competition between Alice and Jos, indeed incentives are only on Alice's side.

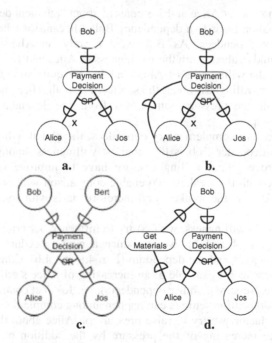

Fig. 3. Scenarios with Substitutes Dependees

Now, if we also create incentives for Jos to personally achieve "payment decision", the competition becomes full. Configurations of competition between substitute dependees may considerably reduce chances of dependency failure for the depender.

If it is not possible to increase criticality or not enough, then we could try to increase pressure on the dependees. As for the criticality factor, we can reemploy the measure used in example 4: introducing an additional depender, Bert (Fig.3c). Such measure will always affect all dependees while its respective impact is based on the position criteria. Therefore, we have not only achieved increasing of pressure on Alice but also on Jos.

Finally, if previous measures are not possible or enough, we could act on the reciprocity factor. Like in example 4, we create an internal procedure that implies the creation of a reciprocal dependency Alice-Bob about the dependum "get office material" (Fig.3d). The reciprocity factor of Alice has increased while Jos' one is unchanged. A situation of substitute dependees does not affect measures related to the reciprocity factor.

As a conclusion, we have demonstrated that a situation of substitute dependees does not influence measures on pressure and reciprocity factor. Yet, it affects measures related to the criticality factor.

In a dependency with substitute dependees, the global willingness about the dependum is the maximum of the willingness of the dependees.

5.3 One Depender-Complementary Dependees

In Example 6, Bob seek for Alice and Jos consent about "payment decision". In the i* SD model, the situation leads to a dependency Bob-AliceandJos where Alice and Jos are complementary dependees. As Bob have to rely on Alice and Jos for its dependum, we should evaluate both the willingness of Alice and Jos.

The analysis of the willingness of Alice and Jos are quite similar and lead to the conclusion of a poor willingness about the service. For both Alice and Jos, the service is not critical at all, the pressure comes only from one depender and there is no reciprocal relationship.

As Alice and Jos are complementary dependees, the global willingness about the dependum for the depender Bob is the smallest willingness among the dependees. Therefore to improve global willingness, we have to improve willingness of all dependees, starting with the weakest. To enable comparison with previous examples, we consider that Alice is the weakest and therefore starts with solutions to increase Alice's willingness.

To increase Alice's willingness, we first try to influence her criticality factor. Like in previous examples (4 and 5), we introduce a new procedure to create a link between one of her goals and the dependum (Fig. 4.a and 4.b). Consequences of this measure are the same as for example 5: an increasing of Alice's criticality factor and an increasing of the pressure on other dependee(s), i.e. Jos. Yet contrary to example 5, by definition, no competition settings can happen among complementary dependees.

After criticality factor, we try to raise pressure on Alice about the dependum. As for example 5, the increasing of the pressure by the addition of a new depender impacts all dependees, i.e. Alice and Jos (Fig. 4.c).

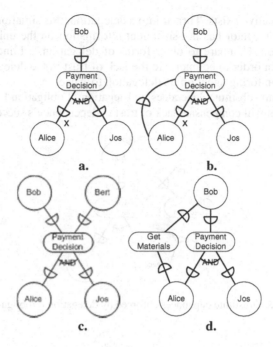

Fig. 4. Complementary Dependees

Finally to increase the reciprocity factor of Alice, we create a new relationship between Alice and Bob (Fig. 4.d). It affects Alice's reciprocity factor without any impact on Jos' willingness factors.

In a dependency with complementary dependees, the global willingness about the dependum is the minimum of the willingness of the dependees. Consequently, measures to improve it should try to increase factors for dependee(s) with the lowest willingness.

6 Delegation Measures

In the previous section, we have analyzed measures to improve willingness through its different constituent elements. If these measures are still not enough to ensure minimum trust of the depender in dependee's success, the depender may transform its dependency into a constraining delegation: delegation of obligation.

A delegation of obligation gives an imperative order from the delegator on the execution, the access to or the fulfillment of the delegatum [4]. The delegator corresponds to the depender of the dependency and the delegatum is an expression of the dependum.

In example 4, if all measures to improve willingness of Alice have failed, we can set up a delegation between Alice and Bob about the dependum. Concretely, Bob makes a positive delegation of obligation on Alice about the service "give payment decision". A positive obligation means that Alice is forced to do something, opposite to negative obligation force to not do. Moreover, in example 4, Bob has only one dependee, no alternative exists. Turned into a delegation, this situation leads to a blind delegation as the delegator has not sufficient information on the unique delegatee to form a trust opinion. Compare to other forms of delegation, a blind delegation will require a monitor in order to compensate the lack of trust in the delegatee. Bob would therefore add a monitoring agent on its delegation to Alice.

In example 5 with substitute dependees, a delegation of obligation from Bob on Alice about the dependum will compensate lack of trust in dependency's success (Fig. 5).

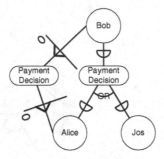

Fig. 5. Substitute dependees enforced by delegation of obligation

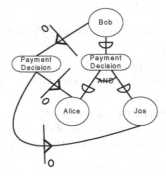

Fig. 6. Complementary dependees enforced by delegation of obligation

In example 6 with complementary dependees, the delegation of obligation must target all dependees, i.e. Alice and Jos, in order to compensate lack of trust in dependency's success. Indeed, imposing a delegation only on some dependees would be inefficient as the trust in dependency's success corresponds to the weakest willingness of the group of dependees (Figure 6).

7 Related Work

In the i* SD model, it is assumed throughout the analysis that the dependee will honour the dependency. However, this is not always the case meaning that the depender becomes vulnerable to the failure of the dependency [9]. As a consequence to the presence of such "down-side" of a dependency, evaluation of trust in the dependee about the dependum is crucial.

The line of work initiated by Castelfranchi and Falcone [3] has highlighted the importance of a cognitive view of trust (particularly for Belief-Desire-Intention agents [8]). To evaluate the trust an actor place in another actor about a service, different beliefs related to the motivations of the agent are considered: competence, willingness, persistence and motivation. For example, the competence belief refers to the agent capability to deliver the service. Additionally, in recent work, Giorgini et al. [5, 6], borrow the notion of capability to address the problem of trust in dependency. Their approach states that if an agent has both permission and capability about a service, than the depender can be confident about dependency's success. Permission can be the result of ownership or delegation while capability could also be delegated. While this approach is quite interesting, it just gives a partial view on trust in dependency, because, as noticed by Castelfranchi and Falcone, capability is only a pre-requisite to trust. Our work complements this approach by dealing with the impact of the other beliefs (willingness, persistence and motivation) on dependency's failure. For sake of simplicity, we use the notion of agent's willingness that regroups through its different determinants the characteristics of these beliefs.

In the original work on i* SD model [9], the "down-side" of a dependency has been treated mainly through the concept of vulnerability. Surprisingly, this concept has not been clearly defined. More recent papers [7, 10] state that dependency relationships bring vulnerabilities to the system and the depending actor (the depender). However, our work has demonstrated that vulnerability of the depending actor is not a consequence of the dependency but rather an intrinsic property of the agent. Therefore, to clarify the situation, we have suggested a new definition for the concept of vulnerability. Moreover, we have suggested that the measures presented by Yu [9] to mitigate vulnerability were in fact measures to fortify the dependency by influencing dependee's behaviour.

8 Conclusion and Future Work

In this paper we have argued that in order to fully reason about trust during the development of multiagent systems, developers should consider the willingness of a dependee to fulfill the dependum. We have also described an approach to reason about willingness of agents based on the concepts of criticality, pressure and reciprocity. Our approach provides a first solution to the vulnerability limitation demonstrated by the i* SD model, and therefore allows developers to reason about trust in a structured way.

Our work is still at an exploratory stage. The proposed approach has been applied to various examples of application domains from the literature but it still remains to be applied in a large-scale real-life case study.

It is worth commenting on the scope and the domain characteristics for which we believe the presented approach is appropriate. It is intended that the proposed process is performed by a software engineer (or software team), during design time, and not from software agents during run-time. We envisage the approach to be suitable for a large number of agent-based applications, where it is possible to identify stakeholders and their dependencies and where vulnerabilities of actor dependencies play an important role for the realization of the system's goals. As such, we believe that our approach is not suitable for the development of embedded software or system software (operating systems for instance) since in such systems there are no identifiable stakeholders. Moreover, due to lack of automated tool support, and the difficulty in considering manually all the possible conflicts identified during the vulnerability analysis, we believe that our approach is suitable for analyzing small to medium size agent based systems of up to 100 agents. We anticipate however that tool support will extend the applicability of the presented approach to large-scale real world agent-based applications.

As a result, future work includes the implementation of automatic tool support for the proposed approach as well as the development of a methodology to help computation of the willingness determinants based on refined formulae. We also plan to investigate solutions at the SD or SR levels that mitigate depender's vulnerability. In particular, we believe it would be interesting to consider the introduction of new goals or softgoals that could impact depender's vulnerability.

References

1. M. Blaze and J. Feigenbaum and A. D. Keromytis: The Role of Trust Management in Distributed Systems Security, In *Proc. of Secure Internet Programming* (1999) 185-210
2. J. Carter and E. Bitting and A. A. Ghorbani: Reputation Formalization within Information Sharing Multiagent Architectures, In *Proc. of Computational Intelligence* (2002) 45-64
3. C. Castelfranchi and R. Falcone: Principles of trust for MAS: cognitive anatomy, social importance, and quantification, In *Proc. of Int. Conf. of Multi-Agent Systems (ICMAS'98)* (1998) 72-79
4. S. Faulkner and S. Dehousse: A Delegation Model for Designing Collaborative Multi-agent Systems, In *Proc. of 9th Int. Conf. on Knowledge-Based Intelligent Information and Engineering Systems (KES'05)*, R. Khosla, R. J. Howlett, L. C. Jain (Ed.), Lecture Notes in Computer Science, Vol. 3682, Springer-Verlag GmbH, Melbourne, Australia (September, 2005) 858.
5. P. Giorgini and F. Massacci and J. Mylopoulos and and N. Zannone: Filling the gap between Requirements Engineering and Public Key/Trust Management, In *Proc. of 2nd Int. Conf. on Trust Management (iTrust'04)* (2004).
6. P. Giorgini and F. Masscci and J. Mylopoulos and and N. Zannone: Modeling Security Requirements Through Ownership, Permission and Delegation, In *Proc. of 13th IEEE Int. Conf. on Requirements Engineering (RE'05)*, IEEE Computer Society Press, Los Alamitos, California (2005).
7. L. Liu and E. S. K. Yu and J. Mylopoulos: Security and Privacy Requirements Analysis within a Social Setting, In *Proc. of 11th IEEE Int. Conf. on Requirements Engineering (RE'03)* (2003) 151-161.
8. M. Wooldridge: *An Introduction to MultiAgent Systems*. John Wiley and Sons, Chichester, England, (2002).

9. E. S. K. Yu and J. Mylopoulos: From E-R to "A-R" - Modelling Strategic Actor Relationships for Business Process Reengineering, In *Proc. of 13th Int. Conf. on the Entity-Relationship (ER'94)*, Pericles Loucopoulos (Ed.), Lecture Notes in Computer Science, Springer (1994) 548-565.
10. E. S. K. Yu and L. Liu: Modelling Trust for System Design Using the i* Strategic Actors Framework, In *Proc. of Trust in Cyber-societies: Integrating the Human and Artificial Perspectives*, R. Falcone, M. Singh, Y.-H. Tan (Ed.), Lecture Notes in Computer Science, Vol. 2246, Springer-Verlag GmbH (2000) 175-194.

Towards Compliance of Agents in Open Multi-agent Systems

Jorge Gonzalez-Palacios and Michael Luck

School of Electronics and Computer Science
University of Southampton
Southampton SO17 1BJ
United Kingdom
jlgp02r@ecs.soton.ac.uk, mml@ecs.soton.ac.uk

Abstract. With the introduction of large-scale open systems, the need for managing interactions between agents, and in particular for managing the entry of a new agent into an existing system, becomes an increasingly more important objective. Without such management, there may be significant implications for the performance of such systems, negating the benefits to be gained from openness. In this paper, we sketch a process by which open multi-agent systems may be *engineered*, through the establishment of a system specification to be used by designers of agents that will enter the system, and by the system itself to check that an agent entering a system complies with the system constraints. While not fully detailed, the paper provides an initial model and a clear direction as to how such a system may be constructed, offering a new way of developing open multi-agent systems.

1 Introduction

The number of computers and computational devices has increased significantly in the last few years and, since these devices rarely work on their own, the number of networks has also exploded. In software, new technologies such as pervasive computing and the Grid are also emerging and take advantage of these networks. These technologies have brought challenging problems in computer science and software engineering, since they demand systems that are highly distributed, proactive, situated and *open.*

An open system is one that allows the incorporation of components at run-time that may not be known at design time. Usually, the components of an open system are not designed and developed by the same group, nor do they represent the same stakeholders. In addition, different groups may use different development tools and may follow different policies or objectives, thus leading to *heterogeneous* systems. Regardless of how and by whom a component is developed, it typically has the same rights to access the facilities provided by the system, as well as the obligation to adhere to its rules.

The introduction of large-scale open systems of this kind is likely to lead to a new set of problems, however, relating to the effects of interactions between

R. Choren et al. (Eds.): SELMAS 2006, LNCS 4408, pp. 132–147, 2007.
© Springer-Verlag Berlin Heidelberg 2007

agents. Indeed, what we are beginning to witness is the emergence of computational societies, of electronic organisations, and of all the variety of good and bad consequences that they bring with them. Just as in human societies, we need to consider the impact of regulations and their absence, of opportunistic and malicious behaviour, and we need to find ways to organise and manage systems in order to mitigate their potential deleterious effect on a system as a whole. While some work has been done on each of these concerns, their combination in large-scale open systems has not been addressed, yet they are fundamental requirements if the visions of Grid computing, for example, are to be realised.

However, traditional approaches (e.g., object-oriented and component-based computing) have fallen short in *engineering* this type of application because they operate at too low a level of abstraction. For example, object-oriented computing decomposes a system into entities (or *objects*) that encapsulate information and functionality. This information, however, usually refers to basic data structures or to other objects. Similarly, the functionality of objects relies on simple procedures like those normally found in most programming languages. Elaborated object decompositions, although possible, tend to make it difficult to understand and design applications that involve high-level concepts such as grid services and workflows.

In response, different approaches have been attempted to facilitate the development of such complex applications. In particular, some evidence suggests that the multi-agent approach provides adequate abstractions to successfully develop this type of system [6], and this has resulted in the appearance of several agent-oriented software methodologies which claim to support the construction of open systems. Although agent-oriented software methodologies exist to support the development of open systems, they are lacking when dealing with the incorporation of new components (or agents) to an existing system. In particular, these methodologies do not address two different but very related problems:

- how to specify the facilities provided by the existing system for those interested in the development of new agents; and
- how to design and construct mechanisms to ensure that the integrity of the system is not violated at run-time by new agents.

Solving these problems requires the accomplishment of some non-trivial tasks. In order to solve the first problem of specifying the facilities provided by the system, we must first accomplish the selection of appropriate abstractions on which to base the specification. For the second problem of ensuring that the integrity of the system is not violated at run-time, mechanisms for monitoring the behaviour of the system and evaluation of its characteristics must be provided.

Although complete solutions to these problems are highly application and platform dependent, we can, nevertheless, separate more general problems from more specific ones and provide partial solutions. In particular, in order to create agents that are eventually incorporated into an existing system, developers need to know what facilities are provided by the system, and the way in which they can access them, so that they can design new agents in accordance with these characteristics. In addition, developers must be aware of the rules of behaviour of the system, and design new agents in such a way that those rules are observed at run-time. From the perspective of maintaining the integrity of the system, this is particularly important in the case of multi-agent systems, because the autonomy and pro-activity exhibited by agents can easily lead to unexpected behaviour.

In this paper we present an initial model for the specification of open multi-agent systems based on organisational concepts, and then take some first steps in applying it to create a mechanism for checking that a specification is observed at run-time. In Section 2, we analyse the characteristics of a specification in open multi-agent systems, that is, *what* must be included, and *how* to express it. Then, in Section 3 we formalise such a specification. The next sections address the problem of how to check that such a specification is observed at run-time, focussing in particular on checking that the protocol used complies with the system specification. Finally, we present some conclusions.

2   Specification of Open Multi-agent Systems

We now move to a consideration of creating specifications of open systems, in such a way that potential participants can determine the requirements and benefits of joining the system. In our case, the targets of such a description are the designers of the agents, so we do not address the problem of *adaptive* agents, although some of the considerations presented here may also apply in the case that the new agents automatically adapt to the specification at run-time.

Such a specification must be as neutral as possible, since the agents might be developed with varied techniques. However, at least some basic assumptions must be made; in particular, the use of some common, appropriate concepts is required. We use *role*, *protocol* and *organisation* as the basic concepts on which a specification can be constructed. In general, these abstractions appropriately model the characteristics found in multi-agent applications, and they give rise to a set of models that provide the documentation necessary both for developers and for automatic compliance monitoring in order for agents to join open systems in effective and managed ways. (Other approaches for controlling the behaviour of open multi-agent systems are based on fewer abstractions, for example agent interaction or protocols [8,7]. Although this might result in less restrictions about how agents are implemented, it tends to complicate the specification of certain type of restrictions, such as those referring to the number of times a role is permitted to be enacted.)

2.1   Participants Model

The participants model contains the description of each agent of the system, referring only to those individual characteristics that do not involve interaction with other agents, and that are independent of how the agent is implemented. Since we model agents by means of roles then, according to the characterisation of roles we employ, the participant model consists of the set of roles in the system and, for each of them, a list of their services and non-functional requirements.

Services are tasks that a role can perform without interacting with other roles. We propose a simple characterisation of a service consisting of a name, the role to which the service belongs, its input and output parameters, and a description of the task itself. Since the actual implementation of the process is not restricted by the specification, its description can be text, pseudocode or any formal description. Regarding the non-functional requirements, we follow a simple approach consisting of representing each requirement by an identifier-value pair, for example $(memory, 40)$, where the identifiers and their possible values have previously been defined.

$Role_1$
$\quad service_1 \; (list\_of\_parameters)$ $\qquad$ //description
$\qquad ...$
$\quad service_n \; (list\_of\_parameters)$ $\qquad$ //description

$\quad [(id_1, value_1)]$
$\qquad ...$
$\quad [(id_m, value_m)]$
$\quad ...$
$Role_k$

Fig. 1. The general form of the participants model

The general form of the participants model is shown in Figure 1, in which requirements identifiers are denoted by id_i and their corresponding value by $value_i$. The square brackets indicate that the use of non-functional requirements is optional. As an example, Figure 2 presents a fragment of the participants model corresponding to a Conference Management System (for which no explanation is needed), but lack of space prevents us from presenting the complete example. This simple example shows three participants, each one having a service. (Note that in this section we use different fonts in figures, to differentiate the general form of a model from the corresponding example.)

2.2 Interactions Model

The interactions model describes the way roles interact by means of protocols. Our protocol characterisation is inspired by a simplified version of *sequence diagrams* similar to those of AUML, and represents the participating roles in the protocol, the messages they exchange, and the sequence of those messages. The messages are labelled with their communicative act and content, or with an identifier (whose communicative act and content are defined elsewhere, e.g. in [4]). The communicative acts must be described in the agent communication language

```
Author
      write(Paper)                         //an original paper is written

ProgramCommittee
      select(Papers, Reviews)              //select the conference papers

Reviewer
      review(Paper, Review)                // review a paper
```

Fig. 2. The application of the Participants Model to the CMS example

$$
\begin{aligned}
&Protocol_1 \\
&\qquad participant_1 \ldots participant_n \\
&\qquad parameter_1 \ldots parameter_m \\
&\qquad message_1 \\
&\qquad \ldots \\
&\qquad message_k \\
&\quad \ldots \\
&Protocol_r \\
&\qquad \ldots
\end{aligned}
$$

Fig. 3. The general form of the interactions model

specified in the Agent communication language layer. In the same way, the content must belong to the content language specified in the Content language layer and the specification of general concepts.

Figure 3 shows the general form of the interactions model, in which each of the messages in the protocol is formed of a sender, a receiver, a communicative act and a content. An example showing a fragment of the interactions model for the Conference Management System is presented in Figure 4, which contains two protocols, *SubmitPaper* and *ReviewPaper*. For each protocol, the first line contains the list of participants, the second line its parameters, and from the third line on, the messages. The *ReviewPaper* protocol, for instance, involves roles *ProgramCommittee* and *Reviewer*, has parameters *paper* and *review*, and employs two messages.

2.3 Social Constraints Model

The specification of social constraints contains the restrictions imposed on the agents' social behaviour. Such restrictions are represented by means of organisational concepts, more specifically by organisational rules. Organisational rules

SubmitPaper
    Author, ProgramCommittee
    paper, confirmationNumber
    Author, ProgramCommittee, inform_paper, paper
    ProgramCommittee, Author, inform_confirmation, confirmationNumber
ReviewPaper
    ProgramCommittee, Reviewer
    paper, review
    ProgramCommittee, Reviewer, request_review, paper
    Reviewer, ProgramCommittee, inform_review, review

Fig. 4. The application of the Interactions Model to the CMS example

are key to the definition of the organisation and thus of the system itself. For this reason, an agent attempting to join an existing system must be provided with the set of rules it must adhere to. The specification of social constraints is formed from the list of organisational rules of the system, expressed in some appropriate language (which we will not consider in this paper because of space constraints). The general form of this model is represented in Figure 5, and an example consisting of two rules is shown in Figure 6. In the latter figure, the first rule states that there must be at least five reviewers, while the second rule states that the program committee must not assign a paper for review, to the same reviewer, more than once.

$$organisational\_rule_1$$
$$\ldots$$
$$organisational\_rule_n$$

Fig. 5. The general form of the social constraints model

2.4 Summary

Up to this point, in this paper, we have focused on the creation of a system specification. Based on the results obtained here, in the following sections we explore the problem of ensuring that what is stated in the specification is observed at run time. Roughly, our approach consists of checking that the actions performed by an agent do not violate any of conditions stated in the sections of the specification. However, before proceeding, we formalise a specification and consider the problem of examining that the specification is complete and free of inconsistencies.

```
card(Reviewer) >= 5

For all p:paper, r: Reviewer, w: review
        card(ReviewPaper(ProgramComittee, r, p, w)) <= 1
```

Fig. 6. The application of the Social Constraints Model to the CMS example

3 A Model of Open Systems

In an open multi-agent system specification the details of the internal structure of the agents are not important, but only their functionality. This is because the agents in the system may be constructed by different developers and following different techniques. For the same reason, the implementation details of the protocols are not relevant, but only their patterns of interaction. This ensures that the agents can be developed according to different tools if they comply with the rules of the system. In this section we present a formal model for open multi-agent systems, based on organisational concepts, and that abstracts the functionality of the agents and the way they interact, regardless of implementation issues.

We define a model for an open multi-agent system as a tuple $\langle \mathcal{E}, \mathcal{N}, \mathcal{P}, \mathcal{S}, \mathcal{O} \rangle$, where:

1. $\mathcal{E}$ is a 4-tuple of set of elements of the system;
2. $\mathcal{N}$ is the set of the *roles' non-functional requirements*;
3. $\mathcal{P}$ is the set of *protocols*;
4. $\mathcal{S}$ is the set of *services*; and
5. $\mathcal{O}$ is the set of *social constraints*.

3.1 Elements of an Open System

$\mathcal{E}$, the tuple of elements in the system, has the form $\langle R, P, S, D \rangle$, where each entry is a set whose elements are identifiers, as follows:

1. R is the set of role identifiers;
2. P is the set of protocol identifiers;
3. S is the set of service identifiers; and
4. D is the set of identifiers of general concepts, which are resources and entities of the environment that are used in the description of other parts of the model, such as protocols, services and social constraints.

3.2 Non-functional Requirements

The elements of the set $\mathcal{N}$ have the form (r, n, v), where $r \in R$, n denotes a type of non-functional requirement, and v represents a possible *value* of n. The interpretation of this is that such a role requires at least that value for the non-functional requirement in order to be played. For example, in the conference management system,

$$(ProgrammeCommitteeChair, confidentiality, 1)$$

indicates that the role *Chair* must comply with the highest (1) confidentiality. However, it must be noted that the list of non-functional requirements and their associated values are highly dependent on the application and platform used.

3.3 Protocols

Each element of $\mathcal{P}$, the set of protocols, is a 5-tuple of the form (p, I, C, A, M), where:

1. $p \in P$ is a unique protocol name,
2. $I \in R$ is the initiator of the protocol,
3. $C \subset R$ is the set of collaborators, that is, the roles that participate in the protocol, apart from the initiator,
4. $A \subset D$ is the set of input and output parameters,
5. M is the allowed sequence of messages, expressing the order the messages must follow during the execution of the protocol. This is a sequence of instructions, each of which is either a message or a *compound message*. A compound message encompasses a *connector* and a *set* of messages, and represents the concurrency connectors of AUML. Concurrency connectors are used as a means to express that multiple messages are sent at the same time, and are of three types: *and* (AND), *inclusive or* (OR), and *exclusive or* (XOR). In the first case all the messages are sent in parallel, while in the second zero or more messages are sent and in the last case only one message is sent.

Finally, each element of M, the set of messages of a protocol, has the form (r_s, r_r, b), where:

$r_s \in R$ is the sender;
$r_r \in R$ is the receiver; and
b is the body of the message.

3.4 Services

$\mathcal{S}$, the set of services, consists of elements of the form (s, r, B), where:
$s \in S$ is a unique service name, and
$r \in R$ is the role to which the service belongs,
$B \subset D$ is the list of parameters of the service.

3.5 Social Constraints

$\mathcal{O} \subset \mathcal{L}$, the set of social constraints, contains the expressions that govern the function of the system.

Table 1 summarises this notation. For simplicity, we do not include the part corresponding to the sequence of messages, but only the structure of each message.

Table 1. Summary of notation

$\mathcal{E}$ element identifiers		
R	role identifiers	
P	protocol identifiers	
S	service identifiers	
D	concept identifiers	
$\mathcal{N}$ non-functional reqs.		
r	role to which applies	
n	non-functional reqs. identifier	
v	value	
$\mathcal{P}$ protocols		
p	protocol identifier	
I	initiator	
C	collaborators	
A	protocol parameters	
M	sequence of messages	
	For each message:	
	s_e	sender
	s_r	receiver
	b	body
$\mathcal{S}$ services		
s	service identifier	
r	role	
B	service parameters	
$\mathcal{O}$ social constraints		

4   Compliance Monitoring

A specification describes a system from different perspectives; for example the specification of protocols deals with the interaction aspects while the specification of participants focuses on the individual aspect of roles. However, it is essential that these perspectives are not in contradiction, but describe the system in a *consistent* form. For instance, an organisational rule cannot reference a protocol that has not been defined in the specification of interaction protocols. For this reason, we need a mechanism for checking consistency in the specification. Such a mechanism can be implemented in different ways; for example, by means of a software tool the consistency can be checked every time the specification is updated. Whatever the mechanism used, the following conditions must be checked.

1. The name of roles, protocols, responsibilities and general concepts must be unique.
2. All the protocols mentioned in the specification must be described in the specification of interaction protocols.

3. All the roles mentioned in the specification participate in at least one protocol and have at least one responsibility.
4. All the resources mentioned in the specification must be defined in the specification of general concepts.

5   Static Analysis on Agent Entry

As mentioned above, our approach to the problem of ensuring the integrity of an open system is to check, at run-time, that what is stated in the specification is not violated. In other words, we are assuming that the integrity of a system is ensured if all the conditions expressed in the specification are observed. On the other hand, since organisational rules form a part of a specification, and the purpose of organisational rules is to ensure the correct behaviour of the system, it follows that the observance of the specification can also ensure that the system behaves as expected at run-time. This is particularly helpful when no other methods of verification or validation are used.

Another assumption that we make deals with how agents enter a system. We assume that each time an agent attempts to enter the system, a mechanism is used to decide whether its entry is accepted. Also, if they are accepted, and during their lifetime, agents can play roles, or quit playing roles. Both actions are notified to the system, and the former needs authorisation too.

Based on the assumption above, and with the aim of monitoring their behaviour, we divide the functionality of an agent into *static* and *dynamic*. Static functionality occurs during the entry of the agent or when a role is assigned to the agent, whereas dynamic functionality occurs (perhaps additionally) at any other moment, for example a protocol initiation.

To illustrate this point, suppose that an agent intends to enter the system. It must first receive approval from a run-time component, hereafter called the *monitor* and depicted in Figure 7. As suggested in the figure, the only way for an agent to access the system is by getting approval from the monitor, based on the *characteristics* of the agent, and the specification of the system. By developing such a monitor, we provide a means to verify statical functionality, for example to detect if an agent's protocol has an incorrect *initiator role*, in the sense that it does not match what is stated in the specification. However, the monitor does not consider aspects that are not verifiable statically, such as if a protocol is executed at the wrong moment.

With these considerations in mind, we proceed to analyse how to check the observance of a specification.

5.1   Run-Time Participants Analysis

The run-time analysis for the participants has the aim of ensuring that the agents comply with the participants model of the specification. This can be done statically, at the moment the agent requests authorisation to play a role. Note that the agent can be playing other roles, or no role at all before attempting

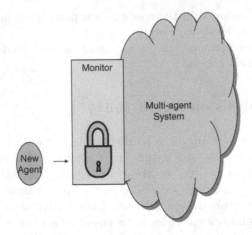

Fig. 7. The function of the monitor

to play a specific role. When an agent requests authorisation to play a role, the monitor must check that the characteristics of the agent, and the way it implements the role, match the conditions stated in the participants model. More specifically, given the role in question, the services as implemented by the agent, and the resources that the agent possesses, the monitor must check that the following conditions hold.

- The role that the agent intends to play exists and is available; that is, the role has not exceeded its cardinality.
- The agent has enough resources to satisfy each of the non-functional requirements specified in the participants model.
- The agent implements all the services specified in the model, and in the way they are specified, in terms of name and parameters.
- Optionally, for a stricter checking, the agent does not implement other services apart from those specified in the model.

Note, however, that checking the services in this way only offers a guarantee that their interfaces have been correctly implemented, but does not say anything about whether their implementation is *semantically* correct; for example, if instead of adding two numbers, they are multiplied.

5.2   Run-Time Protocol Analysis

During the entry of an agent to the system, we can also check, to some extent, whether the protocols implemented by the agent correspond to those specified. Essentially, the procedure is a matter of matching the characteristics of both protocols: those of the agent implementation and those specified in the system. Most of the checking is straightforward, except the part regarding the sequence of messages of the protocol, which depends on how many features of the sequence diagrams are considered. According to this, the algorithm is divided into two parts: matching the head and matching the messages. Protocols are accepted only if they are accepted in both parts. However, it must be noted that this procedure does not check the dynamic characteristics of the protocol, such as the *actual* sequence in which the messages are sent, nor the actual content of the messages, since there is no mechanism to guarantee that the characteristics of the protocol, as were checked, are observed during the operation.

In the following, such a procedure, together with its inputs and outputs, is presented.

Algorithm for Matching the Head. The matching the head part deals with checking that the role exists and that the protocols correspond to those specified in the interactions model. The interactions model was presented in Section 2.2, and is refined below using a notation that is more appropriate for expressing the algorithm.

Let $R = \{r_1, r_2, \ldots, r_k\}$ be the set of roles of the system (where k is the number of roles), and

Q_i the set of protocols associated to role r_i.

Since Q_i contains the protocols associated with role r_i, it can be expressed as $Q_i = \{q_1^i, q_2^i, \ldots, q_{m_i}^i\}$, where m_i is the number of protocols associated with role i, and each q_j^i denotes a protocol and thus have the form

$q_j^i = (p_j^i, I_j^i, C_j^i, A_j^i, M_j^i)$, where:

p_j^i is the name of the protocol,

$I_j^i \in R$ denotes the initiator,

$C_j^i \subset R$ denotes the collaborators,

A_j^i is the (ordered) sequence of parameters of the protocol, each consisting of a *name* and a *type*, so we can express it as

$A_j^i = \left\langle (a_1, t_1), (a_2, t_2), \ldots, \left(a_{m_j^i}, t_{m_j^i}\right) \right\rangle$, where m_j^i is the number of parameters of the protocol, and finally

M_j^i is the sequence of messages.

The algorithm is presented in Figure 8 and, as can be observed, is straightforward and consists of checking the compliance of the protocol name, the initiator, the collaborators and the sequence of parameters of the protocol.

Algorithm for Matching the Messages. In the second part of the procedure, matching the messages, the objective is to check that the sequence of messages stated in the specification is equivalent to the sequence of messages implemented by the agent, so that any possible difference in the expression of the protocol is not important for the execution. (From this perspective, we can ignore several features of sequence diagrams, but we do have to consider some others which are relevant when describing a sequence of messages.)

Before proceeding with the algorithm, it is worth mentioning the extent of the algorithm in terms of how the sequence of messages is formed. Our representation of protocols is based on AUML sequence diagrams, which are rich in features, some inherited from UML sequence diagrams and some exclusive to agents.

Inputs:

    r the role in question; and

    $Q \subseteq \mathcal{P}$, the set of protocols involving r, as implemented by the agent

Output:

    acceptance:

        true if the header of the protocol complies with the specification;

        false otherwise

Algorithm:

    $acceptance = false$

    $r \notin R \Rightarrow$ **exit**

    $\exists e$ such that $r = r_e \wedge 1 \leq e \leq m$

    $\forall (p, I, C, M) \in P_r$

        $p \notin \{p_1^e, p_2^e, \ldots, p_{m_e}^e\} \Rightarrow$ **exit**

        $\exists t$ such that $p = p_t^e \wedge 1 \leq t \leq m_e$

        $I \neq I_t^e \Rightarrow$ **exit**

        $C \neq C_t^e \Rightarrow$ **exit**

        $\forall (a, y) \in M$

            $(a', y') = nextElement\,[M_t^e]$

            $a' \neq a \vee y' \neq y \Rightarrow$ **exit**

    $acceptance = true$

Fig. 8. Algorithm: MATCHING THE HEAD

Specifically, we must check the multiplicity of the messages — that the number of messages sent and the number of receivers of the messages must correspond to those of the specification — and the type of message delivery — that whether it is synchronous or asynchronous, it must match that specified in the system. We consider two types of structures: conditions and concurrency connectors. A condition is a logical expression that determines if a message is sent or not. As was mentioned before, concurrency connectors are used as a means to express that multiple messages are sent at the same time and are of three types: *and* (AND), *inclusive or* (OR), and *exclusive or* (XOR).

However, for our purpose (checking whether two sequence diagrams represent essentially the same protocol) not all the features are relevant. While we need to consider the roles involved in the protocol and their existence in the system, and the *and, or* and *exclusive or* parallel connectors, the conditions of messages can be ignored since they are meaningful only at execution time. In particular, we do not consider: agents, since we only allow roles as participants of protocols; lifelines and threads of interaction, since they are not relevant in the functionality of the protocol; nested and interleaved protocols, since they are not considered in our definition of protocol; and protocol templates, for the same reason.

Since this algorithm is meant to be executed statically, it simply checks that the sequence of messages matches the sequence specified in the system, but in the case of messages joined by a concurrency connector, the messages can appear in any order. Conditions are just ignored as they are relevant only at run-time.

To describe this algorithm we make use of the following functions. The first two functions operate on a message instruction, while the last two operate on a compound message. The *message* function returns *true* if and only if the message instruction is a simple message, and not joined to other messages by a concurrency connector. The *compound_message* function returns *true* if and only if the message instruction is a compound message, (a set of messages joined by a concurrency connector). The *connector_of* function denotes the concurrent operator of a compound message ($\in \{AND, OR, XOR\}$). Finally, the *set_of_messages* function denotes the set of messages of a compound message. Note that this function denotes a set, not a sequence, since the order of the messages is not important.

The algorithm is presented in Figure 9. As can be observed, for the protocol to be accepted, the messages are compared. Simple messages are examined for equality, whereas for compound messages of type OR and XOR, equality is not required, but being a subset is enough. We have implemented this algorithm by translating the sequences of messages into non-deterministic finite state machines and then checking their equivalence.

Inputs:
> $S = \langle m_1, m_2, \ldots, m_n \rangle$, the sequence of specified messages
> $S' = \langle m'_1, m'_2, \ldots, m'_n \rangle$, the sequence of implemented messages

Output:
> acceptance

Algorithm:
acceptance = **false**
$\forall i \in \{1, \ldots, n\}$
  $message(m_i) \Rightarrow$
    $m_i \neq m'_i \Rightarrow$ **exit**
  $compound\_message(m_i) \Rightarrow$
    $connector\_of(m_i) = \textbf{AND} \wedge$
        $set\_of\_messages(m'_i) \neq set\_of\_messages(m_i) \Rightarrow$ **exit**
    $connector\_of(m_i) \in \{\textbf{OR}, \textbf{XOR}\} \wedge$
        $\neg (set\_of\_messages(m'_i) \subseteq set\_of\_messages(m_i)) \Rightarrow$ **exit**
acceptance = **true**

Fig. 9. Algorithm: MATCHING THE MESSAGES

6   Related Work and Conclusions

It has been argued by many [2,3] that agents interacting in a common society need to be constrained in order to avoid and solve conflicts, make agreements, reduce complexity, and in general to achieve a desirable social order. This is the role of norms, or organisational rules, which represent what ought to be done by a set of agents, and whose fulfilment can be generally seen as a public good when their benefits can be enjoyed by the overall society, organisation or group [1]. Research on norms and agents has ranged from fundamental work on the importance of norms in agent behaviour—[3], to proposing internal representations of norms [10], considering their emergence in groups of agents [13], and proposing logics for their formalisation [9]. Despite such efforts to understand how and why norms can be incorporated into agents and multi-agent systems, there is still much work to do, particularly in relation to the engineering of such norm-based or organisation-based systems.

The easiest way to represent and reason about norms is by seeing them as built-in constraints where all the restrictions and obligations of agents are obeyed absolutely without deliberation. In this view, the effort is left to the system designer to ensure that all agents respond in the required way and, consequently, that the overall system behaves coherently. However, this may result in inflexible systems that must be changed off-line when either the agents or the environment change. By contrast, if a dynamic view of norms is taken, the flexibility of the overall system can be assured [14]. We have considered the role of norms in the design of agent architectures and their reasoning processes elsewhere, but in this paper we have focussed on the *engineering* of such systems through the use of organisational rules, specification and compliance. It is precisely the use of organisational rules that distinguishes our specification from other organisational models such as [11,12,5].

In contrast to other models for the development of multi-agent systems based on organisational concepts, the model presented in this paper excludes any reference to particular implementation issues, and so is suitable for *open* multi-agent systems. In addition, this model uses organisational rules, which makes it capable of handling situations that other approaches leave unconsidered, such as restrictions about the number of times a role must be enacted. Finally, our model also describes the facilities provided by a system, and they way they are accessed, which is essential for the development of new components, and their eventual incorporation into the system.

In other work, in addition to considering compliance with protocols, we also consider other elements of the specification that can be checked at the entrance of an agent to the system, which are the participants model, and a specific subset of organisational rules. The former includes checking the services and non-functional requirements of the roles in the system. The latter refers to checking the compliance of those rules that refer only to static properties of role assignment such as the number of times a roles must be played, sequence in which roles must be played, and conflicts in playing more that one role at the same time.

Also, in other work, we consider the compliance of a more general type of organisational rules, this is, those rules that need to be checked continually, not only at the entrance of an agent to the system. For this, we have designed a mechanism that collects the relevant information from the system and analyses the corresponding rules. This work presents some similarities to works on law enforcement [8,7], being the main difference (in addition that we use *organisational rules* and they use *laws*) that our work consists in monitoring compliance, while theirs consists in preventing violation.

References

1. C. Castelfranchi, R. Conte, and M. Paolucci. Normative reputation and the cost of compliance. *Journal of Artificial Societies and Social Simulation*, 1(3), 1998.
2. R. Conte. Emergent (info)institutions. *Journal of Cognitive Systems Research*, 2:97–110, 2001.
3. R. Conte, R. Falcone, and G. Sartor. Agents and norms: How to fill the gap? *Artificial Intelligence and Law*, 7(1):1–15, 1999.
4. FIPA. http://www.fipa.org/, 1999.
5. D. Grossi, F. Dignum, V. Dignum, M. Dastani, and L. Royakkers. Structural aspects of the evaluation of agent organizations. In *Proceedings of the Workshop on Coordination, Organization, Institutions and Norms in Agent Systems*, 2006.
6. Nicholas R. Jennings. An agent-based approach for building complex software systems. *Communications of the ACM*, 44(4):35–41, 2001.
7. Naftaly Minsky. Law governed interaction (lgi): A distributed coordination and control mechanism. Technical report, Rutgers University, 2005.
8. R. Paes, G. Carvalho, C. Lucena, P. Alencar, H. Almeida, and V. Silva. Specifying laws in open multi-agent systems. In *Agents, Norms and Institutions for Regulated Multi-agent Systems (ANIREM)*, 2005.
9. A. Ross. *Directives and Norms*. Routledge and Kegan Paul Ltd, 1968.
10. R. Tuomela and M. Bonnevier-Tuomela. Social norms and agreements. *European Journal of Law, Philosophy and Computer Science*, 5:41–46, 1995.
11. Wamberto Vasconcelos, Mairi McCallum, and Tim Norman. Modelling organisational change using agents. Technical Report AUCS/TR0605, Department of Computing Science, University of Aberdeen, 2006.
12. Luis Erasmo Montealegre Vzquez and Fabiola Lpez y Lpez. An agent-based model for hierachical organizations. In *Proceedings of the Workshop on Coordination, Organization, Institutions and Norms in Agent Systems*, 2006.
13. A. Walker and M. Wooldridge. Understanding the emergence of conventions in multi-agent systems. In V. Lesser and L. Gasser, editors, *Proceedings of the International Conference on Multi-Agent Systems*, pages 384–389, 1995.
14. F. Zambonelli, N. Jennings, and M. Wooldridge. Organisational abstractions for the analysis and design of multi-agent systems. In *Proceedings of the First International Workshop on Agent-oriented Software Engineering*, 2000.

Towards an Ontological Account of Agent-Oriented Goals

Renata S.S. Guizzardi[1], Giancarlo Guizzardi[2,3],
Anna Perini[1], and John Mylopoulos[4]

[1] ITC-irst, Trento-Povo, Italy
{souza,perini}@itc.it
[2] Department of Computer Science, UFES, Vitória-ES, Brazil
[3] Laboratory of Applied Ontologies (ISTC-CNR), Trento, Italy
guizzardi@loa-cnr.it
[4] Department of Computer Science, University of Toronto, Canada
jm@cs.toronto.edu

Abstract. The software agent paradigm has received considerable attention recently, both in research and industrial practice. However, adoption of this software paradigm remains elusive in software engineering practice. We claim that part of the adoption problem lies with the fact that mentalistic and social concepts underlying agents are subjective and complex for the average practitioner. Specifically, although there are many efforts related to the topic coming from philosophy, cognitive sciences and computer science, a uniform and well-founded semantic view on these concepts is currently lacking. This work extends an existing upper-level ontology and offers it as a foundation for evaluating and designing agent-oriented modeling languages. In particular, the paper focuses on the concept of goal, aiming at disambiguating its definition, discussing its different manifestations, and clarifying its relation to other important agent-related concepts. For that, we examine how goals are conceived and used according to some relevant literature on agent-orientation. In addition, related work on akin fields, especially philosophy and AI are used as a basis for the proposed ontological extensions.

1 Introduction

The agent paradigm is shaped by developments from several research areas, such as Distributed Computing, Software Engineering (SE), Artificial Intelligence (AI), and Organizational Science [Wooldridge and Jennings, 1995]. An AI perspective of agents focuses on their cognitive (or mentalistic) properties, e.g. beliefs, goals and commitments. On the other hand, an SE perspective emphasizes its potential for designing open, distributed, dynamically reconfigurable software, with only lip service paid to mentalistic or cognitive underpinnings. However, given the potential of using agents both for conceptual modeling and system development, such properties may indeed be central to both domain analysis and system development. For instance, understanding agent goals, perceptions and beliefs leads to a deeper understanding of values and strategies

R. Choren et al. (Eds.): SELMAS 2006, LNCS 4408, pp. 148–164, 2007.
© Springer-Verlag Berlin Heidelberg 2007

adopted in an organization, thereby contributing to the conception of effective information systems [Guizzardi, 2006] [Dignum, 2004].

Several agent cognitive models are proposed in the AI literature, the best-known among them being the BDI model [Rao and Georgeff, 1991]. This model focuses on three basic mental components of agents: belief, desire and intention. *Belief* refers to knowledge the agent has about the environment and about other agents with whom she interacts. *Desire* refers to the "will" of an agent towards a specific goal, although she might never actually pursue these goals. Finally, *intention* entails specific plans and commitments to achieve specific goals. A different model characterizes the state of an agent as a combination of mental components such as *beliefs, capabilities, choices,* and *commitments* [Shoham, 1993]. Besides these well-known models, much work related to AI theory, philosophy and cognitive sciences underlies the definition of such cognitive notions, guiding their practical use for modeling and developing multi-agent systems. Among them is the early work of Bratman [Bratman, 1987] on goals, beliefs, intentions and related mental models, and the contribution of Castelfranchi and colleagues on delegation [Castelfranchi and Falcone, 1998], dependency [Conte and Castelfranchi, 1995] and commitments [Castelfranchi, 1995]. In addition to these, work on conceptual formalization through the use of ontologies also provides valuable contribution in this respect [Guizzardi, 2006] [Bottazzi and Ferrario, 2005] [Masolo et al., 2003].

This work constitutes a follow-up to earlier efforts on defining a uniform conceptualization for agent-oriented systems. We aim at investigating diverse definitions and treatments of the agent mentalistic concepts and - where possible - merge these through amalgamation or compromise. In [Guizzardi, 2006], we propose an ontology of agent and related concepts, based on previous results and guidelines presented in [Guizzardi, 2005]. In this earlier work, we use the proposed ontology to guide the understanding and evaluation of modeling languages adopted in the development of agent-oriented knowledge management systems. Regarding the use of ontologies to support the evaluation and re-design of software engineering modeling languages, the role of the ontology is threefold:

- clarify modeling language concepts;
- evaluate and re-design the notation in order to avoid construct *overload, excess, redundancy* and *incompleteness* [Guizzardi, 2005];
- in cases where different notations A and B are used, assist in the transformation from one notation to the other, by guiding the mapping between the concepts of language A to those of language B.

In this paper, we specifically focus on the concept of *goal*, aiming at clarifying its meaning and finding out its relations to other basic agent-inspired concepts. Goals are widely used in agent-orientation and related fields, ranging from conceptual goal modeling in Agent Organizations and Requirements Engineering to goal execution in AI Planning and Agent Teamwork. In Agent Organizations, for instance, goals are used to describe the objectives of the organization as a whole, being generally associated with roles, which are then assigned to agents that act on behalf of the organization [Hubner et al., 2002]

[Dignum, 2004] [Esteva et al., 2002]. In a few Requirements Engineering approaches, on the other hand, the concept of goal is the basis for requirements analysis, representing the objectives of different stakeholders, and rationalizing strategic dependencies among these stakeholders [van Lamsweerde, 2000] [Yu, 1995] [Bresciani et al., 2004]. In AI Planning [Ghallab et al., 2004], goal is an essential concept, since this area mainly focuses on computational approaches to the problem of reasoning and deliberating about actions that are intended to fulfill a goal. Finally, the research area of Agent Teamwork generally makes extensive use of Planning techniques to support the cooperation of the team agents in the pursuit of a common goal [Boella et al., 1999] [Yen et al., 2001].

It is important to emphasize that although being the result of careful investigation, this work still represents the first steps in the direction of providing uniform semantics to the concept of goal. The remaining of this article is organized as follows: section 2 focuses on the main motivations behind this research initiative; section 3 describes this work's main contribution, by presenting an excerpt of our agent ontology (named UFO-C) and discussing it in comparison with related work; section 4 presents applications of the use of UFO-C to support agent-oriented software engineering; and section 5 finally concludes the paper.

2 Motivation

Concerns with the definition of syntactic and semantic properties of agent-oriented concepts have contributed to the proliferation of research initiatives on metamodels. Many of these works focus on: a) defining organization-centered concepts such as agent, group and roles in order to enable modeling of heterogeneous systems [Odell et al., 2004] [Ferber and Gutknecht, 1998]; b) interoperating and/or unifying modeling methodologies [Henderson-Sellers et al., 2005] [Perini and Susi, 2005][Bernon et al., 2004]; and c) enabling agent-oriented modeling through the use of CASE tools [Perini and Susi, 2005]. These works have been generally based on a bottom-up strategy, constructing their conceptualizations by abstracting concepts that are present in existing languages, methodologies and formalisms. Modeling Language are sometimes the result of a negotiation process, and commonly incorporate features motivated by reasons other than being truthful to the domain in reality being represented (e.g., increasing computational efficiency, providing compatibility to a computational paradigm, facilitating the translation to a specific implementation environment). Thus, one of the disadvantages of a bottom-up approach such as the ones just mentioned is to incorporate in the produced metamodel many of these improper features.

In contrast, the objective of our research is to employ theories developed in disciplines such as cognitive science, philosophy, as well as social sciences to uncover the kinds of individuals that constitute the social reality as well as to understand the ontological nature of these entities. As a result we aim at producing a Foundational Ontology that explicitly represents these entities.

As argued in [Guizzardi, 2005], the quality of a conceptual modeling language can be systematically evaluated by comparing, on one hand, a metamodel of this language, and on the other hand, an explicit representation of the subject domain this language is supposed to represent, i.e., a domain ontology. In the ideal case, these two entities are isomorphic and share the same set of logical models. To put it simple terms, in this ideal situation the language is not only able to represent all the relevant concepts of the subject domain at hand, preserving all their properties, but the user of the language can identify in an unambiguous manner what are the domain concepts represented by each of the language's modeling constructs. Thus, if we have a concrete model representing the subject domain, this model can be used for evaluating and (re)designing modeling languages in that domain.

The work described here can then be seen as complementary to the effort of developing metamodels for agent-oriented concepts. First, it can be used to systematically evaluate and perhaps propose modification to these metamodels so that they become isomorphic to this ontology. Second, once the mapping between elements in a metamodel (syntactic elements) and in an ontology are established, the elements of the latter can be used to provide real-world semantics for the elements of the former. In other words, the interpretation mapping from a language construct to a category in an ontology establishes the meaning of that construct in terms of the real-world element represented in that ontology. If the ontology itself is described in a formal language (see [Guizzardi, 2005], this linking also enables the definition of a formal semantics for this language. In this article, however, we do not intend to formally characterize the proposed ontology and, for this reason, the UML diagrams depicting fragments of this ontology are intended here for presentation only. This is mainly due to the fact that this ontology (UFO-C) is still in preliminary stage of development and that we defend the position that we should first concentrate on understanding a certain conceptualization before formally describing it.

3   The UFO Ontology

In this section, we present our conceptualization of goal and related concepts. We base this conceptualization on the *UFO (Unified Foundation Ontology)* defined in [Guizzardi, 2005] [Guizzardi and Wagner, 2005] [Guizzardi, 2006], extending it when necessary.

The UFO ontology is divided into three incrementally layered compliance sets: 1) UFO-A defines the core of UFO, as a comprehensive ontology of *endurants*; 2) UFO-B defines - as an increment to UFO-A - terms related to *perdurants* [1]; and 3) UFO-C defines - as an increment to UFO-A and UFO-B - terms related to the spheres of *intentional and social entities*. In this paper, we focus on the UFO-C ontology, referring to the other ontologies only to provide definitions when needed. The ontologies are described here in natural language, and illustrated with the aid of UML class diagrams. Thus, UML is not intended here for formalization purposes but rather for facilitating the visualization of the concepts.

---

[1] Endurants and perdurants intuitively correspond to *objects* and *events* (respectively) as understood in natural language.

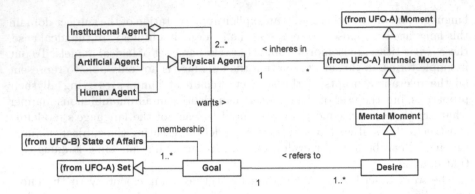

Fig. 1. UML diagram representing a fragment of UFO-C

For an in depth discussion and formal characterization of UFO-A, one should refer to [Guizzardi, 2005]. The formalization of UFO-B and UFO-C is planned as future work, once the semantics of the concepts comprising these ontologies is fully comprehended.

Figure 1 shows an excerpt of UFO-C defining a *goal* in relation to two other important concepts, namely *desire* and *physical agent*. In general, we say that a physical agent has a goal, and this goal is related to the agent's desire. *Desire* here is defined as a *mental moment*, which specializes the concept of intrinsic moment from UFO-A. UFO-A defines a *moment* as an entity whose existence is existentially dependent on another entity. This Husserlian notion of moments is akin to what is termed trope, abstract particular, property instance, or mode in the literature. An intrinsic moment is a special kind of moment that is existentially dependent on one single individual (e.g., the color of an apple depends of the existence of the apple itself). Examples of intrinsic moments of a physical agent are age, height and address. Mental moment is a specialization of intrinsic moment referring to mental components of a physical agent, such as belief, desire, intention, and perception. Summing up, a desire is conceived as a mental moment, which is existentially dependent on a particular agent, being an inseparable part of its mental state.

Fig. 1 also defines goal as a set of states of affairs (i.e. a set of world states). This choice has some important implications that deserve debate. We noted two main views on goals in the AI and agent-orientation literature. On one hand, a goal may be seen as a specialization of the concept of mental moment. On the other hand, a goal may be treated as a state of affairs (or set of state of affairs). However, in agent-orientation, both views are possible. In fact, it is common to find works that treat them interchangeably [Conte and Castelfranchi, 1995] [Rao and Georgeff, 1991]. We believe that the reason behind this confusion is the fact that in artificial systems, both the mental states of the agents composing the system and the state of the world are explicit and sometimes treated as the same thing. This approach is illustrated in the context of the CAST architecture supporting Agent Teamwork, where the authors affirm that the team agents develop an "overlapping shared mental model, which is the source for team members to reason about the states and the needs of others" [Yen et al., 2001]. However, when we consider hybrid systems involving artificial and human agents, we cannot assume anymore the explication of mental moments. Instead, beliefs, intentions and perceptions remain inside the human agent's mind. With this discussion, however, we do not intend to say that mental moments cannot be considered and represented in an agent-oriented model. What we find important is the realization that there are two distinct concepts involved here: one external and another one internal to the agent. The external concept regards a state of affairs desired by an agent (here called goal), and the internal one is the desire itself, which is part of the agent's mental state.

In this work, we commit to the definition of goal as a set of states of affairs because we find it more flexible from several different perspectives. For instance, it allows a more flexible view of organizational goals. For now, UFO-C views an organization as an institutional agent constituted by a number of other (physical, artificial or institutional) agents (refer to Fig. 1). Thus, a goal could be seen as a mental moment associated with a sort of collective mind, in the sense of Searle. Nevertheless, [Bottazzi and Ferrario, 2005] see an organization as an abstract social concept, which is separate from the collective body of agents that composes it. Taking this approach leads to the impossibility of considering a goal as a mental moment, since an organization here cannot be conceived as having a mind. Defining goal as a set of states of affairs accommodates both views, i.e. it is always possible to say that an organization (or institutional agent) has a goal. Since our account for organization and related concepts is still preliminary, we prefer to take this more flexible approach[2].

Another reason for this choice comes from the fact that some ontological theories do admit part-of relations applied to states of affairs but not to moments. Thus, having goal as a mental moment would disallow *goal decomposition* (defined in to Figure 2). However, several approaches foresee the need to refine goals by decomposing it into sub-goals. This is applied, for instance, by some Agent Organization methodologies (e.g. MOISE+ [Hubner et al., 2002] and OperA [Dignum, 2004]) to understand the goals of particular roles by refining general organizational goals. Moreover, this is also common practice for some Requirements Engineering approaches, which use goal decomposition to analyze objectives of particular stakeholders and/or to derive the requirements of supporting information systems [van Lamsweerde, 2000] [Bresciani et al., 2004] [Yu, 1995].

Fig. 2 shows that according to UFO-C a goal decomposition is a kind of *basic formal relation* (from UFO-A) between goals, which is defined in terms of a binary mereological (part-of) relation between these goals. A Goal decomposition groups several sub-goals related to the same super-goal. In other words, suppose

---

[2] We do not include here an in depth discussion on organizational goals. In order to be complete, the concepts of roles, commitments/claims and norms would have to be considered. [Guizzardi, 2006] presents our initial views on this topic. However, more remains to be done in the future and is out of the scope of this paper.

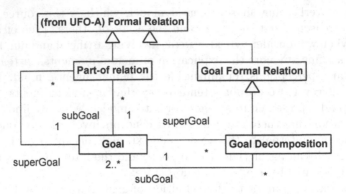

Fig. 2. Goal decomposition

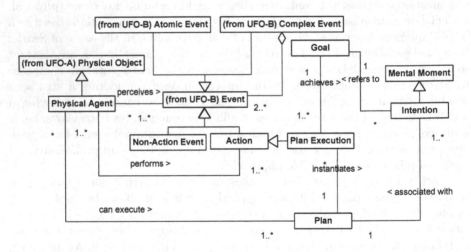

Fig. 3. Differentiating between Goal and Plan

that goals G1 and G2 are *parts of* the super-goal G. Thus, we can say that there is a *goal decomposition relation* between G (as a super-goal) and G1 and G2 (as sub-goals).

Figure 3 focuses on the relation of goal to the actual plan executed to achieve this goal. This leads us to the distinction made in UFO-B between *action* and *non-action events*. The former refers to events created through the action of a physical agent, while the latter are typically events generated by the environment itself and perceived by the agents living in it.

A *plan execution* is an intended execution of one or more actions, and is therefore a special kind of action event. In other words, a plan execution may be composed of one or more ordered action events, targeting a particular outcome of interest to the agent. These action events may be triggered by both action and non-action events perceived by the agent. Besides, a plan execution instantiates

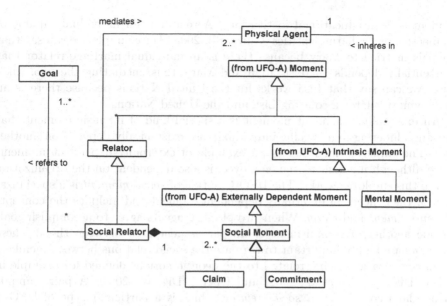

Fig. 4. Commitments and Claims

a plan (or plan type). Thus, when we say that a physical agent executes a plan, we actually mean this agent creates the action events previously specified in the plan. Furthermore, such plan is connected to the agent through a mental moment referred to as *intention*. Agent's intention directly leads to the adoption of certain goals, and is associated with a plan, i.e. a specific way of achieving this specific goal. In fact, the association to a plan is the main differentiation between desire (as in Fig. 1) and intention. To put it differently, while a desire refers to a wish of the agent towards a particular set of state of affairs, an intention actually leads to action towards achieving this goal [Rao and Georgeff, 1991] [Conte and Castelfranchi, 1995] [Boella et al., 1999].

The difference between goal and plan is an important one, not always clear in existing works. For instance, some AI Planning techniques define goals as tasks the system must perform [Ghallab et al., 2004]. MOISE+ [Hubner et al., 2002] also adopts a more operational view on goals as being the tasks performed by the agents of an organization. Examples of work that do make this differentiation include the KAOS [van Lamsweerde, 2000] and i*/Tropos [Yu, 1995] [Bresciani et al., 2004] requirement engineering approaches.

Figure 4 clarifies UFO-C's view on the social concepts of commitment and claim, highly associated with the concept of goal and thus, presenting important contribution to enable the understanding and modeling goal adoption.

First, it is important to have a more detailed view of how UFO-A specializes the concept of moment. Moments can be specialized into intrinsic moments and relators. The former refers to a moment that is existentially dependent on one single individual. In contrast, a relator is a moment that is existentially depen-dent on more than one individual (e.g., a marriage, an enrollment between a student and an educational institution). A relator is an individual capable of connecting or mediating entities [Guizzardi, 2005]. For example, we can say that John is married to Mary because there is an individual marriage relator that existentially depends on both John and Mary, thus, mediating the two. Likewise, we can say that Lisa works for the United Nations because there is an employment relator mediating Lisa and the United Nations.

An externally dependent moment is a special kind of intrinsic moment that although inhering in a specific individual, also existentially depends on another one. The employee identifier is an example of externally dependent moment, since although inherent to the employee, is also dependent on the organization where this employee works. The UFO-C notion of *social moment* is a specialization of the concept of externally dependent moment and includes the concepts of *commitment* and *claim*. When two physical agents agree to accomplish goals to one another, a commitment/claim pair is generated between them. These concepts are highly important to regulate the social relations between members of an organization, being related to the deontic notions defined for example in ISLANDER [Esteva et al., 2002] and OperA [Dignum, 2004]. A pair commitment/claim constitutes a *social relator*, which is a particular type of UFO-A *relator*. Fig. 4 also shows that a social relator refers to a goal. When a physical agent A commits to a physical agent B, this means that A adopts a goal of B. Conversely, the social relator created between A and B state that B has the right to claim the accomplishment of this specific goal to A.

Dependency is a common relation explored in Requirements Engineering approaches (e.g. i* [Yu, 1995] and Tropos [Bresciani et al., 2004]) and Agent Organization methodologies (e.g. OperA [Dignum, 2004]). However, the distinction between *dependency* and *delegation* is usually not made. Figure 5 depicts this important distinction. The first difference regards the fact that while a dependency constitutes a *formal relation*, a delegation consists of a *material relation* [Guizzardi, 2005]. This distinction between formal and material relations is elaborated in UFO-A. A formal relation is either an internal relation holding directly between two entities (e.g., instantiation, parthood, inherence), or it is reducible to an internal relation between intrinsic moments of involved relata. Examples of formal relations of the latter type is Lisa 'is older than' Mike, and John 'is taller than' Mary. In both of cases, these relations are reducible to comparative formal relations between intrinsic moments of the involved relata (individual heights and ages). A material relation, in contrast, cannot be reduced in such a way and has real material content. For a material relation to take place between two or more individuals, something else needs to exist, namely, a relator connecting these entities. The relations 'married to' and 'works for' aforementioned are examples of material relations founded by relators of type marriage and employment, respectively.

Let us examine this difference in further detail. Fig. 5 shows that a dependency connects two physical agents (a depender and a dependee) and a goal (a dependum). An agent A (the depender) depends on an agent B (the dependee) regarding a goal G if G is a goal of agent A, but A cannot accomplish G, and

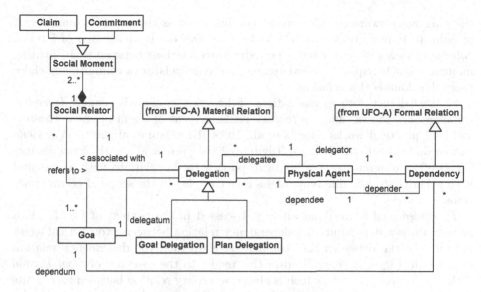

Fig. 5. Goal Delegation and Dependency

agent B can accomplish G. A delegation is associated with a dependency but it is more than that. As a material relation, it is founded on something more than its connected elements. In this case, the connected elements are two physical agents (delegator and delegatee) and a goal (delegatum), and the foundation of this material relation is the social relator (i.e. a commitment/claim pair) established between the two physical agents involved in this delegation. In other words, when agent A delegates a goal G to agent B, besides the fact that A depends on B regarding G, B commits herself to accomplish G on behalf of A, thus adopting the goal of A. Goal and plan delegation refer to what Castelfranchi and Falcone define as open and close delegation [Castelfranchi and Falcone, 1998], meaning that the former leaves the decision regarding the strategy towards goal accomplishment to the depender. The latter rather prescribes a specific strategy (i.e. a plan) the depender should adopt towards achieving the delegated goal.

To illustrate the difference between dependency and delegation, consider the following case. Suppose John is a program committee member of a certain conference and that he received from Paul (the conference program chair) an article X to review. Suppose that John cannot review this article by himself, since there are some aspects of the article which are outside his field of competence. Now, suppose that George is a colleague of John who is knowledgeable exactly in those aspects that John needs to review article X. In this case, we could say that John depends on George to review article X. Notice, however, that this relation between John and George can be reduced to relations between the goals and capabilities of these individual agents. Moreover, this relation does not even require that the related agents are aware of this dependence. This is certainly not the case for the relation between Paul and John. As the program committee chair, Paul depends on John to review article X. However, in this case, not only they are both aware of this dependence but there is the explicit commitment of John to Paul to review article X. In other words, the delegation of Paul to John to review article X cannot be reduced to relations between their intrinsic moments, but it requires the existence of a certain relator (a commitment/claim pair) that founds this relation.

Figure 6 depicts four specializations of the category of goals, namely *depended, collaborative, shared,* and *conflicting* goals, typical of agent-oriented theoretical and practical works [Boella et al., 1999] [Bresciani et al., 2004] [Yu, 1995] [Conte and Castelfranchi, 1995] [Dignum, 2004] [Yen et al., 2001]. Such distinctions reflect different ways a goal can participate in relations with agents and with other goals, i.e., different roles a goal can play in the scope of certain relations.

Depended goal is the kind already discussed in the context of Fig. 5, i.e. a goal which is a dependum of a dependency relation between two physical agent individuals: the depender and the dependee. In fact, the dependency relation depicted in Fig. 5 is generalized in this model to the category of *Goal Formal Relation involving agents,* which is always a ternary relation between two agents and a goal. A *shared goal* is a set of states of affairs intended at the same time by two different physical agent individuals. In other words, two agents share a goal if they both have individual desires that refer to that same goal. A *collaborative goal* is a special kind of shared goal. A collaborative goal G is the subject of a potential collaboration relation between agents A and B if: (i) G is shared by A and B; (ii) there are at least two sub-goals G1 and G2 of G such that A wants G1 but depends on B to accomplish it, and B wants G2 but depends on A to accomplish it. In other words, a collaborative goal is always composed of at least two depended goals. To illustrate collaborative goals, suppose agents A and B have a shared goal of "taking a heavy table out of the room". This goal can be decomposed in two sub-goals referring to carrying out each side of the table, which can be respectively adopted by A and B. In this case, one agent depends on the other to accomplish their shared super-goal, thus this goal can only be attained in collaboration. Finally, two goals are *conflicting* if they cannot be achieved at the same time. For instance, taking two conflicting goals G1 and G2, the accomplishment of goal G1 would preclude the achievement of goal G2 and vice-versa. In other words, if we take any two state of affairs S1 and S2, such that S1 satisfies G1 and S2 satisfies G2, we have that S1 and S2 cannot obtain simultaneously (i.e., in the same world or world history).

Note that the definition of these different types of goal also influenced our choice for preferring the definition of goal as a set state of affairs rather than a mental moment. Such definitions are actually facilitated by this choice. For example, a shared goal can be seen as a state of affairs referenced (i.e. intended) at the same time by two physical agents. If it were to be defined as a mental moment, we would have to be careful to talk about shareability, since each agent has its own mental moment and thus, the goals would not be effectively shared. Instead, we would have anyway to assume that these two agents having distinct goals would aim at the same set of state of affairs.

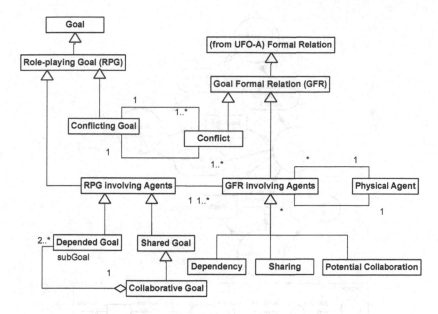

Fig. 6. Different Roles played by Goals in Goal Formal Relations

4   Applications of UFO-C to Support Agent-Oriented Software Engineering

The UFO-C ontology is aimed at providing a consistent understanding of the concepts involved in agent-orientation. In particular, with respect to agent-oriented software engineering, we hope to provide support to: i) clarifying the concepts underlying modeling languages; ii) evaluating and (re)designing modeling languages to make it more consistent and accessible to the user; and iii) interoperating different modeling languages. Figures 7 and 8 present applications of the UFO-C ontology to achieve all these aims.

The Tropos actor diagram of Fig. 7 depicts the main agents and dependencies of a paper review scenario. In the Tropos original language, dependencies and delegations were overloaded in the concept of dependency. In other words, an analysis of this language in light of UFO-C has shown that in many Tropos models, what is called dependency is actually a delegation. In these cases, besides a dependency between agents A and B, the relationship also implies that agent B commits to deliver the dependum (e.g. a goal) to agent A. The diagram of Fig. 7 illustrates this difference. Most relationships shown in the diagram are delegation, for instance, the **PC Chair** depends on the **PC Member** to accomplish the goal of **reviewing papers**. And in this case, the **PC Member** commits herself to this goal. Thus, this is a case of delegation. We can then say that the **PC Chair** delegates the goal of **reviewing papers** to the **PC Member**. On the other hand, the relationship between the **Conference Chair** and the **Paper Author** is an example of dependency. While the former depends on the

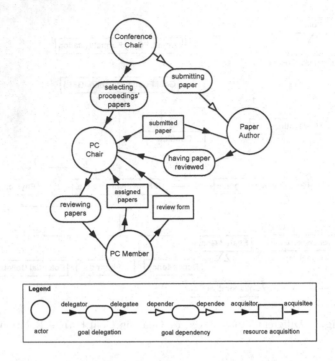

Fig. 7. Tropos actor diagram illustrating a paper review scenario

latter to submit papers in order to guarantee the realization of the conference, she cannot assume that the **Paper Author** will actually do it. In other words, it is possible that no paper is submitted to the conference because there is no commitment from specific paper authors to do so.

Understanding both concepts of dependency and delegation with the aid of UFO-C led to the decision of redesigning Tropos to incorporate both dependency and delegation. This has solved a problem of construct overload, which could prevent the correct understanding of the nature of the relationships while at the same time, has given more expressivity to the language. Benefits gained by considering both concepts are for instance:

- supporting analysts to reason about different *degrees of vulnerability*. In general, a dependency makes the depender more vulnerable than a delegation. This happens because in a delegation, the dependee has an explicit commitment toward the depender in respect to the goal to be accomplished. In a dependency, however, this is not the case. In fact, sometimes, the dependee is not even aware of this dependency (e.g. the dependency between **Conference Chair** and **Paper Author** mentioned above). Consequently, if a goal is depended but not delegated, the depender is less certain of its accomplishment.
- allowing the understanding when the dependee can be *subjected to sanctions*. In the case of a delegation, which assume a commitment from the dependee

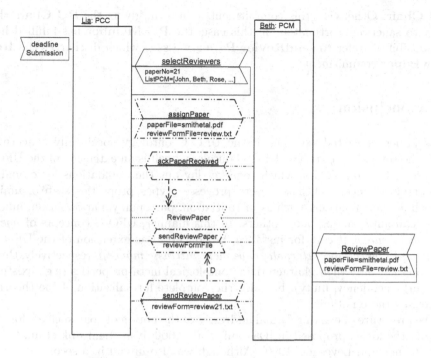

Fig. 8. AORML's interaction sequence diagram

towards the depender, sanctions may be applied in case the dependee fails to accomplish the goal she had committed to.

– enabling the analyst to find during the analysis, dependencies which can be *opportunities for the establishment of latter delegations*. In other words, if there are dependencies that are critical for the accomplishment of the goals of an agent, then this agent can seek to obtain a commitment from the dependee, lowering her degree of vulnerability. Also in organizational modeling, this analysis can be helpful in the (re)design of the commitments of organizational roles in order for organizational goals to be accomplished more efficiently.

Fig. 8 depicts an AORML (Agent-Object-Relationship Modeling Language) interaction sequence diagram, showing the interactions between **PC Chair** and **PC Member** to accomplish the goal of reviewing papers. This diagram illustrates how UFO-C may assist the interoperation of two notations, namely Tropos and AORML. The delegation between the **PC Chair** and **PC Member** previously analyzed is mapped into an AORML commitment construct during interaction modeling. The **ReviewPaper** commitment is created after the **PC Member** acknowledges that she has received the papers assigned to her for review (view create arrow coming from the **ackPaperRecieved** message to the **ReviewPaper** commitment). The **ReviewPaper** commitment has a message attached to it (i.e. a **sendReviewPaper** message), indicating that this commitment is fulfilled if the **PC Member** submits a message of this kind to the

PC Chair. Otherwise, this commitment is broken, giving the **PC Chair** the right to sanction. Fortunately, in this case, the **PC Member** has fulfilled her responsibility (refer to **sendReviewPaper** message which discharges the **ReviewPaper** commitment).

5   Conclusion

This paper presented excerpts of the UFO-C ontology specifically concerned with the concept of *goal*. The UFO-C ontology itself is an extension of the UFO-A and UFO-B ontologies, which together lay out the foundations for domain-independent concepts such as objects, processes, types, properties, state of affairs as well as their relations, such as instantiation, partonomy, participation, inherence, causality, among many others. In this manner, UFO-C concepts of *agent* and *social moment* can, for instance, be conceived as extension of the UFO-A concepts of *object* and *externally dependent intrinsic moment*, respectively, thus, inhering not only their characterizing ontological meta-properties (e.g., existential (in)dependency, unity), but also the complete formalization of the theories regarding these notions.

We are aware of existing formal addresses of the notion of goal, such as, for example, the logics proposed in [Dastani et al., 2006] [van Riemsdijk et al., 2005] and [Cohen and Levesque, 1990]. Although we also intend in a second stage of this enterprise, to completely formalize the theories put forth here, this work differs from these "logics of goals" in a manner of emphasis. The aim in this particular paper is not to define a formal language that can be used to reason about goals. In contrast, the focus is on the real-world semantics of this concept, i.e., to understand the meaning of the notion of goal by making explicit its ontological meta-properties as well as its relations to other ontological categories (such as state of affairs, mental and social moments, social commitments and claims, objects, processes, etc.) for which a number of formal theories have already been developed in areas such as philosophy and cognitive science.

Several research areas permeating the agent-oriented paradigm make use of the term *goal*. Examples of these areas include Agent Organizations, Requirements Engineering, AI Planning and Agent Teamwork. However, further analysis of these different usages of the term goal in these areas shows that it has been used to represent a number of different and sometimes incompatible notions. In this article, we make use of a comprehensive network of ontological categories to make explicit which ontological elements are referred by these different senses of the term goal used in the literature, as well as the relations they bear to each other.

Finally, although several related works have already been analyzed and discussed, our research agenda for the future includes the study of other works that may provide valuable input to enhance the present conceptualization. In parallel, we aim at extending UFO-C even further, deepening our understanding of other important concepts (for instance, those of action and event, and especially communicative action and communicative event, commitment and claim, etc.). Moreover, we intend to apply UFO-C to evaluate and re-design diverse modeling languages, proceeding with our previous effort in this direction, while profiting from the advances in the ontology to provide more consistent and semantically uniform languages.

References

[Bernon et al., 2004] Bernon, C., Cossentino, M., Gleizes, M., Turci, P., and Zambonelli, F. (2004). A Study of some Multi-agent Meta-models . In Odell, J., Giorgini, P., and Mller, Jrg, P., editors, *Agent-Oriented Software Engineering V*, volume 3382 of *LNCS*, pages 62–77. Springer-Verlag, Berlin, Germany.

[Boella et al., 1999] Boella, G., Damiano, R., and Lesmo, L. (1999). A Utility Based Approach to Cooperation among Agents. In *Proceedings of the Worskhop on Foundations and applications of collective agent based systems (ESSLLI'99)*, Utrecht, The Netherlands.

[Bottazzi and Ferrario, 2005] Bottazzi, E. and Ferrario, R. (2005). A Path to an Ontology of Organizations. In *Proceedings of the Workshop on Vocabularies, Ontologies and Rules for The Enterprise (VORTE'05)*, Enschede, The Netherlands. Centre for Telematics and Information Technology (CTIT).

[Bratman, 1987] Bratman, M. E. (1987). *Intentions, Plans, and Practical Reason*. Harvard University Press.

[Bresciani et al., 2004] Bresciani, P., Giorgini, P., Giunchiglia, F., Mylopoulos, J., and Perini, A. (2004). Tropos: An Agent-Oriented Software Development Methodology. *International Journal of Autonomous Agents and Multi Agent Systems*, 8(3):203–236.

[Castelfranchi, 1995] Castelfranchi, C. (1995). Commitments: From Individual Intentions to Groups and Organizations. In *Proceedings of the First International Conference on Multi-Agent Systems*, Cambridge, MA, USA. AAAI-Press and MIT Press.

[Castelfranchi and Falcone, 1998] Castelfranchi, C. and Falcone, R. (1998). Towards a Theory of Delegation for Agent-Based Systems. *Robotics and Autonomous Systems*, 24(24):141–157.

[Cohen and Levesque, 1990] Cohen, P. R. and Levesque, H. J. (1990). Intention is Choice with Commitment. *Artificial Intelligence*, 42(3):213–261.

[Conte and Castelfranchi, 1995] Conte, R. and Castelfranchi, C. (1995). *Cognitive and Social Action*. UCL Press.

[Dastani et al., 2006] Dastani, M., van Riemsdijk, M. B., and Meyer, J.-J. (2006). Goal Types in Agent Programming. In *Proceedings of the 17th European Conference on Artificial Intelligence*, pages 220–224, Riva del Garda, Italy. IOS Press.

[Dignum, 2004] Dignum, V. (2004). *A Model for Organizational Interaction: Based on Agents, Founded in Logic*. PhD thesis, Utrecht University, The Netherlands.

[Esteva et al., 2002] Esteva, M., Padget, J., and Sierra, C. (2002). Formalizing a Language for Institutions and Norms. In Meyer, J.-J. C. and Tambe, M., editors, *Intelligent Agents VIII*, volume 2333 of *LNAI*, page 348 to 366. Springer-Verlag, Berlin, Germany.

[Ferber and Gutknecht, 1998] Ferber, J. and Gutknecht, O. (1998). A meta-model for the analysis and design of organizations in multi-agent systems. In *ICMAS '98: Proceedings of the 3rd International Conference on Multi Agent Systems*, page 128, Washington, DC, USA. IEEE Computer Society.

[Ghallab et al., 2004] Ghallab, M., Nau, D., and Traverso, P. (2004). *Automated Planning: Theory and Practice*. Morgan Kaufmann, Sao Mateo, CA, USA.

[Guizzardi, 2005] Guizzardi, G. (2005). *Ontological Foundations for Structural Conceptual Models.* PhD thesis, University of Twente, The Netherlands.

[Guizzardi and Wagner, 2005] Guizzardi, G. and Wagner, G. (2005). Some Applications of a Unified Foundational Ontology in Business Modeling. In Rosemann, M. and Green, P., editors, *Ontologies and Business Systems Analysis*, pages 345–367. Idea Group, London, UK.

[Guizzardi, 2006] Guizzardi, R. S. S. (2006). *Agent-oriented Constructivist Knowledge Management.* PhD thesis, University of Twente, The Netherlands.

[Henderson-Sellers et al., 2005] Henderson-Sellers, B., Debenham, J., Tran, N., Cossentino, M., and Low, G. (2005). Identification of Reusable Method Fragments from the PASSI Agent-Oriented Methodology. In Kolp, M., Bresciani, P., Henderson-Sellers, B., and Winikoff, M., editors, *Agent-Oriented Information Systems III*, volume 3529 of *LNCS*, pages 95–110. Springer-Verlag, Heidelberg, Germany.

[Hubner et al., 2002] Hubner, J. F., Sichman, J. S., and Boissier, O. (2002). A Model for the Structural, Functional, and Deontic Specification of Organizations in Multiagent Systems. In Bittencourt, G. and Ramalho, G. L., editors, *Advances in Artificial Intelligence: 16th Brazilian Symposium on Artificial Intelligence (SBIA'02)*, volume 2507 of *LNAI*, pages 118–128. Springer-Verlag, Berlin, Germany.

[Masolo et al., 2003] Masolo, C., Borgo, S., Gangemi, A., Guarino, N., and Oltramari, A. (2003). Ontology Library, WonderWeb Deliverable. Technical Report D18, LOA-CNR, Trento, Italy.

[Odell et al., 2004] Odell, J., Nodine, M., and Levy, R. (2004). A Metamodel for Agents, Roles, and Groups. In Odell, J., Giorgini, P., and Mller, Jrg, P., editors, *Agent-Oriented Software Engineering V*, volume 3382 of *LNCS*, pages 78–92. Springer-Verlag, Berlin, Germany.

[Perini and Susi, 2005] Perini, A. and Susi, A. (2005). Automating Model Transformations in Agent-Oriented modeling. In Mller, J. P. and Zambonelli, F., editors, *Agent Oriented Software Engineering VI*, volume 3950 of *LNCS*, pages 167–178. Springer-Verlag, Berlin, Germany.

[Rao and Georgeff, 1991] Rao, A. S. and Georgeff, M. P. (1991). Modeling Rational Agents within a BDI-Architecture. In *Proceedings of the Second International Conference on Principles of Knowledge Representation and Reasoning (KR'91)*, pages 473–484, Cambridge, MA, USA. Morgan Kaufmann Publishers.

[Shoham, 1993] Shoham, Y. (1993). Agent-oriented Programming. *Artificial Intelligence*, 60:51 to 92.

[van Lamsweerde, 2000] van Lamsweerde, A. (2000). Requirements Engineering in the Year 00: A Research Perspective. In *Proceedings 22nd International Conference on Software Engineering*, pages 5–19. ACM Press.

[van Riemsdijk et al., 2005] van Riemsdijk, M. B., Dastani, M., and Meyer, J.-J. (2005). Semantics of Declarative Goals in Agent Programming. In *Proceedings of the Fourth International Joint Conference on Autonomous Agents and Multiagent Systems*, Utrecht, The Netherlands.

[Wooldridge and Jennings, 1995] Wooldridge, M. J. and Jennings, N. (1995). Intelligent Agents: Theory and Practice. *Knowledge Engineering Review*, 10(2):115–152.

[Yen et al., 2001] Yen, J., Yin, J., Ioerger, T. R., Miller, M. S., Xu, D., and Volz, R. A. (2001). CAST: Collaborative Agents for Simulating Teamwork. In *Proceedings of the Seventeenth International Joint Conference on Artificial Intelligence (IJCAI'01)*, pages 1135–1144, Seattle, WA, USA. Morgan Kaufmann.

[Yu, 1995] Yu, E. (1995). *Modeling Strategic Relationships for Process Reengineering.* PhD thesis, University of Toronto, Canada.

Improving Multi-Agent Architectural Design

Carla Silva[1], Jaelson Castro[1,2,*], Patrícia Tedesco[1], João Araújo[3], Ana Moreira[3],
and John Mylopoulos[4]

[1] Centro de Informática, Universidade Federal de Pernambuco, Recife-PE, Brasil, 50732-970
{ctlls, jbc, pcart}@cin.ufpe.br
[2] Istituto Trentino di Cultura – ITC, Istituto per la Ricerca Scientifica e Tecnologica – IRST,
Trento-Povo, Italy
jaelson@itc.it
[3] CITI/Dept. Informática, FCT, Universidade Nova de Lisboa, 2829-516 Caparica, Portugal,
{ja, amm}@di.fct.unl.pt
[4] Department of Computer Science, University of Toronto, Ontario, Canada, M5S 2E4
john@cs.toronto.edu

Abstract. Agents provide developers with a flexible way to structure systems
around autonomous, communicating elements. To support the efficient
development of such systems, design techniques need to be introduced. In this
context, we propose an extension of the UML 2.0 metamodel to support agency
features and UML-based diagrams which can be used to capture four views of
multi-agent systems architecture (Architectural, Intentional, Environmental and
Communication). The approach also provides heuristics to guide the description
of multi-agent systems according to the proposed diagrams in the context of the
Tropos framework. To illustrate the approach we present an Electronic
Newspaper example.

Keywords: Multi-Agent Systems, Architectural Design.

1 Introduction

Agents offer a new and often more appropriate manner to develop complex systems,
which executes in open and dynamic environments. To support the development of
such systems, tools and techniques need to be introduced such as methodologies to
guide analysis and design, and proper abstractions to enable developers to deal with
the complexity of agent-oriented systems [11].

Tropos [3, 7] is a framework which offers an approach to guide the development of
multi-agent systems (MAS). It relies on the i* notation to describe both requirements
and architectural design. However, the use of i* as an architectural description
language (ADL) is not suitable, since it has some limitations with respect to capturing
some information required for designing MAS architectures, such as ports,
connectors, protocols and interfaces. To address this issue, in this work we present an
approach for using UML 2.0 based notation to describe MAS architecture in Tropos.
This proposal includes (i) an agency metamodel, which defines the constructs
required to specify structural and dynamic features of MAS according to the Belief-
Desire-Intention model [16], and Foundation for Intelligent Physical Agents (FIPA)

R. Choren et al. (Eds.): SELMAS 2006, LNCS 4408, pp. 165–184, 2007.

standards [6]; (ii) four views of MAS architectural design modeled by four UML-based diagrams; (iii) some guidelines to help the specification of MAS according to those diagrams. This proposal is an improvement of our previous work [23] in that we now extend the UML 2.0 metamodel [28] to address agency features and a UML profile to enable MAS modeling by using UML constructs [24]. In particular, both the agency metamodel and the UML-based diagrams introduced in [24] have been redefined to include the following constructs: agent role, intention, commitment, trust, agent communication language and degree of dependency. Moreover, we refine the heuristics presented in [23, 24] to guide the specification of MAS according to the UML-based diagrams which now address these new constructs. Differently from [23, 24], our approach is now illustrated through an Electronic Newspaper example.

The rest of this paper is organized as follows. Section 2 presents the agency metamodel. Section 3 shows the modeling diagrams based on the agency metamodel and a guide to specify MAS according to these diagrams. Section 4 describes an Electronic Newspaper example. Section 5 discusses related works. Finally, section 6 summarizes our work and points out still open issues.

2 Agency Constructs

Aiming at providing a notation which supports MAS specification at the architectural level, in [24] we have decided to extend the UML metamodel to support agency concepts such as agent, goal, belief and resource. However, at that stage we did not include in the agency metamodel the following concepts: agent role, intention, commitment, trust, agent communication language and degree of dependency. This paper is a step towards a notation for MAS design which includes such concepts.

2.1 An Agency Metamodel

For the sake of simplicity, the metamodel defining the agency features is divided into two categories: intentional and interaction. The intentional category concepts are described in Fig. 1 while the interaction category concepts are described in Fig. 2. Although there is not much consensus yet in the literature regarding the properties required to specify MAS, in previous work [20, 23] we have established some agent concepts and relationships which were used to create the agency metamodel.

In the intentional category, a MAS can be conceived as an Organization [5] which is composed of a number of AgentRoles as well as of other Organizations. The AgentRole concept extends the UML metaclass Class from the StructuredClasses package which extends the metaclass Class (from the Kernel package) with the capability of having an internal structure and ports. Norms are required for the Organization to operate harmoniously and safely. They define a policy and constraints that all the organizational members must comply with [12]. The Organization is typically immersed in exactly one Environment that the Agents may need to interact with to play their AgentRoles [21]. An AgentRole has *rights* to access resources which belong to the environment [32]. The Right metaclass possesses four boolean properties: *create*, *destroy*, *read* and *write*. The *Agent, Organization, Norm,*

Environment and *Resource* concepts extend the UML metaclass *Class*, since they represent information that needs to be encapsulated into a class.

Each Agent can play one or more AgentRoles, and an Agent which plays an AgentRole has the Intention to achieve the AgentRole's goals. An agent commits itself to achieve goals and to execute plans. Thus, the Intention metaclass has the *commit* property. Based on [2] we consider two commitment strategies, defined as the enumeration class Commitment: (i) *single-minded:* an agent may drop commitments when it believes they can no longer be attained, regardless of changes in its goals; (ii) *open-minded:* an agent may drop commitments when it believes they can no longer be attained or when the relevant goals are no longer desired. After committing to a goal and an associated plan, an agent starts the plan realization. The *Right* and *Intention* concepts are extensions of the UML metaclass *AssociationClass*, since they represent information that appear just because there is a relationship between two other elements and that information needs to be encapsulated into a class.

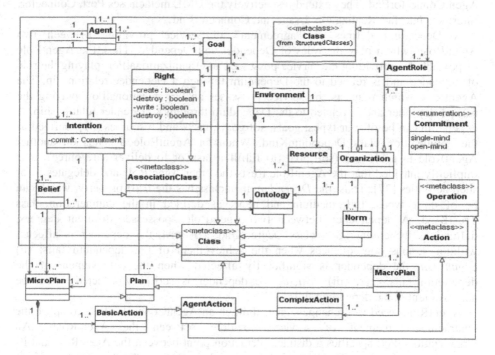

Fig. 1. Agency metamodel reflecting intentional concepts

A Goal is a condition or state of affairs in the world that the Agent has committed itself to achieve. How the goal is to be achieved is not specified, allowing alternatives to be considered [14]. A Plan encapsulates a recipe for achieving some goal. An AgentAction determines the steps to perform a plan and extends both the Action and Operation UML metaclasses. The AgentAction has two subclasses: the ComplexAction, which can be further refined and the BasicAction, which cannot be decomposed. A Plan has two subclasses: a MacroPlan if the Plan is defined by the AgentRole and a MicroPlan if the Plan is defined by the Agent. The difference between MacroPlan and

MicroPlan is that the former is a partial plan and, therefore, is composed of ComplexActions, and the latter is the complete and final plan and, therefore, is composed of Basic Actions. Beliefs represent the information the Agent has about itself and its current environment [30]. These are preconditions for both executing its plans and ordering the plans' actions (i.e., the MicroPlans). These concepts also extend the UML metaclass Class. The description of both Beliefs and Goals must comply with the Ontology used in the Organization, i.e., the vocabulary of concepts which belongs to the system domain. We define the MAS Ontology by extending the UML metaclass Class. The rationale is that the UML class diagram has been employed to describe ontology in MAS [22].

Since AgentRoles are going to be used in the system architectural design, we will define them by using the organizational architectural features defined in [4]. These features, defining the interaction category, are depicted in Fig. 2 and include: OrganizationalPort, AgentConnector, Dependum, Dependee, Depender and AgentConnectorEnd. They extend respectively the UML metaclasses Port, Connector, Interface, InterfaceRealization, Usage and ConnectorEnd.

A Dependum defines an "agreement" of service providing between two AgentRoles which play the roles of Depender and Dependee. Thus, the AgentRole responsible for providing the service possesses an OrganizationalPort playing the role of dependee and is related to the Dependum through a Dependee relationship. The AgentRole which requests the service possesses an OrganizationalPort playing the role of depender and is related to the Dependum through a Depender relationship. A dependum can be of four types: goals, softgoals, tasks and resources [31], defined as the enumeration class DependumKind. When an AgentRole depends on another AgentRole to achieve a (soft)goal (to fulfill a task or to deliver a resource), it is implicitly intended that the AgentRole trusts the other AgentRole and delegates it for such activities [27]. Thus, the *Dependum* metaclass has the *trust* property, which can be of three types: full, medium and none, as defined in the enumeration class TrustKind. A dependency between two AgentRoles possesses different degrees, defined as the enumeration class DegreeKind: (i) *open*, the depender is affected without serious consequences when the achievement of the dependum fails; (ii) *committed*, the depender is significantly affected when the achievement of the dependum fails, and; (iii) *critical*, the depender is seriously affected when the achievement of the dependum fails [31].

AgentRoles need to exchange signals through an AgentConnector to accomplish the contractual agreement of service providing between the AgentRoles. An OrganizationalPort specifies a distinct interaction point between the AgentRole and its environment. An AgentConnectorEnd is an endpoint of an Agentconnector, which attaches the AgentConnector to an OrganizationalPort. Each AgentRole can interact with other AgentRoles according to an *InteractionProtocol*. An *InteractionProtocol* describes a sequence of *CommunicationMessages* that can be sent or received by Agents playing certain AgentRoles through the execution of their AgentActions. In addition, the *InteractionProtocol* must comply with an *Ontology* and an *Agent Communication Language (ACL)*. The Ontology is the vocabulary of the terms used in the message contents and their meaning (both the sender and the receiver must ascribe the same meaning to symbols for the communication to be effective). The ACL defines the format of each *CommunicationMessage* which composes the *InteractionProtocol*. The

ACL concept extends the UML metaclass Class, while the *InteractionProtocol* concept extends the UML metaclass Interaction. The *CommunicationMessage* concept extends the UML metaclass Message and can be of several types including REQUEST, INFORM and REFUSE, among other performatives defined by the FIPA [6] (defined as the enumeration class MessageKind). These indicate what the sender intends to achieve by sending the message.

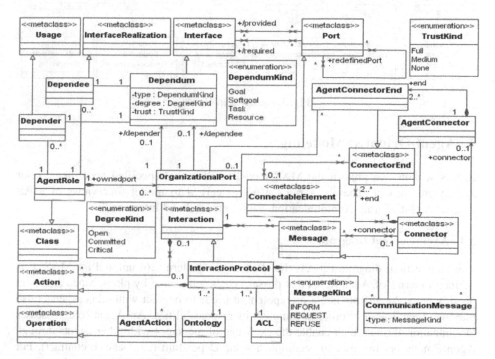

Fig. 2. Agency metamodel reflecting interaction concepts

2.2 An Agency Profile

A Profile has been defined in the UML 2.0 specification to give a straightforward mechanism for adapting an existing metamodel with constructs that are specific to a particular domain, platform, or method. For example, in our approach we have created an agency metamodel by extending some UML metaclasses to address agent-oriented concepts. To enable MAS modeling by using UML constructs and tools, we use the profile mechanism to adapt the UML metamodel with constructs that are specific to the agent paradigm according to the agency metamodel defined in Fig. 1 and Fig. 2. Such adaptation is grouped in a profile, called *Agency Profile*. An extension (a kind of association) is used to indicate that the properties of a metaclass are extended through a stereotype.

Fig. 3 presents some extensions we have made according to the agency metamodel defined in Figs. 1 and 2, such as the stereotype *Agent* extending the UML metaclass *Class*, the stereotype *OrganizationalPort* extending the UML metaclass *Port*, the stereotype *Dependum* extending the UML metaclass *Interface*, the stereotype *Depender* extending the UML metaclass *Usage*, the stereotype *Dependee* extending the UML metaclass *InterfaceRealization* and the stereotype *AgentConnector* extending the UML metaclass *Connector*.

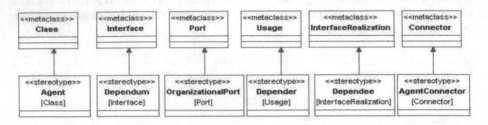

Fig. 3. Agency stereotypes

3 Agent-Oriented Modeling

In this section, we present the MAS modeling diagrams specified according to our agency metamodel. These diagrams were conceived to model four views of MAS design: Architectural, Communication, Environmental and Intentional.

3.1 Architectural Diagram

The architectural diagram reflects the client-server pattern [26] tailored for MAS. It is defined in terms of AgentRoles that possess goals achievable by plans. Since an Agent playing some AgentRole is not omnipotent, it needs to interact with other Agents (also playing AgentRoles) in order accomplish its responsibilities. An AgentRole possesses OrganizationalPorts which enable the exchange of messages with other agents through AgentConnectors in order to accomplish some Dependum (i.e., service contract). For example, Fig. 4 shows the Provider AgentRole, responsible for performing the service defined in the Dependum. This AgentRole aims at achieving the ServicePerformed goal by executing the PerformPlan MacroPlan, which, in turn, consists of performing the service() ComplexAction.

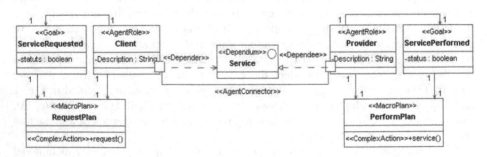

Fig. 4. MAS Architectural Diagram

The Client AgentRole aims at achieving the ServiceRequest goal by executing the RequestPlan MacroPlan, which, in turn, consists of performing the request() ComplexAction. Therefore, the Client AgentRole is responsible for requesting the service defined in the Dependum. Both the message for requesting the service execution and the message for confirming whether the service was successfully concluded are sent through the AgentConnector. Information such as *type:DependumKind*, *degree:DegreeKind* and *trust:TrustKind* are part of the Dependum specification (similarly to the isAbstract:Boolean property which is part of the Class specification in UML 2.0) and cannot be graphically modeled. This information could be added to the model element through tagged values [28], which are used to define model element's properties which are not predefined in UML.

3.2 Communication Diagram

The communication diagram is defined in terms of Agents playing given AgentRoles and the messages exchanged between them to achieve a service providing. For example, Fig. 5 shows an interaction involving the agents playing the Client and Provider AgentRoles. The interaction specified using the communication diagram is asynchronous. The expression *client : Client* indicates an Agent *client* which plays the *Client* AgentRole. Information such as *Ontology* and *ACL* cannot be graphically modeled since they are part of the InteractionProtocol specification.

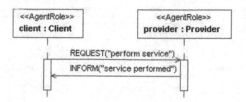

Fig. 5. MAS Communication Diagram

3.3 Environmental Diagram

The environmental diagram is defined in terms of AgentRoles composing an organization, situated in an environment. This environment is composed of resources, which are accessed by the AgentRoles according to their rights in order to accomplish their responsibilities. For example, Fig. 6 shows the *Provider* AgentRole composing the *Org* organization which is situated in the *Env* environment.

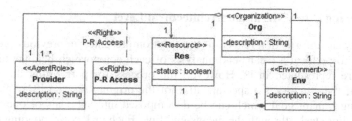

Fig. 6. MAS Environmental Diagram

The Provider AgentRole needs to access a *Res* resource available in the *Env* environment to fullfil its responsibilities. The *Provider* AgentRole can only read the *Res* resource, according to its *P-R Access* right (read *Provider-Res Access* right)). Information such as *create:Boolean, destroy:Boolean, read:Boolean* and *write: Boolean* cannot be graphically modeled since it is part of the Right specification.

3.4 Intentional Diagram

The intentional diagram is defined in terms of agent roles, agents, their beliefs, goals, plans, as well as the norms and the ontology used in the organization. For example, Fig. 7 shows the *Provider* AgentRole composing the *Org* organization which must comply with the OrganizationalNorm norm. The AgentY Agent, which plays the Provider AgentRole, has a belief about if some request message has been received (depicted as RequestReceived belief). Information such as *commit:CommitmentKind* cannot be graphically modeled since it is part of the Intention specification.

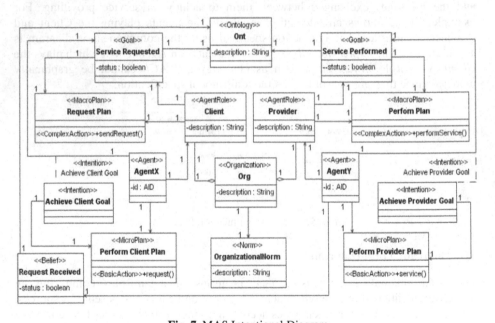

Fig. 7. MAS Intentional Diagram

3.5 Mapping i* to UML at the Architectural Level

To identify the information related to the notation presented in previous sections, it is necessary to perform a means-end analysis of each actor which belongs to the MAS architecture represented in i*. However, the process for performing the means-end analysis of these actors is a specialization of the original process [31]. We begin by establishing a main goal which can be decomposed into subgoals or operationalized by one or more tasks through the means-end link. Each task corresponding to a means element in some means-end relationships must be decomposed into other tasks, (soft) goals and resources. Subtasks cannot be further decomposed. The end element in the means-end relationship can only be a (soft)goal. Each (soft)goal must be operationalized by a means-end relationship or decomposed by a task-decomposition link. The means element in the means-end relationship can only be a task.

In [23], we have presented some heuristics to map the i* concepts to both agency and UML-RT concepts [17]. However, at that stage we did not take into account the architectural concepts supported by UML 2.0. Hence, in [24], we have redefined these heuristics to consider the MAS architectural concepts (Fig. 4) extended from UML 2.0. Here, we define other heuristics to address the derivation of the new concepts we have added to agency metamodel. These heuristics include mapping guidelines for agent role, intention, macro plan, complex action and degree of dependency:

H1. Each role in the i* model becomes an «AgentRole» class in the architectural diagram.

H2. Each agent in the i* model becomes an «Agent» class in the intentional diagram.

H3. Each play relationship between an agent and a role in the i* models becomes an association class relationship «Intention» between the correspondent «Agent» and «AgentRole» in the intentional diagram. In this work we do not provide guidelines to define the commit property of the «Intention».

H4. Each dependum in the i* model becomes a «Dependum» interface in the architectural diagram. Note that a «Dependum» can be of four types (goals, softgoals, tasks and resources) according to the metamodel in Fig. 2. These types are not provided explicitly in the model since it is a property of the model element.

H5. In an i* model, a dependency is: (i) open if it has the symbol "o"; (ii) committed if it has no symbol, and; (iii) critical if it has the symbol "x". Thus this information can be captured in the degree property of the «Dependum». Here guidelines to define trust of the «Dependum» are not provided.

H6. Each depender in the i* model becomes a «Depender» usage in the architectural diagram.

H7. Each dependee in the i* model becomes a «Dependee» interface realization in the architectural diagram.

H8. Each dependency (depender -> dependum -> dependee) in the i* model becomes a «Connector» association in the architectural diagram. Ports are added to the agents to enable the link through the connector.

H9. Each resource related to the actor in the i* model becomes a «Resource» in the environmental diagram. It represents an environmental resource which the agent needs to access to perform its responsibilities. In this work we do not provide guidelines to define the agent rights to access each «Resource».

H10. Each goal (or softgoal) in the i* models which is not decomposed becomes a «Goal» in both the architectural diagram and intentional diagram. It represents the objectives the agent playing a specific role intends to achieve.

H11. Each task in the i* models becomes a «MacroPlan» in both the architectural diagram and intentional diagram. It represents the means through which a goal is going to be achieved.

H12. Each sub-task in the i* models becomes a «ComplexAction» in the architectural diagram. It represents each step which composes a «MacroPlan».

H13. A «Belief» is some condition for performing a task (i.e, a «Plan» or an «AgentAction»). It represents the knowledge the agent has about both the environment and itself.

H14. The «Organization» is the MAS the agent roles and other organizations compose.

H15. Each (soft)goal that is part of a task becomes a «Goal» and creates a «ComplexAction» responsible for generating that goal in the «MacroPlan» correspondent to the task.

A preliminary mapping of i* concepts into agent, goal, belief, plan and resource concepts was originally proposed in [3]. However, here we did not provide a guide or a notation to capture the mapped information. This paper introduces a notation to be used in the MAS specification at the architectural level. Finally, we define a specialization of the original means-end analysis process which is appropriate for refining the rationale of each agent role before the mapping of the i* concepts to the agency concepts. However, we have not defined yet the heuristics to derive MAS ontology and norms. Furthermore, the specification of the Communication diagrams, «MicroPlan» and «BasicAction» are still performed in an ad hoc fashion. These issues will be addressed in future work.

4 An Example

To illustrate our approach, we consider the Electronic Newspaper example, introduced and modeled using the Tropos framework in [22]. The e-News system (Fig. 8) enables a user to read news by accessing the newspaper website maintained by a Webmaster AgentRole which is responsible for updating the published information. The information to be published is provided by the Chief Editor AgentRole. The Chief Editor depends on the Editor to have the news of a specific category. For example, an Editor may be responsible for political news, while another one may be responsible for sports news. Each Editor contacts one or more Photographers-Reporters to find the news of specific categories (e.g., sport news). The Chief Editor then edits the Editor' news and forwards them to the Webmaster to publish them. The e-News system (Fig. 8) is composed of four AgentRoles: Editor, Webmaster, Chief Editor and Photographer-Reporter. The *Joint Venture* architectural style [10] has been chosen and applied to the MAS architectural design, but due to lack of space we will not elaborate on the reasons for that choice. Here, our focus is on the design of the MAS architecture according to agent modeling diagrams (Section 3).

4.1 From i* to UML

We start this activity by using the heuristics presented in Section 3.5 to produce MAS UML-based models at the architectural level in the context of Tropos. We begin by performing the means-end analysis for each actor which belongs to the MAS architecture described using the i* notation. Then, we rely on the mapping heuristics to specify each diagram presented in Section 3.5.

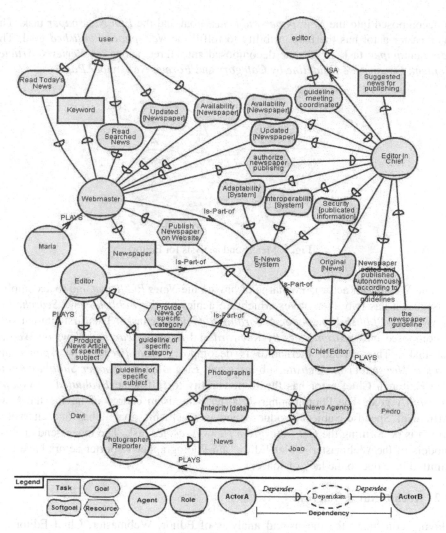

Fig. 8. e-News System Architecture

For example, in our example, we perform the specialized means-end analysis of the Editor, Webmaster, Chief Editor and Photographer-Reporter actors in order to capture their rationale when pursuing their goals and dependencies.

The Editor expects to obtain *News of Specific Category Edited*. One alternative to satisfy this goal is to perform the *Edit News of Specific Category* task. This task is decomposed into five sub-tasks (see the refined model in Fig. 9): *Format News Article*; *Select Unknown, Recent, Important and Accurate News*; *Review Photos Quality*; *Review News Content*; *Get News;* and *Provide Specific Subject Guideline*.

Analogously, the Chief Editor actor expects to get hold of *Newspaper Edited and Published According to the Guideline* and, to achieve this goal, it has the alternative of performing the *Edit and Publish Newspaper According to Guideline* task. This task is decomposed into the *Newspaper Published* goal and the *Edit Newspaper* task. The Webmaster actor has the responsibility to fulfill the *Newspaper Published* goal. The *edit newspaper* task is further decomposed into three subtasks: *Reviews Articles Content, Decompose Guideline by Category* and *Format Newspaper Pages*.

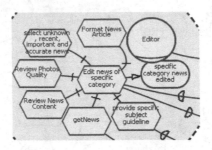

Fig. 9. Means-end analysis for Editor

The Webmaster actor is in charge of having the *News Published* and to accomplish this goal it has two alternatives which are achieving the *Publish News Searched by Keyword* or *Publish Newspaper According to Guideline* tasks. This first alternative is decomposed into *Search News by Keyword* and *Release Searched News on Website* sub-tasks. This second alternative is decomposed into *Preview Newspaper* and *Update Newspaper on Website* sub-tasks and *Evaluated Newspaper Suitability* goal. The Editor in Chief actor has the responsibility to fulfill the *Evaluated Newspaper Suitability* goal. The Photographer-Reporter actor is in charge of having the News Article of Specific Subject Produced and to reach this goal it has one alternative which is performing the *Get News from News Agencies* task. The means-end analysis models of the Webmaster, Chief Editor and Photographer-Reporter actors have been omitted here due to the lack of space.

4.2 Architectural Diagram

Having concluded the means-end analysis of Editor, Webmaster, Chief Editor and Photographer-Reporter actors, we can now move on to identifying the properties that characterize that MAS according to the agent modeling diagrams (Section 3). The heuristics presented at Section 3.5 can be of some assistance to describe the Editor, Webmaster, Chief Editor and Photographer-Reporter actors according to the architectural diagram (Fig. 4). For example, the *News of Specific Category Edited* goal present in the means-end analysis of the Editor actor becomes a «Goal» associated to the Editor «AgentRole» (shaded area of Fig. 10). The *Edit News of Specific Category* task becomes a «MacroPlan» associated to both the Editor «AgentRole» and Papers Reviewed «Goal». Each of the *Format News Article, Select Unknown, Recent, Important and Accurate News, Review Photos Quality, Review News Content, Get News* and *Provide Specific Subject Guideline* tasks becomes an «ComplexAction» in the *Edit News of Specific Category* «Plan».

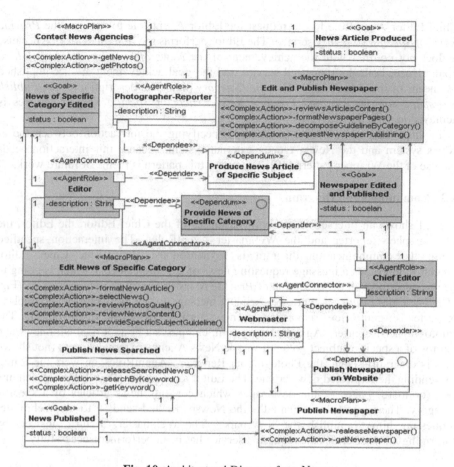

Fig. 10. Architectural Diagram for e-News

Each dependum of the Editor actor's dependencies becomes a «Dependum». For example, the dependum of the *Provide News of Specific Category* task dependency, between Editor «AgentRole» and Chief Editor «AgentRole», becomes a *Provide News of Specific Category* «Dependum», typed as a task (shaded area in Fig. 10). The depender and dependee roles of the *Provide News of Specific Category* dependency become the «Depender» dependency from Chief Editor «AgentRole» and the «Dependee» realization from Editor «AgentRole», respectively. The *Provide News of Specific Category task* dependency itself becomes a «Connector» between Editor «AgentRole» and Chief Editor «AgentRole». Ports are added to these «AgentRole» classes to enable the link through the «Connector». The same guidelines are applied to the other actors present in the i* model. As a result several classes are incorporated in the MAS architectural diagram depicted in Fig. 10.

The shaded area corresponds to the interaction between the Chief Editor and Editor AgentRoles to achieve the Provide News of Specific Category service. The Chief Editor AgentRole intends to achieve the *Newspaper Edited and Published* goal by means of the *Edit and Publish Newspaper* plan. However, to edit the newspaper the

Chief Editor AgentRole has to request the Editor AgentRole to perform the *Provide News of Specific Category* service. The Editor performs the requested service because it does not conflict with the achievement of the *News of Specific Category Edited* goal. Hence, both the requested service and the goal achievement are accomplished by means of the *Edit News of Specific Category* plan. The description of the *Publish Newspaper on Website* and *Produce News Article of Specific Subject* services is achieved in a similar way.

In this work, we are not concerned in specifying the interaction between the e-News system and the News Agency external system, because this interaction needs the use of the Wrapper pattern [10]. The use of this pattern is theme of future work.

4.3 Communication Diagram

Fig. 11 shows an interaction involving instances of the Chief Editor, the Editor, the Photographer-Reporter and the Webmaster AgentRoles. The interaction specified using the communication diagram is asynchronous. Hence, the Chief Editor «AgentRole» sends a message requesting news of specific category which is going to be provided through the execution of *Provide News of Specific Category* service (Fig. 10). Then, the Editor «AgentRole» sends a message to one (or more) Photographer-Reporter «AgentRole» requesting a news article of a specific subject. The Photographer-Reporter «AgentRole», in turn, composes a news article with news and photos of a specific subject gotten from the News Agency external system (not shown in this diagram). Then, the Photographer-Reporter «AgentRole» answers the Editor by sending the requested news article. The Editor answers the Chief Editor by sending one (or more) pages of the newspaper which contents news articles of a specific category. The Chief Editor then edits the Newspaper and sends it to the Webmaster requesting him to publish the Newspaper. The Webmaster, in turn, answers by informing whether or not the requested service has been performed successfully.

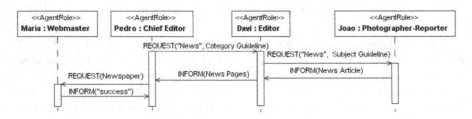

Fig. 11. e-News Communication Diagram

4.4 Environmental Diagram

The heuristics presented in Section 3.5 continue to be used here to identify the properties which characterize MAS according to this diagram. Hence, all *News Pages, News Article, Subject Guideline, Category Guideline* resource elements related to the Editor actor (Fig. 9) become a «Resource» associated to the Editor «AgentRole» in the environmental diagram presented in the shaded area of Fig. 12.

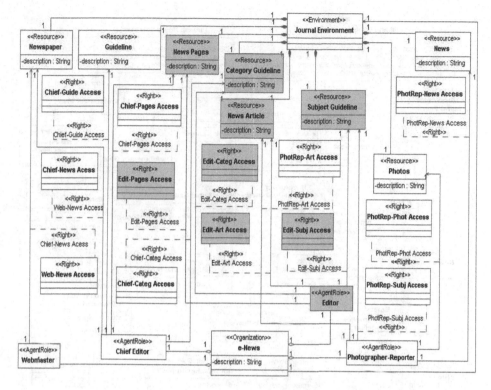

Fig. 12. e-News Environmental Diagram

In this diagram we have the *Editor, Chief Editor, Webmaster and Photographer-Reporter* AgentRoles composing the *e-News* organization which is situated in the *Journal* environment. The *Editor* «AgentRole» needs to access the *News Pages, News Article, Category Guideline and Subject Guideline* resource available at the *Journal* environment to achieve the *News of Specific Category Edited* goal. The *Editor* «AgentRole» can read, write, create or destroy the *News Pages and Subject Guideline* resources, according to its *Edit-Pages Access* and *Edit-Subj Access* rights, respectively (read *Editor-News Pages Access* right and *Editor- Subject Guideline Access* right). The *Editor* «AgentRole» can only read the *News Article and Category Guideline* resources, according to its *Edit-Art Access* and *Edit-Categ Access* rights, respectively (read *Editor-News Article Access* right and *Editor-Category Guideline Access* right). The description of the agent roles' rights to access resources is achieved in a similar way.

4.5 Intentional Diagram

The intentional diagram is defined in terms of agent roles, agents, beliefs, goals, plans, intentions, norms and ontology (see Fig. 13).

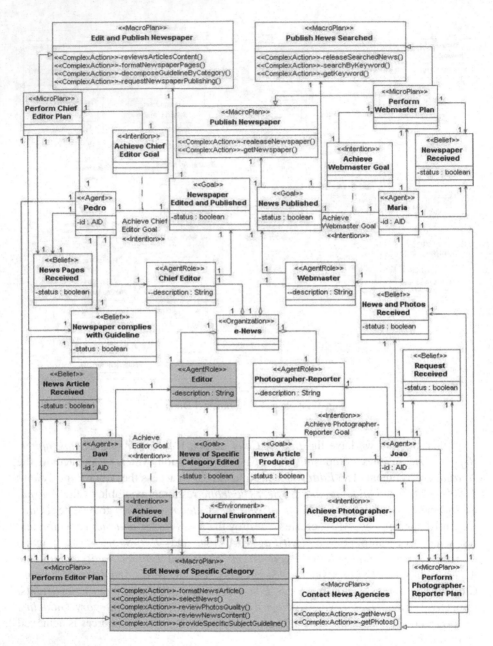

Fig. 13. e-News Intentional Diagram

The heuristics presented in Section 3.5 are used here to identify some properties which characterize that MAS according to this diagram. Hence, the agent Davi, which plays the Editor agent role in Fig. 8, becomes an «Agent» in the intentional diagram (shaded area of Fig. 13). The relationship between the Davi «Agent» and the Editor

«AgentRole» creates an intention to *Achieve the Editor Goal.* To accomplish this, Davi «Agent» has to execute the *Perform Editor Plan* «MicroPlan». The condition to perform the *Edit News of Specific Category* task (Fig. 9) is that the News Article has been received. Hence, the Davi «Agent» has the *News Article Received* «Belief» which is the condition to execute the *Perform Editor Plan* «MicroPlan». The description of the intentional elements associated to the other agent roles is achieved in a similar way.

5 Related Work

[8] presents an agent ontology based on the unified foundational ontology (UFO) and shows how it can be used as a foundation of agent concepts and for evaluating agent-oriented modeling methods. UFO is stratified into three ontological layers in order to distinguish its core, UFO-A, from the perdurant (i.e. process) extension layer UFO-B and from the agent extension layer UFO-C. Although this work provides a foundation for conceptual modeling, including agent-oriented modeling, it does not propose a modeling language for MAS based on this ontology. However, the proposed ontology can be used as a type of 'mirror' for our modeling language, i.e. for verifying how clear and expressive our language is.

[9] proposed an agent-oriented approach named ARKnowD (Agent-oriented Recipe for Knowledge Management Systems Development) to guide the creation and evolvement of knowledge management solutions. It has extended the UFO-C to create an ontology to evaluate, adjust and combine the notations adopted in ARKnowD, i.e. Tropos [7] and AORML [29] notations. However, that approach is tailored for the development of knowledge management information systems.

In the other hand, several languages for MAS modeling have been proposed in the last few years, such as AUML [15], MAS-ML [19] and SKwyRL-ADL [13].

The work presented in [13] proposes a metamodel which defines an architectural description language (ADL) to specify secure MAS. In particular, SKwyRL-ADL includes an agent, a security and an architectural models and aims at describing secure MAS, more specifically those based on the BDI (belief-desire-intention) model. Moreover, the Z specification language is used to formally describe SkwyRL-ADL concepts. Our approach also supports MAS specification according to the BDI model. Furthermore, our notation supports architectural features, such as ports, connectors, interfaces and protocols and provides diagrams which enable the specification of MAS in four views. Our approach also provides a guide to specify design using the proposed diagrams. Since we have both extended an agency metamodel from UML 2.0 metamodel and created an agency profile, we can use the UML constructs and tools to model MAS architectural design.

The proposal of a multi-agent system modeling language called MAS-ML is presented in [19]. It extends the UML metamodel according to the TAO (Taming Agents and Objects) metamodel concepts [18]. TAO provides an ontology that defines the static and dynamic aspects of MAS. The MAS-ML includes three structural diagrams – Class, Organization and Role diagrams – which depict all elements and all relationships defined in TAO. The Sequence diagram represents the dynamic interaction between the elements that compose a MAS — i.e., between objects, agents, organizations and environments. Compared with that approach, our proposal improves the MAS specification because our notation supports architectural features, such as ports, connectors, interfaces and protocols and its use is guided by some heuristics.

AUML [15] provides extensions of UML, including representation in three layers of agent interaction protocols, which describes the sequence of messages exchanged by agents as well as the constraints in messages content. However, AUML does not provide extensions to capture the agent's reasoning mechanisms (individual structure) or the agent's organization (system structure). On the other hand, we provide UML-based diagrams to capture the agent internal structure and the MAS structure, as well as a guide to use these diagrams in MAS specification.

In summary, we are concerned with the detailed specification of MAS design by providing a standard notation which captures four views of MAS architecture and heuristics to guide the use of this notation. Furthermore, our approach explicitly models the purpose - resource delivery, task performing or (soft)goal achievement - associated to an interaction between two agent roles. This information is derived from actor dependency in i* models. Our approach is being developed in the context of the Tropos framework, aiming at supporting all phases of the MAS development lifecycle.

6 Conclusions and Future Work

This work aims to address current issues related to the lack of proper techniques and notation to specify MAs architectural design. We propose both the agency metamodel and the UML-based diagrams to capture four views of MAS at architectural level and, therefore, support specification of MAS architectural design in more detail. Besides supporting the BDI model and FIPA standards, the proposed diagrams also address MAS architectural constructs (ports, connectors, interfaces and protocols) and constructs such as agent role, intention, commitment, trust, agent communication language and degree of dependency. Finally, these diagrams may be used in other frameworks/methodologies, facilitating the development and design of MAS. In particular, we outline a guide to design MAS according to our notation in the context of the Tropos framework. We also applied our approach to an Electronic Newspaper example to illustrate the feasibility of both the proposed notation and heuristics.

Our proposal is under development and consequently much work is still required to improve both the notation and the heuristics to specify MAS in detail. In fact, we still need to define diagrams to model the deployment and action views of MAS. Moreover, some information associated to MAS is not yet addressed by the current heuristics. For example, a strategy to derive both the system ontology and organizational norms from i* models is still required. Therefore, we intend to address these open issues by applying our approach to real case studies as well as comparing our approach with other related works (e.g. [29]). By now, we are proposing a standard notation based on the agency metamodel to describe organizational architectural styles [25].

Future work also includes investigating whether other UML 2.0 diagrams are useful for designing MAS. For example, the work presented in [21] could be used to complement our approach to model agent plans and actions using UML 2.0 activity diagrams in Tropos.

Acknowledgments

This work was supported by several research grants (CNPq Proc. 142248/2004-5, CAPES Proc. BEX 1775/2005-7 & CAPES/ GRICES Proc. 129/05).

References

1. Bellifemine, F., Caire, G., Poggi, A., Rimassa, G.: JADE - A White Paper. In: Special issue on JADE of the TILAB Journal EXP (2003)
2. Brazier, F., Dunin-Kęplicz, B., Treur, J., Verbrugge, R.: Modelling Internal Dynamic Behaviour of BDI Agents. In: Gabbay, D., Smets, Ph. (eds.): Dynamics and Management of Reasoning Processes. Series in Defeasible Reasoning and Uncertainty Management Systems, Vol. 6. Kluwer Academic Publishers (2001) 339 – 361
3. Castro, J. Kolp, M., Mylopoulos, J.: Towards Requirements-Driven Information Systems Engineering: The Tropos Project. Information Systems Journal, 27. Elsevier (2002) 365 – 89
4. Castro, J., Silva, C., Mylopoulos, J.: Detailing Architectural Design in the Tropos Methodology. In: 15th Conference Advanced Information Systems Engineering (CAiSE'03). Klagenfurt/Velden, Austria (2003) 111 – 126
5. Ferber, J.: Multiagent Systems: An Introduction to Distributed Artificial Intelligence. Addison Wesley (1999)
6. FIPA. FIPA (The Foundation for intelligent agents), Available: http://www.fipa.org (2004)
7. Giorgini, P., Kolp, M., Mylopoulos, J., Castro, J.: Tropos: A Requirements-Driven Methodology for Agent-Oriented Software. In: Henderson-Sellers, B. et al. (eds.): Agent-Oriented Methodologies. Idea Group (2005) 20 – 45
8. Guizzardi, G., Wagner, G.: Towards Ontological Foundations for Agent Modeling Concepts using UFO. In: Lecture Notes on Artificial Intelligence (LNAI) 3508, Springer-Verlag (2005)
9. Guizzardi, R.: Agent-oriented Constructivist Knowledge Management. PhD Thesis. University of Twente. The Netherlands (2006)
10. Kolp, M., Giorgini, P., Mylopoulos, J.: Information Systems Development through Social Structures. In: 14th Software Engineering and Knowledge Engineering (SEKE'02). Ischia, Italy (2002)
11. Luck, M., McBurney, P. and Preist, C.: Agent technology: Enabling Next Generation Computing (A Roadmap for Agent Based Computing). AgentLink (2003)
12. Minsky, N and Muarata, T.: On Manageability and Robustness of Open Multi-Agent Systems. In: Lucena, C. et al. (eds.): Software Engineering for Multi-Agent Systems II: Research Issues and Practical Applications. LNCS, 2940, Springer-Verlag (2004) 189 – 206
13. Mouratidis, H., Faulkner, S., Kolp, M., Giorgini, P. A Secure Architectural Description Language for Agent Systems. In: 4th Autonomous Agents and Multi-Agent Systems (AAMAS'05). The Netherlands (2005)
14. Mylopoulos, J., Kolp, M., Castro, J.: UML for agent-oriented software development: The Tropos proposal. In: 4th Unified Modeling Language (UML'01), Toronto, Canada (2001)
15. Odell, J., Parunak, H. V. D, Bauer, B.: Extending UML for agents. In: AOIS'00 at the 17th National Conference on Artificial Intelligence, Austin, USA. iCue Publishing (2000) 3 – 17
16. Rao, A.S. and Georgeff, M.P.: BDI agents: from theory to practice. Technical Note 56, Australian Artificial Intelligence Institute (1995)
17. Selic, B., Rumbaugh, J.: Using UML for Modeling Complex Real - Time Systems. Rational Whitepaper, www.rational.com (1998)

18. Silva, V., Garcia, A., Brandão, A., Chavez, C., Lucena, C., Alencar, P.: Taming Agents and Objects in Software Engineering. In: Garcia, A. et al. (eds.): Software Engineering for Large-Scale Multi-Agent Systems. LNCS, Vol. 2603. Springer-Verlag (2003) 1 – 25
19. Silva, V., Lucena, C.: From a Conceptual Framework for Agents and Objects to a Multi-Agent System Modeling Language. In: Sycara, K. et al. (eds.): Journal of Autonomous Agents and Multi-Agent Systems. Kluwer Academic Publishers, 9, 1-2 (2004) 145 – 189
20. Silva, C., Tedesco, P., Castro, J., Pinto, R.: Comparing Agent-Oriented Methodologies Using a NFR Approach. In: 3rd Software Engineering for Large-Scale Multi-Agent Systems (SELMAS'04). Edinburgh, Scotland (2004) 1 – 9
21. Silva, V. T., Noya, R. C., Lucena, C. J. P.: Using the UML 2.0 activity diagram to model agent plans and actions. In: 4th Autonomous Agents and Multi-Agent Systems (AAMAS'05). The Netherlands (2005) 594 – 600
22. Silva, I. G. L.: Design and Implementation of Multi-Agent Systems: The Tropos Case (in portuguese). Master Thesis. CIn, Universidade Federal de Pernambuco, Brazil (2005)
23. Silva, C., Castro, J., Tedesco, P., Araújo, J., Moreira, A., Mylopoulos, J.: Improving the Architectural Design of Multi-Agent Systems: The Tropos Case. In: 5th Software Engineering for Large-Scale Multi-Agent Systems (SELMAS'06) in conjunction with 28th International Conference on Software Engineering (ICSE'06). Shangai, China (2006)
24. Silva, C., Araújo, J., Moreira, A., Castro, J., Tedesco, P., Alencar, F., Ramos, R.: Modeling Multi-Agent Systems using UML. In: 20th Brazilian Symposium on Software Engineering (SBES'06). Florianópolis, Brazil (2006) 81 – 96
25. Silva, C., Araújo, J., Moreira, A., Castro, J., Alencar, F., Ramos, R.: Organizational Architectural Styles Specification. In: Jornadas de Ingeniería del Software y Bases de Datos, 2006, Barcelona (2006)
26. Shaw, M. and Garlan, D. Software Architecture: Perspectives on an Emerging Discipline. Prentice Hall (1996)
27. Susi, A., Perini, A., Giorgini, P., Mylopoulos, J.: The Tropos Metamodel and its Use. In: Informatica, 29, 4 (2005) 401 – 408
28. Unified Modeling Language (UML) Specification: Infrastructure Version 2.0. www.omg.org/docs/formal/05-07-04.pdf (2005)
29. Wagner, G.: The Agent-Object-Relationship Meta-Model: Towards a Unified View of State and Behavior. In: Information Systems, 28, 5 (2003) 475 – 504
30. Wooldridge, M.: An Introduction to Multiagent Systems. John Wiley and Sons, Ltd. England (2002)15 – 103
31. Yu, E.: Modelling Strategic Relationships for Process Reengineering. Ph.D. thesis.Department of Computer Science. University of Toronto, Canada (1995)
32. Zambonelli, F., Jennings, N. R. and Wooldridge, M.: Developing Multiagent Systems: the Gaia Methodology. In: ACM Transactions on Software Engineering and Methodology, 12, 3 (2003) 317 – 370

Objects as Actors Assuming Roles in the Environment

Tetsuo Tamai[1], Naoyasu Ubayashi[2], and Ryoichi Ichiyama[3]

[1] The University of Tokyo, Tokyo, Japan
tamai@acm.org
[2] Kyushu Institute of Technology, Fukuoka, Japan
ubayashi@acm.org
[3] The University of Tokyo, Tokyo, Japan
ir@bellbind.net

Abstract. To achieve the goal of realizing object adaptation to environments, a new role-based model *Epsilon* and a language *EpsilonJ* are proposed. In Epsilon, an environment is defined as a field of collaboration between roles and an object adapts to the environment assuming one of the roles. Objects can freely enter or leave environments and belong to multiple environments at a time so that dynamic adaptation or evolution of objects is realized. Environments and roles are the first class constructs at runtime as well as at model description time so that separation of concerns is not only materialized as a static structure but also observable as behaviors. Environments encapsulating collaboration are independent reuse components to be deployed separately from objects. In this paper, the Epsilon model and the language are explained with some examples. The effectiveness of the model is illustrated by a case study on the problem of integrated systems. Implementation of the language is also reported.

1 Introduction

Considerable research efforts have been devoted to make objects in object-oriented systems more flexible and adaptable. The recent interest in self-managed (or autonomic, self-healing, adaptive) systems/computing indicates renewed attention on this target [16].

Research on multi-agent systems(MAS) started with objectives of constructing systems composed of autonomous agents that possess independent proactive behaviors. Agents are by nature dynamic and adaptable to environments. Now, the MAS technology is getting to be applied to real complex software systems [11].

Thus, objectives and approaches of OO and MAS are getting closer. Our work has its root in software engineering, particularly in object-oriented technology, but is expected to be useful in designing and implementing multi-agent systems.

Our motivation stems from the observation that objects in the real world reside in various environments, which may not be stable due to various reasons. If objects are workers or manufacturing equipment, their environment changes periodically between the day and the night and between weekdays and weekends. When an object moves, the surrounding environment naturally changes. Or an object stays at the same place but the environment may dynamically change. Corresponding to such environmental change, objects adaptively change themselves. Conversely, objects may spontaneously

R. Choren et al. (Eds.): SELMAS 2006, LNCS 4408, pp. 185–203, 2007.

evolve, causing change in their relation to the environment. Moreover, there generally exist multiple environments around an object and the object may selectively belong to a subset of them at a time and the selection of environments may also change dynamically.

Motivation of our research is to build a computational model that is flexible enough to cope with future changes but simple enough to describe and reason about the design validity. For that objective, we have a good reason to believe that a role-based model is a highly promising candidate.

Examples that imply appropriateness of role-based approaches can be found in a variety of existing work, with which we share similar motivations. Following are three of such examples.

Y. Honda et al. [8] gave an example of adaptation. A woman Hanako, modelled as an object, marries with Taro and adapts to the environment *family*. She then gets employed as a researcher by a company and adapts to the environment *laboratory*. The adaptation is made dynamically, while object Hanako preserves its identity when she enters a new environment like the laboratory or even after she quits the job for some reason.

M. Fowler [3] gave an example of personnel roles in a company to be assumed by employees. He listed up engineers, salesmen, directors and accountants as roles and put a question how to deal with situations such that a person plays more than one role or a person changes his or her role in the lifetime. He showed several patterns that solve this problem and gave a generic name *role pattern*. Those patterns employ ad hoc techniques, revealing the difficulties of describing such situations naturally in the conventional object-oriented framework.

E. Kendall [13] gave an example of the bureaucracy pattern. There are five roles in the pattern: Director, Manager, Subordinate, Clerk and Client. A client deals with a clerk. Manager and Subordinate are subclasses of Clerk. A manager supervises subordinates and reports to a director. There exist two environments: a bureaucracy of a sales company and a trading relation between clients and clerks. A clerk or a manager may belong to both environments.

These examples suggest a role model where an environment is defined as a field of collaboration between roles and an object adapts to the environment assuming one of the roles. There have been proposed a number of role models but our model has been designed aiming at the following challenging objectives.

1. Support adaptive evolution
2. Describe separation of concerns
3. Advance reuse

In this paper, we introduce our role model *Epsilon* and a language based on the model *EpsilonJ* with examples. We also explain language implementation.

2   Role Model

2.1   Collaboration and Role Model

The history of object-oriented technology is abundant with role models [30]. The major objective of considering roles has been to describe collaboration of objects and identify clear and solid boundary of each object. An object may take part in multiple collaborations assuming different roles in different collaborations. Thus, the characteristics of an object may be clarified by consolidating roles the object plays in multiple collaborations.

A typical way of describing a collaboration is by specifying use cases or behavioral scenarios as observable behaviors of the collaboration. Originally advocated by I. Jacobson [10] as a method OOSE and inherited by the Unified Modeling Process [9], the use case approach is now well practised. In the context of use case approaches, the word *role* is not necessarily used but either a role or its corresponding concept is captured as an aspect of objects engaged in collaboration. The granularity roles in this case is smaller than objects and conceptually comparable to functions or methods.

In some other OO development methodologies, the concept of roles is given a higher position so that the term *role modelling* is created and extensively used. A typical example is the *OOram* methodology [21], which not only defines role models but also integrates them with OO models through the step of role model synthesis. D. Riehle extended the approach of role modelling to deal with object migration [33] and to design composite patterns [22] and frameworks [23]. B. Kristensen et al. also presented a conceptual framework of role modelling [15].

In these methodologies, roles play an important part in the phases of analysis and design but usually become invisible in the implementation phase. However, there are some work that aim at preserving roles explicitly in programs. For example, VanHilst & Notkin [32] used class templates of C++ to implement roles. Smaragdakis & Batory [25] introduced a construct of *mixin layers* where collaboration fields are described as layers composed of roles, and roles are filled by objects a la mixin style. Multi-Dimensional Separation of Concerns (MDSOC) [19] has a longer history but the idea of describing collaboration fields in separate dimensions and defining classes by consolidating roles in those dimensions is similar. All these approaches are class based and composition of objects consolidating roles is done statically.

Role models have been explored in the agent-oriented modelling community as well [1,18]. Particularly, in designing multi-agent systems, it is quite natural to bring in a framework of behavior interaction between multiple roles. In the MAS setting, agents behave concurrently and adaptively, which fits well to the notion of dynamic role assignment to agents.

So far, there do not seem to exist an established consensus on how to employ the role modelling concept in MAS design at the concrete level, e.g. whether roles should be used as components from which agents are to be built or rather agents and roles are basically on equal terms, whether roles should be defined as a group within which interaction takes place between the roles or roles can be defined first and grouping of roles can be created afterward, etc.

Efforts are being made to bridge the software engineering (SE) community and the MAS community. Gaia, for example, was proposed as a methodology for developing multi-agent systems but has been matured as "a software engineering paradigm for designing and developing complex software systems" [34]. The concept of roles is also one of the key factors in Gaia. In Gaia, an agent is considered as an active software entity playing a set of agent roles. Roles are identified in the analysis phase and precisely defined composing a role model in the architectural design phase but absorbed into agents within an agent model in the detailed design phase.

Our work is starting from SE but features such as roles as first class citizens at runtime and dynamic binding of roles and objects as explained in the following sections will be complementary to MAS approaches like Gaia.

2.2 Epsilon Model

Our aim is to support description of collaboration not just at the model level but also at the programming level. Collaboration model is built not for identifying objects but for manipulating collaboration environments and their roles directly and reusing them as program components. Up to that point, we share the same objective as VanHilst & Notkin, Smaragdagis & Batory, or Hyper/J, a language for MDSOC.

However, as we stated in the previous section, the major motivation for our research is to devise a mechanism for object adaptation to environments. An environment in the context of role model is regarded as a collaboration field and objects enter collaboration environments by playing roles as actors or leave environments by discarding roles dynamically. At this point, our approach parts from the above other OO methods and comes closer to the notion of agent-oriented systems.

The basic elements of our model *Epsilon* are as follows.

Collaboration Field and Roles. In our model, an environment is regarded as a collaboration field where a set of roles interact each other to collaborate. A collaboration field coupled with a set of roles is a basic element of the model. Roles are like objects exchanging messages between them to realize collaboration. Roles are encapsulated in the collaboration field and cannot be accessed directly from the outside of the field. A collaboration field with roles can be regarded as a unit of concern and reuse that can be deployed independently from ordinary objects.

Object and Role Binding Mechanism. Objects belonging to a class are defined as in the conventional object-oriented framework. An object participates in a collaboration field as an actor playing one of the roles defined in the field. This mechanism is called binding of an object and a role instance. Through the binding, the object acquires functions and properties of the role. The object can also discard the role dynamically so that it leaves from the collaboration field. An object can assume multiple roles of different collaboration fields at a time.

2.3 Language

We designed a language named *EpsilonJ* that supports the model features described above. EpsilonJ is an extension of Java, basically following the Java syntax. Recently, some new languages with similar objectives have been appearing, e.g. ObjectTeam/Java [7] and Chameleon [4] but some of their basic design concepts look fairly different. For example, although there is a notion of role instance in ObjectTeam/Java, the combination of a role class and a base class is statically fixed and only attachment/detachment of a role instance to an object can be changed dynamically. Attachment of a role to a class in Chameleon is like static aspect weaving in AspectJ. Both mechanisms are significantly different from the approach of EpsilonJ, where role-object binding is executed dynamically at the instance level as will be seen below.

Declaration of Environments and Roles. In EpsilonJ, environments or collaboration fields are called "contexts." Declaration of `context` and `role` can be made with attributes and methods just like object classes. Declaration of `role` is placed inside of `context` declaration, similar to inner classes of Java but the coupling between a context and its roles is stronger than that of an outer class and inner classes as we will see later. Instances of contexts and roles are created dynamically.

Encapsulation of Roles in Environments. As declaration of roles is confined in a context, their interaction is encapsulated within the context. Roles in a context can communicate with each other but cannot access to other contexts and roles in other contexts directly. Collaboration is naturally described on the role instance basis.

Following is an example program to show how `context` and `role` are declared and collaboration between roles are described.

```
context Company {
    static role Employer {
        int salary = 100;
        void pay() {Employee.getPaid(salary);}
    }
    role Employee {
        int save;
        void getPaid(int salary) {save += salary;}
    }
}
```

When the qualifier "static" is declared in a role definition, there is exactly one instance of that role in a context instance and it is created at the time of the context instance creation. Note that this semantics of "static" is different from that of the Java nested classes. In Java, a static class declared in a class is not an inner class; it has no current instance of the enclosing class. On the other hand, a "static" role in a context is associated with its enclosing context instance. It only means the role instance is a singleton in the context. The singleton role instance can be referred by the role name within the context and by the role name qualified with the context instance reference from the outside of the context.

For example, after a context instance is created as:

```
Context c = new Company();
```

the role instance of Employer can be referred by `c.Employer`.

Role Instance Creation. When a role is not declared "static" its role instances can be created by an indefinite number, using the keyword "new" and a constructor. For example:

```
context C {
  static role R1 {
    void m1() {
      R2 y = new R2(); //create a role instance of R2
      y.m2();
      ...
    }
  }
  role R2 {
    void m2() { ... }
  }
}
```

It is also possible to create a role instance from the outside of the context. For example:

```
Context x = new C();
C.R2 y = new x.R2();
```

As this example shows, a role instance is necessarily associated with the enclosing context instance and thus the constructor should be qualified by a context instance reference, not by context type (i.e. you have to write new x.R2() rather than new C.R2()).

A set of instances of a role is called a role group. A role group is associated with a context instance and it is referred by the role name. A method of a role is called just as a method of an object is called but when a role has multiple instances, there is a shorthand for calling the same method of all role instances by qualifying the method name just with its role name. Then, the method is invoked for all the role instances in nondeterministic order and when the method has a return value, the one from the last invocation will be returned. Thus, the method call Employee.getPaid(salary) in the method declaration of pay() in Employer role is interpreted as calling the getPaid method of all the Employee instances.

If you want to control the order of invocation and the returned value, you should call the method of role instances individually. If you use the given order but want to control over each invocation, a method Iterator iterate() is available. It is applied to a role group and returns an Iterator that iterates over the current role instances.

Binding of Objects with Roles. An object can be dynamically bound to a role of a context and can be unbound later. An object may be bound to multiple roles of different contexts. When an object is bound to a role, it acquires the functions of the role, i.e. it can call the role's methods as the following example shows.

```
class Person {
  int money;
}
Person tanaka = new Person();
Person sasaki = new Person();
Company todai = new Company();
todai.Employer.bind(sasaki);
todai.Employee.newBind(tanaka);
(todai.Employer)sasaki.pay();
(todai.Employee)tanaka.getPaid();
```

A method `bind(Object o)` is defined in all roles, meaning to bind the Object o to the role instance whose `bind` method is being invoked. A method `newBind(Object o)` is defined in all non-static roles, meaning to create a new role instance and bind the Object o to it. The `newBind` method is actually a two step process: `todai.Employee.newBind(suzuki)` being equivalent to `(new todai.Employee()).bind(suzuki)`.

After the binding, the object bound to a role acquires the functions of the role and thus role methods can be invoked through casting as shown in the above program piece. This mechanism of role method access through the binding to an object can be regarded as a kind of delegation.

Our design choice of defining the binding operation between an object and a role instance, not between an object class and a role class, is intentional and has rationale. We could have characterized a role as a slot or a template where a binding object is inserted. We did not do so, because in some cases, it would be useful for a role instance to retain its own state after detaching from the binding object. For example, suppose a person object Tanaka took a role of the account department head at the company Todai but then the role was replaced by Suzuki. It would be appropriate that the role instance of the account head still retains the state of the work left unfinished by Tanaka and lets Suzuki succeed it.

Instead of `(todai.Employer)sasaki.pay()`, one may want to write just:

```
sasaki.pay();
```

but it is not allowed for the following reasons.

1. Since an object can be bound to multiple role instances, the above expression can be ambiguous.
2. By indicating casting, static type checking gets possible.

However, even with this casting mechanism, whether the object is really bound to the designated role so that the method can be found without failure should be checked dynamically, because binding and unbinding are dynamic operations. This is a cost we have to pay for realizing dynamic deployment. To help dynamic type checking, a method `Object boundObject()` is predefined to each role instance or a static role that returns the object it is bound to and `null` if no object is bound.

A method `<Role> unbind()` is defined in all roles. This method can be applied to a role instance or a static role. When the role is bound to an object, its binding is dissolved and the reference to the role instance is returned. When the role is not bound to an object, its effect is no operation.

Required Interface. If binding an object with a role just brings about disjoint union of the methods in the object and the role, nothing particularly interesting will happen. There should be some coupling between the object and the role that are bound together so that the state and the behavior of the object should be affected by the binding.

For that purpose, there is a way of defining an interface to a role and it is used at the time of binding with an object, requiring the object to supply that interface, i.e. the binding object should possess all the methods specified in the interface. A required interface can be declared using the `requires` phrase as follows.

```
interface Deposit {void deposit(int);}
context Company {
  role Employee requires Deposit {
    void getSalary(int salary) {
      deposit(salary);}
    ...
}
```

To reduce a plethora of names, there is an anonymous required interface expression as follows.

```
role Employee requires {void deposit(int);} {
  void getSalary(int salary) {
    deposit(salary);}
  ...
}
```

Method Import. When a required interface is declared to a role, methods can be imported to the role from the binding object. For example, suppose the class Person has a method deposit such as:

```
class Person {
  string name; int money;
  void deposit(int s) {money+=s;}
}
```

and the variable tanaka has a reference to its instance. Using the binding operation:

```
todai.Employee.newBind(tanaka)
```

the method deposit(int) of tanaka is imported to the Employee role instance through the interface. The binding object class may explicitly implement the interface like:

```
class Person implements Deposit {
  string name; int money;
  void deposit(int s) {money+=s;}
}
```

but it is not mandatory. It is only necessary to have a method that has the same name and the same signature required by the role. After the binding, whenever the method deposit(int) of the role instance is called, the corresponding method of tanaka is invoked.

The binding object may even have a method with a different name but the same signature as the required method. In that case, binding with the replacing phrase is used to specify the correspondence. For example, suppose the class Person is defined as:

```
class Person {
  string name; int money;
  void save(int s) {money+=s;}
}
```

Then, the binding operation should be given by:

```
todai.Employee.newBind(tanaka)
  replacing deposit(int) with save(int);
```

After this binding, whenever the method `deposit(int)` of the role instance is called, the method `save(int)` of `tanaka` is invoked instead.

In general, when a role has a required interface declaration, every interface method should be explicitly replaced at the time of binding by a binding object method, except when the object possesses a method with the same name and the same signature.

Method Export. All public methods declared in `role` are "exported" in the sense that they can be used from the binding object. But here, we focus on the case where an interface method is overridden in the role body. For example,

```
context Company { ...
  role Employee requires {void deposit(int);} {
    void deposit(int salary) { ... }
  }
}
```

In this case, when the Person object referred by the variable `tanaka` is bound to `Employee` role as before:

```
todai.Employee.newBind(tanaka)
  replacing deposit(int) with save(int);
```

thereafter whenever the method `save` of `tanaka` is called, the overriding role method `deposit` is invoked instead. This can be regarded as method export from the role to the binding object.

Method Import/Export. When an interface method is overridden by the corresponding role method, the replacing method of the binding object becomes hidden. If there is a need for invoking the hidden method in the context, either in the body of the overriding method or in other role (or context) methods, it is possible to invoke it by attaching the qualifier `super` to the method name. For example,

```
context Company { ...
  role Employee requires {void deposit(int);} {
    void deposit(int salary) {
    ...
      super.deposit(salary);
    ...
    }
  }
}
```

Multiple Method Replacement. A role instance, including a static role, cannot be bound to more than one object, i.e. a role is always played by a single actor. This is because if a role instance is bound to multiple objects, there is no unambiguous way of determining which object is affected by invocation of a role method. On the other hand, an object may bind to multiple role instances and thus the same object method may replace multiple role methods. In contrast to the case of a single role instance bound to multiple objects, this case can be given unambiguous semantics.

Suppose replaced methods are all importing the object method, then each call of the role interface method will actually call the replacing object method.

On the other hand, when replaced methods are all exporting (overriding), when the replacing object method is called, all the overriding methods are called. The order of invocation is compiler dependent.

As the third case, suppose some replaced methods are importing the object method and others are exporting themselves. Then, a call to the replacing object method that is overridden will result in the same behavior as stipulated in the second case. A call to an interface method in the role with "super" qualifier will always result in calling the original replacing method of the binding object however it is overridden. When a call to an interface method is not qualified with "super", it calls the current overridden object method, the effect of which is the same as calling the object method being replaced. When more than one role method is overriding it, all of them will be called. This case may look complicated but the principle is very simple. The binding/unbinding mechanism is dynamic in nature and the current status of binding is always respected, except the explicit call of the original method with "super."

3   Case Study

It is straightforward to write the three examples introduced in the introduction with our Epsilon model as they are analogous to the example of the Company context explained above.

3.1   Integrated System

Here, we take the problem of integrated systems for a case study. An integrated system is a system integrating independent but related components. When a component takes an action, related components behave accordingly. For example, a collected system of an editor, a compiler, and a debugger is a typical integrated system. When the compiler detects a syntax error or the debugger stops at a breakpoint, the editor scrolls to the corresponding source statement.

A simplified model of integrated systems was introduced by K. Sullivan et al.[28]. In this model, the components subject to integration are objects that have just a binary state, "on" and "off." We call these objects Bits. An instance of Bit has operations "set" and "clear," that changes the state to "on" and "off", respectively. Binary relations, Equality and Trigger, are defined between Bits. The Equality relation always makes the states of the related Bits the same, while the Trigger relation activates the target Bit to be "on" if the source Bit becomes "on," but takes no actions on the other situations.

For example, let us assume the structure as illustrated in Figure 1. In this system, the four nodes, b1, b2, b3 and b4, represent instances of Bit; b1 and b2 are connected by an Equality relation and so are b2 and b3; b3 triggers b4. If b1 receives a message "set," then the "set" message is also sent to b2, which in turn sends the "set" message to b3.

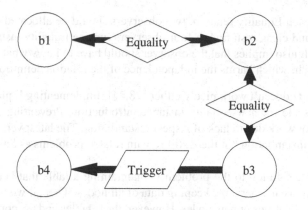

Fig. 1. Bit Relations

Furthermore, the "set" message is sent to b4 because b3 is a trigger of b4. However, no matter what is sent to b4, nothing happens to b3 or to the other nodes. Note that each of b2 and b3 is involved in two different relations, which requires special care. Also, some mechanism of preventing the message propagation reflecting back to the sender is required, otherwise the propagation will continue infinitely.

The problem is to make this system scalable and evolvable, separating the definitions of the Bit objects and the Equality and Trigger relations. More concretely, the questions are:

- Is it easy to add a new node?
- Is it easy to add a new type of nodes?
- Is it easy to add a new relation?
- Is it easy to add a new type of relations?

3.2   Problems with Current OO Approaches

It has been argued that conventional object oriented techniques are not adequate to meet the above requirements [28,12,24]. A simple approach of embedding relations in the Bit class definition obviously harms the independence of Bit from relation definitions. Applying design patterns, particularly the mediator pattern and the observer pattern, may look promising. However, they are not so effective as expected, because:

Mediator Pattern. Bit class must know the mediator that implements Equality, Trigger, etc. and thus it directly depends on the mediator definition.

Observer Pattern. The observer pattern is better than the mediator pattern for dealing with the case where a Bit instance is involved in multiple relations. However, Bit has to accept observers and also has to notify observers when it changes its state. The former is usually implemented by inheriting "Subject" superclass or interface and the latter introduces some change to the Bit method declaration, which makes it impossible to reuse the existing Bit definition entirely. Moreover, an observer should be created for each event distinguishing the event source and the event type.

Thus, for each Equality relation, two observers should be allocated for each operation, set and clear, resulting in four observers for one Equality instance, which is awkward. It also implies that the observer should have to know what kind of events it is to watch, which harms the independence of the relation definition.

Using AspectJ doesn't work nicely either [28,24]. Implementing Equality as an Aspect does not scale for new equality instance introduction. Preventing unbounded recursion does not work due to lack of Aspect instantiation. The latest version of AspectJ allows Aspect instantiation but there still remain related problems as Sakurai et al.[24] shows.

One probable solution to the problem is maintaining a table that keeps data of all relations as well as another table keeping data of all nodes. Then, it would be relatively easy to add new relations or new nodes. However, these tables and the control procedure using them are global by nature, while adding (and deleting) relations and nodes is a local operation. This is a solution that solves a local problem globally, which in general is not desirable.

Sullivan & Notkin [29] treated this problem with ABT (Abstract Behavior Types). In their solution, the Bit class defines operations, "set" and "clear" and also announces events, "justset" and "justcleared." Relations such as Equality are defined as a mediator that listens to events and invokes corresponding operations. Compared to the mediator pattern in the ordinary object-oriented framework, the Bit object doesn't have to know the existence and the interface of the mediator but it is required to explicitly raise events to be used by the mediator.

3.3   Our Solution

We claim that the problem is solved elegantly using EpsilonJ. The definition of Bit is natural and simple, totally independent from the Equality and Trigger relations.

```
class Bit {
  boolean state=false;
  void set() {state=true;}
  void clear() {state=false;}
  boolean get() {return state;}
}
```

The Equality relation is defined as a context, requiring an interface `ActionInterface` that simply declares a method without parameters and return values.

```
interface ActionInterface {void fire();}
context Equality {
  boolean busy=false; // A flag to prevent infinite recursion
  static role Actor1 requires ActionInterface {
    void fire() {
      super.fire();
      if(!busy) {
        busy=true;
        Actor2.fire();
```

```
                // Role instance method "fire" of
                // all Actor2 instances are called
          busy=false;
        }
      }
    }
    static role Actor2 requires ActionInterface {
      // Similar to Actor1
    }
}
```

The Equality definition above is totally independent from that of Bit or any other types of components.

Combining this context and Bit, the integrated system of Figure 1 can be defined exploiting binding operations as follows.

```
Bit b1=new Bit(); Bit b2=new Bit();
Bit b3=new Bit(); Bit b4=new Bit();
Equality e12set = new Equality();
Equality e23set = new Equality();
Trigger t34 = new Trigger();
e12set.Actor1.bind(b1)
   replacing fire() with set();
e12set.Actor2.bind(b2)
   replacing fire() with set();
...
```

In this way, concerns of components and networks are clearly separated and they are explicitly combined by a piece of role-object binding code.

3.4 Results

We have succeeded in separating Bit and Equality; they are totally independent and reusable. As the context Equality must be instantiated, its context variable busy is an instance variable created for each context, which is convenient for implementing the infinite loop prevention mechanism. The method replacement operation of import & export in this case, together with the method renaming capability, was powerful enough to allow a concise description. The design scales to new node(Bit) introduction and new types of nodes introduction as well as new relation instance introduction and new type relation introduction.

Besides the integrated system, we have written various kinds of examples, including the mediator pattern, the observer pattern, the visitor pattern, Kendall's bureaucracy structure, a rental shop business, the contract net protocol([26]) and the dining philosophers problem.

4 Comparison with Other Approaches

4.1 Comparison with AspectJ

Aspect-oriented programming(AOP) with AspectJ has a feature of adding aspects dynamically as well as statically [14]. The main objective of writing aspects is to deal with cross-cutting concerns. It implies that there already exists some structure of module decomposition. Although efforts have been made to design software based on the AOP principle from the beginning, under the name of "early aspects"[20], the normal framework of mind for thinking aspects assumes the existing program code as a target of inserting advices to join points. On the other hand, Epsilon's way of thinking assumes no existing code and designs collaboration contexts independently. The task corresponding to designating pointcuts and attaching advices is executed by binding objects to roles.

It is often argued that *obliviousness* is a fundamental property that characterizes AOP [2]. It means that designers and developers of base functionality need not be aware of, anticipate or design code to be advised by aspects. There also is criticism to this idea, claiming that the obliviousness approach casts a too heavy burden on aspect designers and makes pointcut descriptors too complex and inflexible [27,6].

In our Epsilon approach, both "role" programs and "base object" programs can be written "obliviously," without considering each other. All the necessary adjustment and combining tasks are taken care of by binding programs. This, in our view, is one of the major characteristics and advantages of EpsilonJ.

4.2 Comparison with Caesar

Some research attempts at describing aspects in terms of role models have been reported (e.g. [5]). Among them, the Caesar model [17] is particularly related with our work. The goal of Caesar is to decouple aspect interface, aspect implementation and aspect binding [17]. The aspect interface is called ACI (Aspect Collaboration Interface) with multiple mutually recursive nested types, which roughly corresponds to the context of EpsilonJ, where a role corresponds to a nested type.

For example, the observer pattern is written in Caesar by nested ACI's and their implementation as follows [17].

```
interface ObserverProtocol {
  interface Subject {
    provided void add(Observer(Observer o);
    provided void removeObserver(Observer o);
    provided void changed();
    expected String getState();
  }
  interface Observer {expected void notify(Subject s);}
}
class ObserverProtocolImpl implements ObserverProtocol {
  class Subject {
    List observers = new LinkedList():
    void addObserver(Observer o) {
      observers.add(o);
    }
    void removeObserver(Observer o) {
      observers.remove(o);
    }
    void changed() {
```

```
    Iterator it = observers.iterator();
    while (iter.hasNext())
      ((Observer)iter.next()).notify(this);
  }
 }
}
```

The same pattern can be written in EpsilonJ as:

```
context ObserverPattern {
  static role Subject requires{void changed();} {
    void changed() {
      super.changed();
      Observer.notify(this);
    }
  }
  role Observer requires{void notify(Subject);} {}
}
```

This is more concise, partly because the interface and the implementation is not separated in EpsilonJ. But the essential point of the observer pattern is the interaction that when the subject's state is changed, it notify's the observers. This crucial behavior is not expressed in the interface of ObserverProtocol in Caesar and only given by the "implementation." The other reason the description in EpsilonJ is shorter is that the operations of adding and removing observers can be omitted, because they are taken care of by the innate binding and unbinding mechanism of EpsilonJ.

A more important difference is observed in the way of aspect binding in Caesar and the binding in EpsilonJ. In EpsilonJ, binding and unbinding of roles and objects are normal runtime operations and thus dynamic deployment is naturally realized. On the other hand, deployment in Caesar requires multiple steps.

Firstly, ACI (ObserverProtocol in this case) and its implementation (ObserverProtocolImpl in this case) has to be bound. Secondly, the ACI's (ObserverProtocol and its nested interfaces, Subject and Observer, in this case) have to be bound to concrete classes. It is done by a new construct that employs a wrapping mechanism. As wrapper instantiation raises a couple of issues, the feature of wrapper recycling to prevent wrapping of the same object and the feature of most specific wrappers to handle polymorphism are introduced. In the description of binding, pointcuts and advices in the sense of AOP may also be defined. Thirdly, the ACI, its implementation and binding classes are composed together to make a new unit called *weavelet*. Lastly, the weavelet has to be deployed using another new construct deploy. Moreover, there are two types of deployment, static and dynamic.

All these features are realized without any specific constructs in EpsilonJ owing to the dynamic instance-based binding with type constraint (given by the requires interface). As binding and unbinding are just methods of roles, it is also easy to encapsulate specific binding(/unbinding) of a given set of objects and roles so that virtual "static deployment" can be realized.

5   Implementation

A preliminary implementation of EpsilonJ was done on Ruby by the third author. Ruby, created by Y. Matsumoto, is a full object-oriented language like Smalltalk with the feature of scripting languages like Perl [31]. It has such a nice feature as adding methods to a class and even to an object instance at runtime, which is quite convenient for implementing a language like EpsilonJ.

As it was implemented on Ruby, its syntax is different from EpsilonJ and so we gave a different name *Bunraku* to this implementation. The implementation of Bunraku was made simple by sacrificing static type checking. As the platform Ruby was a type-less language, this design decision was natural.

We also implemented EpsilonJ on Java. The basic idea is to use the annotation feature of Java 5.0 so that it is implemented totally within the scope of standard Java. Context and Role's are declared like:

```
public @Context class Company {
 @StaticRole abstract class Employer extends RoleBase<Employer>{
    ...
 }
 @Role abstract class Employee
       extends RoleBase<Employee> {
    ...
 }
}
```

Context is defined as a class and Role's are defined as inner classes of the Context class but they are annotated by @Context and @StaticRole (in the static case) or @Role, respectively. Role classes are declared abstract, because some method bodies are supplied at runtime when the binding of a role and an object is executed. A set of basic role methods, including bind, newbind, and unbind, are defined in RoleBase class and every role class has to inherit it. The requires phrase is actually designated by the standard interface implements phrase. Creating a new instance of contexts and roles is executed by a special factory method and thus the use of new operator explained in the preceding subsections is modified here. Besides this point, the syntax explained in Section 2.3 is partly modified in this implementation, but the features are essentially the same.

Some annotation types can be read at runtime and with the reflective APIs they can change the program behaviors. This mechanism is employed for implementing dynamic features of EpsilonJ, including binding and unbinding.

The overhead of compilation is negligible. However, as the current implementation is quite naive, runtime overhead is significant: execution time being between 10 times to 20 times slower than hand-coded programs. Performance enhancement is one of our future work.

6   Conclusions

We proposed a new computation model based on the role concept where objects evolve their behavior by playing roles as actors. The aim of this model is to realize object adaptability within a clear conceptual framework. A collaboration field called environment or context can be defined by a set of roles that interact with each other. An object can dynamically participate in a collaboration field and assume one of its roles so that it acquires functions of the role and capability of collaborating with other roles in the field. The object after assuming a role may dynamically throw away the role and quit from the field. An object may assume multiple roles of different collaboration fields at a time so that it grows into a complex object with rich functions but its behavior can be clearly comprehensible from the base behavioral properties of roles.

We also designed a language *EpsilonJ* based on the model. The feature of EpsilonJ is in some way shared by many aspect-oriented languages, typically AspectJ. In AspectJ, behavior of objects will be changed after being woven with aspects, while in EpsilonJ, behavior of objects will be changed after being bound with roles.

Limitations of the current model/language and future work to be done are as follows:

1. Performance of the current implementation is poor and there is a large room for optimization.
2. Many example problems have been written in EpsilonJ but so far they are all small in size. We have to write practical application systems in EpsilonJ and evaluate its usefulness.
3. Compared to AspectJ, where object behavioral change is designated by a fine granularity mechanism of pointcuts and advices, EpsilonJ provides behavioral change at a higher abstraction level of role and object binding. This feature has an advantage of supporting a comprehensible mental model but in some cases brings weaker expressiveness. Such a tradeoff in the language design should be further studied.

The dynamic and flexible feature of our language EpsilonJ will make it a promising tool to be employed by multi-agent system research. To promote it, we have to address the above issues and accumulate experience of using EpsilonJ.

References

1. R. Depke, R. Heckel, and J. M. Kuster. Roles in agent-oriented modeling. *International Journal of Software Engineering and Knowledge Engineering*, 11(3):281–302, 2001.
2. R. E. Filman and D. P. Friedman. Aspect-oriented programming is quantification and obliviousness. In *Aspect-Oriented Software Development*, pages 21–35. Addison-Wesley, 2005.
3. M. Fowler. Dealing with roles. http://www2.awl.com/cseng/titles/0-201-89542-0/apsupp/. supplemental information to *Analysis Pattern*, Addison-Wesley, 1997.
4. K. B. Graverson. The success and failures of a language as a language extension. In *ECOOP 2003 Workshop on Object-oriented Language Engineering for the Post-Java Era*, Darmstadt, Germany, 2003.
5. K. B. Graverson and K. Osterbye. Aspect modelling as role modelling. In *OOPSLA 2002 Workshop on TS4AOSD*, Seattle, Nov. 2002.
6. W. G. Griswold, M. Shonled, K. Sullivan, Y. Song, N. Tewari, and Y. Cai. Modular software design with crosscutting interfaces. *IEEE Software*, Jan/Feb 2006.
7. S. Herrman. Programming with roles in ObjectTeams/Java. In *AAAI '05*, Oct. 2005.
8. Y. Honda, S. Watari, and M. Tokoro. Compositional adaptation: A new method for constructing software for open-ended systems. *Computer Software*, 9(2):122–136, 1992. in Japanese.

9. I. Jacobson, G. Booch, and J. Rumbaugh. *The Unified Software Development Process*. Addison-Wesley, Reading, 1999.
10. I. Jacobson, M. Christerson, P. Jonsson, and G. Övergaard. *Object-Oriented Software Engineering: A Use Case Driven Approach*. ACM press, 1992.
11. N. R. Jennings. An agent-based approach for building complex software systems. *Communications of the ACM*, 44(4), Apr. 2001.
12. T. Kamina and T. Tamai. McJava - a design and implementation of Java with mixin-types. In *2nd ASIAN Symposium on Programming Languages and Systems (APLAS 2004), LNCS 3302*, pages 398–414, Taipei, Taiwan, Nov. 2004. Springer.
13. E. A. Kendall. Role model designs and implementations with aspect-oriented programming. In *OOPSLA' 99*, pages 353–369, Nov. 1999.
14. G. Kiczales, J. Lamping, A. Mendhekar, C. Maeda, C. Lopes, J.-M. Loingtier, and J. Irwin. Aspect-oriented programming. In *Proceedings of the European Conference on Object-Oriented Programming(ECOOP), Finland*. Springer-Verlag, June 1997.
15. B. B. Kristensen and K. Osterbye. Roles: Conceptual abstraction theory and practical language issues. *Theory and Practice of Object Systems*, 2(3):143–160, 1996.
16. J.-P. Martin-Flatin, J. Sventek, and K. Geihs. Self-managed systems and services. *Communications of ACM*, 49(3):37–39, Mar. 2006.
17. M. Mezini and K. Ostermann. Conquering aspects with Caesar. In *Proceedings of the International Conference on Aspect-Oriented Software Development (AOSD 2003)*, pages 90–99, Boston, Mar. 2003.
18. J. J. Odell, H. V. D. Parunak, and M. Fleisher. The role of roles in designing effective agent organizations. In A. Garcia, C. Lucena, F. Zamobnelei, A. Omicini, and J. Carstro, editors, *Software Engineering for Large-Scale Multi-Agent Systems*, Lecture Notes in Computer Science, 2003.
19. H. Ossher and P. Tarr. Using multidimensional separation of concerns to (re)shape evolving software. *CACM*, 44(10):43–50, Oct. 2001.
20. A. Rashid, P. Sawer, A. Moreira, and J. Araujo. Early aspects: a model for aspect-oriented requirements engineering. In *Proceedings of the International Conference on Requirements Engineering (RE 2002)*, pages 9–13, Essen, Germany, Sept. 2002. IEEE.
21. T. Reenskaug, P. Wold, and O. Lehne. *Working with Objects: the OOram Software Engineering Method*. Manning Publications, Greenwich, 1996.
22. D. Riehle. Composite design patterns. In *OOPSLA '97*, pages 218–228, Oct. 1997.
23. D. Riehle and T. Gross. Role model based framework design and integration. In *OOPSLA '98*, pages 117–133, Vancouver, Oct. 1998.
24. K. Sakurai, H. Masuhara, N. Ubayashi, S. Matsuura, and S. Komiya. Association aspect. In *Proceedings of 3rd International Conference on Aspect-Oriented Software Development (AOSD 2004)*, pages 16–25, Lancaster, UK, Mar. 2004.
25. Y. Smaragdakis and D. Batory. Mixin layers: An object-oriented implementation technique for refinements and collaboration-based designs. *ACM Transactions on Software Engineering and Methodology*, 11(2):215–255, 2002.
26. D. R. Smith. The contract net protocol: High-level communication and control in a distributed problem solver. *IEEE Trans. on Computers*, 29(12):1104–1113, 1980.
27. K. Sullivan, W. G. Griswold, Y. Song, Y. Cai, M. Shonle, N. Tewari, and H. Rajan. Information hiding interfaces for aspect-oriented design. In *ESEC-FSE'05*, pages 166–175, Lisbon, Portuga, Sept. 2005.
28. K. Sullivan, L. Gu, and Y. Cai. Non-modularity in aspect-oriented languages: Integration as a crosscutting concern for AspectJ. In *1st Proceedings of 1st International Conference on Aspect-Oriented Software Development (AOSD 2002)*, pages 19–26, Enschede, Holland, Apr. 2002.

29. K. J. Sullivan and D. Notkin. Reconciling environment integration and software evolution. *ACM Transaction on Software Engineering and Methodology*, 1(3):229–268, 1992.
30. T. Tamai. Objects and roles: modeling based on the dualistic view. *Information and Software Technology*, 41(14):1005–1010, 1999.
31. D. Thomas and A. Hunt. *Programming Ruby: A Pragmatic Programmer's Guide*. Addison-Wesley, 2000.
32. M. VanHilst and D. Notkin. Using C++ templates to implement role-based designs. In *JSSST International Symposium on Object Technologies for Advanced Software*, pages 22–37. Springer Verlag, 1996.
33. R. Wieringa, W. de Jonge, and P. Spruit. Using dynamic classes and role classes to model object migration. *Theory and Practice of Object Systems*, 1(1):61–83, 1995.
34. F. Zambonelli, N. R. Jennings, and M. Wooldridge. Developing multiagent systems: The gaia methodology. 12(3):317–370, July 2003.

A Framework for Situated Multiagent Systems

Danny Weyns and Tom Holvoet

DistriNet, Katholieke Universiteit Leuven
Celestijnenlaan 200 A, B-3001 Leuven, Belgium
{danny.weyns, tom.holvoet}@cs.kuleuven.be

Abstract. In this paper, we present an object-oriented framework for situated multiagent systems. The framework integrates various mechanisms for adaptivity we have developed and applied in our research, including selective perception, protocol-based communication, behavior-based decision making with roles and situated commitments, and laws that mediate the activities of agents in the environment. The framework provides a reusable design asset that facilitates the development of new multiagent system applications that share the common base more reliable and cost efficiently. We give an overview of the framework, and we zoom in on two particular features: decision making with a free-flow tree and support for simultaneous actions. Finally, we show how the framework is applied to an experimental robot application.

1 Introduction

In our research, we study the engineering of software systems with two particular characteristics: (1) the systems are subject to highly dynamic and changing operating conditions such as dynamically changing workloads and variations in the availability of resources, and (2) activity in the systems is inherently localized, i.e. global control is difficult to achieve or even infeasible. Example domains are peer-to-peer file sharing systems, wireless sensor networks, and automated traffic and transportation systems.

To deal with the dynamics and the inherent locality of activity, we apply the paradigm of situated multiagent systems. During the last five years, we have developed several mechanisms of adaptivity for situated multiagent systems, including selective perception [33], protocol-based communication [32], behavior-based decision making with roles and situated commitments [22], and laws that mediate the activities of agents in the environment [28]. We have applied these mechanisms in various applications, ranging from experimental simulations [24] and prototypical robot applications [31] up to an industrial transportation system for automatic guided vehicles [30].

Based on these experiences, we have developed an object-oriented framework for situated multiagent systems. The framework aims to support the development of experimental applications with characteristics similar to the systems we target in our research. Particular motivations for the framework development are: (1) it integrates the various mechanisms for adaptivity in an abstract design, (2) it provides a reusable design asset that allows developers to derive new situated multiagent systems that share the common base more reliable and cost efficiently, (3) it provides a tool for investigating, experimenting and evaluating new concepts and mechanisms of situated multiagent systems.

R. Choren et al. (Eds.): SELMAS 2006, LNCS 4408, pp. 204–231, 2007.

In this paper, we give an overview of the framework for situated multiagent systems. We describe the core of the framework (frozen spot) that is common to all applications derived from the framework, and the hot-spots that represent the variable parts which allow a framework to be adapted to a particular application [11]. We provide a more detailed explanation of two particular features: decision making with a free-flow tree and support for simultaneous actions.

The framework allows the development of situated agent systems with a software environment as well as systems with a physical environment. It provides no support for distribution of a software environment. The framework can be classified in the middle between whitebox and blackbox [11]. Some parts of the framework core are completely hidden for the application developer, an example is the synchronization of simultaneous actions. Other parts however, require knowledge of the internals of the framework. The framework is implemented in Java 1.5 and is available for download [1]. [34] provides a detailed documentation of the framework in the form of a cookbook [6].

Overview. The paper is structured as follows. We start with a brief introduction of the Packet-World that we will use to illustrate the explanation of the framework. Section 3 then presents the main packages of the framework and discusses the two basic parts of the framework: agent and application environment. Section 4 zooms in on decision making with a free-flow tree, and Sect. 5 explains how simultaneous actions are supported in the framework. Section 6 explains failure treatment in the framework. In Sect. 7, we show how the framework is applied to an experimental robot application. Section 8 points out the typical differences between the framework and other multiagent system development frameworks. Finally, Sect. 9 draws conclusions.

2   The Packet-World

Before we start with explaining the framework, we briefly introduce the Packet-World that we will use as an illustrative case throughout this paper. The basic setup of the Packet-World consists of a number of differently colored packets that are scattered over a rectangular grid. Agents that live in this virtual world have to collect these packets and bring them to the correspondingly colored destination. Figure 1(a) shows an example of a Packet-World of size 10x10 with 8 agents (symbolized by the little fellows).

Colored rectangles symbolize packets that can be manipulated by the agents and circles symbolize destinations. The battery symbol at the bottom row of the grid symbolizes a battery charger.

In the Packet-World, agents can interact with the environment in a number of ways. Agents can make a step to a free neighboring cell. If an agent is not carrying any packet, it can pick up a packet from one of its neighboring cells. An agent can put down a packet it carries at one of the free neighboring cells, or of course at the destination point of that particular packet. Agents can also pass packets to neighboring agents forming a chain. Such a chain enables agents to deliver packets more efficiently, e.g. in the situation of Fig. 1(a), agent 1 can pass a packet to agent 8 that can deliver the packet directly at the destination. Finally, if there is no sensible action for an agent to perform, it may wait for a while and do nothing. Besides acting in the environment, agents can also send messages to each other. In particular, agents can request each other for information

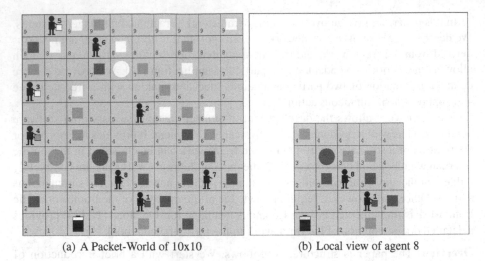

(a) A Packet-World of 10x10   (b) Local view of agent 8

Fig. 1. Example of the Packet-World

about packets or destinations and set up collaborations. The goal of the agents is to perform their job efficiently, i.e. clear up the packets with a minimum number of steps, packet manipulations, and message exchanges.

Agents in the Packet-World can access the environment only to a limited extent. Agents can only manipulate objects in their direct vicinity. The *sensing–range* of the world expresses how far, i.e. how many squares, an agent can perceive its neighborhood. Figure 1(b) illustrates the limited view of agent 8, in this example the sensing–range is 2. Similarly, the *communication–range* determines the scope within which agents can communicate with one another.

Performing actions requires energy. Therefore agents are equipped with a battery. The energy level of the battery is of vital importance to the agents. The battery can be charged at the battery charger. The charger emits a gradient field, i.e. a force field that is spread in the environment and that can be sensed by the agents. The intensity of the field increases further away from the charger. To navigate towards a battery charger, the agents follow the gradient of the field in the direction of decreasing values. The value of the gradient field is indicated by a small number in the bottom left corner of each cell.

In addition to the basic setup, the Packet-World also supports indirect coordination among agents via markers in the environment. A typical example are digital pheromones that agents use to form paths between a cluster of packets and the corresponding destination. For more details about the Packet-World we refer to [24].

3   General Overview of the Framework

Figure 2 shows a general overview of the packages of the framework for situated multiagent systems.

The `Agent` and `Application Environment` packages encapsulate the core of the framework and provide factories to create agents and the application environment.

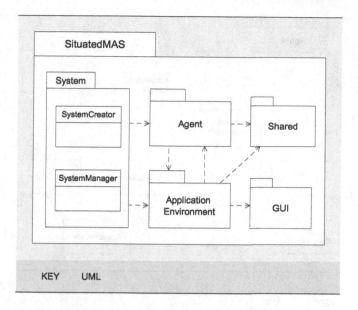

Fig. 2. General overview of the framework

The Shared package encapsulates helper classes for Agent and Application Environment. GUI provides basic support to show the influences invoked by the agents and the messages sent by the agents.

Developing an application with a software environment starts with the implementation of the various hot spots of the Agent and Application Environment package (we discuss the hot spots below). SystemCreator then integrates the hot spots with the framework core to build the application. SystemCreator creates the application environment and populates it with the agents. SystemCreator returns an instance of SystemManager that is used to control the execution of the application. SystemManager allows the user to start the application, to suspend and resume the execution, and to terminate the application.

To develop an application with agents deployed in a physical environment, only the hot spots of the Agent package have to be implemented and integrated with the framework core (Agent package). The integrated software can directly be deployed on the physical machines. To enable the agents to interact with the physical environment, the software has to be connected to sensors and actuators.

3.1 Overview of the Agent Package

Figure 3 shows a general overview of the Agent package. The package is divided in several sub-packages, we briefly explain each of the sub-packages in turn.

KnowledgeIntegration encapsulates the agent's internal state that is modelled as a collection of knowledge objects (KnowledgeObject). Besides basic support for adding and removing knowledge objects, KnowledgeIntegration provides

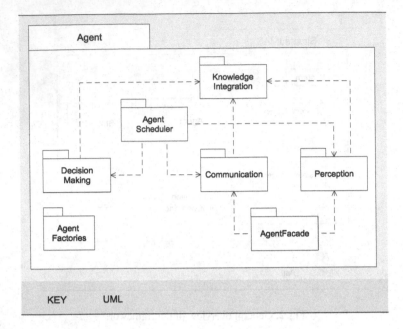

Fig. 3. General overview of the Agent package

various additional features such as support to update the state with a given set of knowledge objects, selection of the knowledge objects of a particular type, registration of an observer to notify changes of a selected type of knowledge objects, etc.

Perception enables the agent to sense the environment. Perception supports selective perception, i.e. agents can sense the environment with a set of selected foci (Focus), interpret representations with descriptions (Description), and filter the resulting Percept with a set of selected filters (Filter) [33]. As an example, VisualFocus that extends Focus enables agents in the Packet-World to visually perceive their environment with a given perception range.

```
public class VisualFocus extends Focus {
  private int range;
  public VisualFocus(int range) {
    setRange(range);
  }
  ...
}
```

Agents can select foci and filters during decision making and communication. The selected foci and filters are registered in KnowledgeIntegration and used by Perception to sense the environment. Perception interacts with the environment via a set of sensors (Sensor). For agents situated in a software environment, a sensor is an abstraction that provides an interface with the application environment. Software agents receive the representation of a perception request via the `AgentFacade`. For agents situated in a physical environment, a sensor is the physical device the agent uses to sense the surrounding world.

Communication deals with the communicative interactions of the agent. Agents communicate according to well-defined communication protocols (`Protocol`) [32]. A protocol consists of a series of protocol steps. We distinguish between three types of protocol steps: conversation initiation, conversation continuation, and conversation termination. A conversation initiation step starts a new conversation according to a particular protocol. An agent initiates a conversation based on its current knowledge, possibly taking into account the data of a message received from another agent that started the interaction. A conversation continuation performs a step in an ongoing conversation. A conversation continuation may deal with a received message without directly responding to it, it may immediately react with a reply message, or it may pick up a conversation after a break. Finally, a conversation termination concludes an ongoing conversation. The termination of a conversation can be induced by changing circumstances in the environment or it can directly result from a preceding step of the conversation. In addition to these protocol steps, the framework provides support for time-outs. The developer can associate a time duration to a conversation, together with a reaction. When no activity has occurred in the conversation for the specified time duration, the accompanying reaction will be executed. For example, if an agent does not receive an answer to a request within a particular time window it can repeat the request, it can discard the conversation, or it can react in some other way. Messages are exchanged in `ExternalMessage` format. An `ExternalMessage` encapsulates a message as a plain string. Internally agents use `AgentMessage` to represent a message. Instances of `AgentMessage` encode messages in terms of domain objects. The conversion of messages is handled by the `SLDecoderEncoder` and is based on a domain `Ontology`. "SL" stands for Semantic Language and is defined by FIPA [16]. For the implementation of the `SLDecoderEncoder`, we reused a package of the Jade libraries [7]. `Ontology` represents the common vocabulary agents use to communicate with one another. Each concept that agents want to use as content of a message needs to be included in their ontology. A concept is stored in the vocabulary as a tuple of the class of the concept and an external name used to refer to the concept (`Tuple<String, Class>`). For example, for agents in the Packet-World, the ontology is defined as:

```
Ontology ont = new Ontology();
ont.addToVocabulary(PacketRepresentation.class, "packet");
ont.addToVocabulary(PositionRepresentation.class, "position");
...
ont.addToVocabulary(Head.class, "head");
...
```

`Communication` is equipped with a `Transceiver` to exchange messages with other agents. For agents situated in a software environment, the transceiver is an abstraction that provides an interface with the application environment. Software agents receive incoming messages via the `AgentFacade`. For agents situated in a physical environment, the transceiver is the physical device the agent uses to communicate with other agents in their neighborhood.

DecisionMaking encapsulates a behavior-based action selection mechanism that supports roles (`Role`) and situated commitments (`SituatedCommitment`) [31,22]. The framework offers the application developer the predefined `FreeFlow` package to instantiate free-flow trees. We elaborate on decision making with a free-flow tree in Sect. 4. Decision making results in the selection of an `Operator` that is passed to `Execution`. An operator is an internal representation used by the agent to represent a selected action. `Execution` decouples the agent's internal representation of actions from the influences that are available to the agent to access and modify the environment. For agents situated in a software environment, the execution module is an abstraction that converts the operator into an `Influence` that is invoked in the application environment. For agents situated in a physical environment, the execution module interfaces with the physical device the agent uses to act in the environment, such as a switch or a motor.

AgentScheduler encapsulates the thread of the agent. `AgentScheduler` determines when the different modules (perception, decision making, and communication) get control. Decision making and communication can select foci and filters that are used by perception to perceive the environment when it gets control. Scheduling of the various activities can be customized according to the requirements at hand. The framework offers a default schema `LTDSchedule` (Look—Talk—Do [25]) that extends `AgentSchedule`. `LTDSchedule` successively activates perception, communication, decision making in an endless loop.

AgentFactories is a package that supports the creation of agents. `AgentFactories` consists of two sub-packages: `SoftwareAgentFactory` and `PhysicalAgentFactory` that can be used to create agents situated in a software environment and a physical environment respectively. In particular, the `PhysicalAgentFactory` supports the instantiation of robot software with the Lego-Mindstorms package [3].

Hot Spots. The hot spots of `Agent` can be divided in two groups: hot spots related to the interaction of the agent with the environment, and hot spots related to the agent's behavior.

Hot spots related to the interaction with the environment are only applicable for agents situated in a physical environment and include `Sensor`, `Transceiver`, and `Execution`. For a concrete application, these hot spots have to be instantiated to interface with the appropriate physical devices. For agents that live in a software environment the core of the framework encapsulates general implementations for sensor, transceiver and execution that are used for the interfacing with the application environment. We illustrate hot spots related to the interaction with the environment for a robot in Sect. 7.

Hot spots related to the behavior of the agent determine how an agent perceives the environment, how it selects actions, and how it communicates with other agents. The hot spots include: KnowledgeObject, Focus, Description, Percept, Filter, DecisionMaking, Role, SituatedCommitment, Operator, Ontology, Protocol, and AgentSchedule. We illustrate a number of instances of these hot spots in Sect. 4.

3.2 Overview of the Application Environment Package

Figure 4 shows a general overview of the application environment package. We briefly look at the various sub-packages.

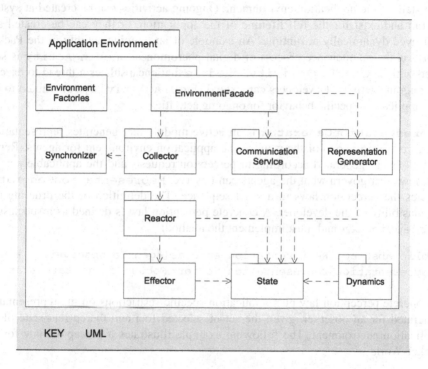

Fig. 4. General overview of the Application Environment package

EnvironmentFacade shields the internals of the application environment to agents. The facade provides an interface to agents to sense the application environment, to invoke influences, and to send messages. EnvironmentFacade dispatches the various activities for processing to the appropriate modules.

State encapsulates the actual state of the application environment. The state of the application environment includes a representation of the topology of the environment, state of static and dynamic objects, external state of agents (e.g., identities and positions), and state of environmental properties that represent system-wide characteristics. An example of an environmental property in the Packet-World is a gradient field that guides agents to a battery charger. State in the framework is set up as a collection of Item objects and a collection of Relation objects. Item is an abstraction for elements in the application environment, with `StaticItem` and `DynamicItem` as specializations. The state of a `StaticItem` is invariable over time, state of a `DynamicItem` may change over time. `Relation` represents a relation between two or more `Item` objects. An example of a relation in the Packet-World is an agent that holds a packet. The framework supports various methods to observe and manipulate `Item` and `Relation` objects.

Dynamics encapsulates a collection of ongoing activities (`OngoingActity`). An ongoing activity defines the behavior of a `DynamicItem` taking into account the current state of the application environment. Ongoing activities can be created at system startup and exist for the full lifetime of the application, or they can be created and destroyed dynamically at runtime. An example of an ongoing activity in the Packet-World is the maintenance process of digital pheromones. `OngoingActity` is supplied with an `OngoingActivitySchedule` that encapsulates a thread to execute the ongoing activity. Developers can extend `OngoingActivitySchedule` to define application-specific behavior for ongoing activities.

RepresentationGenerator is an active module that generates representations (`Representation`) of the state of the application environment for agents. Representations are generated according to perception requests and the applicable perception laws that govern what the agents can observe. `RepresentationGenerator` applies the perception laws in a strict sequence. The definition of the ordering is a responsibility of the developer. A concrete perception law is defined as a subclass of `PerceptionLaw` and must implement the method:

```
public abstract Representation enforce(AgentId observer,
  Representation representation,Vector<Focus> foci,State state);
```

A concrete perception law puts application specific restrictions on the representation generated for an observer, given the set of selected foci and the current state of the application environment. The following example illustrates a perceptual law for the Packet-World:

```
public Representation enforce(AgentId observer,
  Representation representation,Vector<Focus> foci,State state){
  Representation repr=copy(representation);
  Position observerpos=((GridState)state).getPosition(observer);
  if (containsVisualFocus(foci))
    for (int i=0;i<((GridStateRepresentation)repr).nbItems();i++){
    ItemRepresentation item = repr.getItem(i);
    Position itempos = item.getPosition(i);
    if (item.isVisible()
      && ((GridState)state).obstacleBetween(observerpos, itempos))
    removeItem(representation, item);
    }
  return representation;
}
```

This law removes all the visible items in a representation that are out of the view of an observer due to an obstacle.

CommunicationService is an active module that handles message transport through the environment. Messages are delivered first-in-first-out. The application developer can define communication laws that enforce domain specific constraints on the transport of messages. A concrete communication law is defined as a subclass of CommunicationLaw and must implement the method:

```
public abstract ExternalMessage enforce(AgentId sender,
    ExternalMessage message, State state);
```

A typical example is a communication law that restricts the delivering of messages to a specific distance from the sender:

```
public ExternalMessage enforce(AgentId sender,
 ExternalMessage message, State state) {
 ExternalMessage msg = copy(message);
 for (int i=0; i<msg.nbAddressees(); i++) {
 if(!((GridState)state).withinComRange(sender,msg.addressee(i)))
   removeAddressee(message,msg.addressee(i));}
 return message;
}
```

This laws drops all addressees for a given message that are not within communication range of the sender.

Synchronizer determines the type of synchronization of simultaneous actions. Simultaneous actions are actions that happen together and that can have a combined effect in the application environment. An example of simultaneous actions in the Packet–World are two agents that push the same packet in different directions. As a result, the packet moves according to the resultant of the two actions. Ferber and Müller have introduced a model for simultaneous actions in which all the agents of the multiagent system act at one global pace, i.e. the agents are globally synchronized [15]. In this model, the environment combines the influences of all agents in each cycle to deduce a new state of the environment. We have introduced a model for regional synchronization [26,29,27]. With regional synchronization agents form synchronized groups—regions—on the basis of their actual locality. Regions are disjoint sets of agents, i.e. at any time each agent is a member of exact one region. Different regions act asynchronously, while agents act synchronously within their region. Regional synchronization complies with the basic characteristic of locality of situated agents. We elaborate on support for simultaneous actions in Sect. 5.

The framework includes support for three types of synchronization: (1) NoSynchronization, i.e. agents act asynchronously which implies that there is no support for simultaneous actions; (2) GlobalSynchronization, all agents act at a global pace—i.e. the Ferber–Müller model; and (3) RegionalSynchronization, i.e. agents act simultaneously based on their actual locality.

Collector is an active module that collects the influences (`Influence`) invoked by agents. `Collector` uses a `Synchronizer` to determine the sets of synchronized agents. If no synchronization is provided, the collector directly passes the influences to the reactor. With global synchronization, the collector collects the influences of all agents in the system before it passes the complete set to the reactor. With regional synchronization, the collector passes sets of influences per region to the reactor. `Collector` encapsulates its own thread, so that it can execute influences in parallel with other activities in the application environment.

Reactor and **Effector**. `Reactor` is responsible for processing sets of synchronized influences. The reactor *calculates* the effects of the influences according to current state of the application environment and the action laws of the multiagent system. This results in a set of effects (`Effect`). `Effector` is responsible for *executing* the effects of the influences resulting in state changes in the application environment. We elaborate on interaction in the application environment with the `Collector-Reactor-Effector` chain in Sect. 5.

EnvironmentFactory is a package that supports developers with the creation of an application environment for the multiagent system. `EnvironmentFactory` creates the internals of the application environment, it initializes the state of the environment with items and relations between items, it integrates the laws for perception, action, and communication, and it allows the developer to specify a synchronization approach for the application.

Hot Spots. Hot spots of the application environment include: `State` with `StaticItem`, `DynamicItem` and `Relation`, `OngoingActivity`, `Representation`, `Influence`, and `Effect`. Besides, `PereceptionLaw`, `ActionLaw`, and `CommunicationLaw` are hot spots that have to be defined for the application at hand. Finally, `Synchronizer` is a hot spot of the application environment for which the developer can simply select one of the available synchronizers.

4   Decision Making with a Free-Flow Tree

The framework provides the developer with one predefined behavior-based action selection mechanism: free-flow trees. Implementations of other decision making mechanisms are not provided in the current framework implementation and as such have to be defined by the developer. In this section, we explain how free-flow trees extended with roles and situated commitments are supported by the framework. But first, we introduce the notion of a free-flow tree.

4.1   Free-Flow Trees

A free-flow tree is a behavior-based action selection mechanism that was introduced by Rosenblatt and Payton in [21]. Tyrrell [23] has demonstrated that hierarchical free-flow architectures are superior to flat decision structures, especially in complex and dynamic environments. The results of Tyrrell's work are recognized in recent research, for a discussion see [9].

A free-flow tree is a hierarchy composed of *activity nodes* (in short nodes) which receive information from internal and external stimuli in the form of *activity*. The nodes feed their activity down through the hierarchy until the activity arrives at the *action nodes* (i.e. the leaf nodes of the tree) where a winner-takes-all process decides which action is selected. A free-flow tree allows an agent to take different preferences into consideration simultaneously. For example, consider an agent in the Packet-World that spots two candidate packets to be picked at about equal distance. A Packet-World agent also has to maintain its battery. To move to the battery charger, the agent can follow the gradient of the field emitted by the charger. If the agent is only able to take into account one preference at a time it will select one packet and move to it, or alternatively it will follow the gradient towards the battery charger. With a free-flow tree the agent can move towards one packet *while* it moves in the direction of the charge station, i.e. if the agent needs to recharge its battery in the near future, it will move towards the packet that is nearest to the battery charger.

Free-flow trees are developed from the viewpoint of individual agents. To enable agents to exhibit explicit social behavior, we have extended the free-flow architecture with the abstractions of a role and a situated commitment [31,22]. Fig. 5 shows a free-flow tree for an agent in the Packet-World extended with roles and situated commitments.

A role represents a coherent part of functionality of an agent in the context of an organization. Roles provide building blocks for social organization in a multiagent system. Agents are linked to other agents by the roles they play in the organization. A role can consist of a number of sub-roles, and sub-sub-roles of sub-roles etc. A role matches to a sub-tree in the free-flow tree. For the Packet-World agents, three main roles are distinguished: *Individual*, *Chain*, and *Maintain*. In the role Individual, the agent performs work, independent of the other agents. The agent searches for packets and brings them to the destination. The Chain role is composed of two sub-roles: *Head* and *Tail* denoting the two roles of agents in a collaboration to pass packets along a chain. Finally in the Maintain role, the agent recharges its battery.

A situated commitment defines a relationship between one role (the goal role) and a non-empty set of other roles (the source roles) of the agent. When a situated commitment is activated the behavior of the agent tends to prefer the goal role of the commitment over the source role(s). Favoring the goal role results in more consistent behavior of the agent towards the commitment. In a collaboration agents commit relatively to one another, typically via communication. However, an agent can also commit to itself, e.g. when it has to fulfill a vital task. A situated commitment is represented in the free-flow tree by a connector that connects the source roles of the situated commitment with the goal role. When a situated commitment is activated, extra activity is injected in the goal role relative to the activity levels of the source roles. The connector *Charging* in Fig. 5 denotes the situated commitment of an agent to itself to recharge its battery. *Charging* connects the top nodes of the source roles *Individual* and *Chain* with the goal role *Maintain*. The connectors *HeadOfChain* and *TailOfChain* denote the mutual situated commitments of two agents that collaborate to pass packets in a chain.

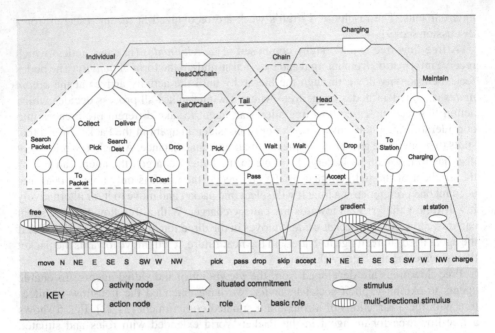

Fig. 5. Free-flow tree for a Packet-World agent with roles and situated commitments (details such as stimuli of activity nodes are omitted; action nodes with the same name—i.e. the move actions—need to be joined together; free and gradient are multi-directional stimuli that have a value for each of the eight directions the agent can move to)

4.2 Support for Free-Flow Trees in the Framework

Figure 6 shows the main classes of the FreeFlow package of the framework. A free-flow tree consists of three types of tree elements (TreeElement): Node, Stimulus, and SituatedCommitment. Tree elements are connected through links (Link). A tree element receives an amount of activity (represented by Activity) of its parent elements and can inject activity in its child elements. Each link has a weight factor that determines how much of the injected activity is passed along that link. Stimulus has no parent elements but calculates its activity based on the internal state of the agent. SituatedCommitment is connected with a non-empty set of nodes that represents its source roles, and one particular node that represents its goal role. A situated commitment can be triggered by two conditions: one that activates the commitment and one that deactivates it. In the activated state, the commitment combines the activity receive from its source roles with an AdditionFunction and injects the resulting activity in its goal role. Node is further specialized in ActivityNode and ActionNode. An ActivityNode is a regular node of the tree, an ActionNode is a leave node of the tree that is associated with an operator. Each Node has a CombinationFunction that determines how the activity received from its parent nodes is combined. Activity nodes that represent top nodes of a role have to implement the Role interface that associates an explicit name with the role. A FreeFlowTree represents the system node

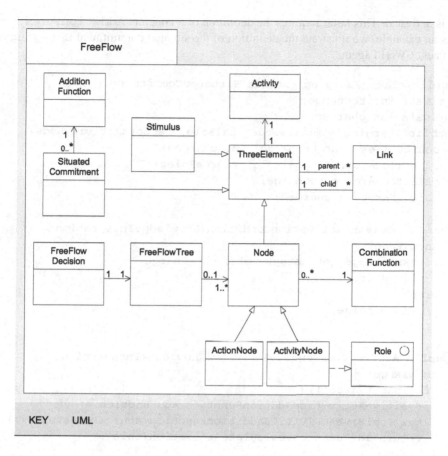

Fig. 6. Overview of the Free-flow package

and is the entry point for `FreeFlowDecision` that implements the action selection algorithm.

Hot Spots. To build a concrete free-flow tree a number of hot spots have to be implemented. In particular, `Activity`, `Stimulus`, `SituatedCommitment`, `AdditionFunction` and `CombinationFunction`, `ActionNode`, `Role`, and `Link` are hot spots. The framework supports the developer with various basic implementations for most of these hot spots. `BasicActivity` is a subclass of `Activity` that represents a basic representation of activity by means of a double value. More advanced implementations have to be defined by the developer. The framework supports the definition of simple stimuli (`SimpleStimulus`) as well as multi-directional stimuli (`VectorStimuli`). A situated commitment has to be defined as a subclass of `SituatedCommitment` and requires the definition of an activation condition, a deactivation condition, and the definition of the outcome of the situated commitment when

it is activated. This latter requires the definition of a concrete `AdditionFunction`.
As an example, we illustrate the definition of the situated commitment `Charging` of
a Packet-World agent:

```
public class Charging extends SituatedCommitment {
private int toCharge;
private int charged;
public Charging(ActivityNode goalRole, Vector<ActivityNode>
  sourceRoles, int toCharge, int charged) {
  super("charging", goalRole, sourceRoles);
  this.toCharge = toCharge;
  this.charged = charged;
}
public boolean activationCondition(KnowledgeIntegration
  knowledge) {
  if (knowledge.getEnergyLevel() < toCharge)
    return true;
  else
    return false;
}
...
public Activity calculateActivity(KnowledgeIntegration
  knowledge) {
  if (isActivated()) {
    PositiveActivitiesAddtionFunction addFunction =
    new PositiveActivitiesAdditionFunction(sourceRoles.size()));
    return addFunction.calculateActivation(this);
  }
  else
    return new BasicActivity(0);
}
...
}
```

For each `Node` a `CombinationFunction` has to be defined. The framework supports various basic functions, including `AddFunction`, `MultiplyFunction`, and `MaximumFunction`. `ActionNode` is a hot spot, for each action node of the tree a subclass of `ActionNode` has to be defined. Such subclass must implement the method `getOperator()`. This method returns the operator that is executed by the agent if that particular node is selected for execution. Each `Link` in the tree has to be assigned a weight factor, except if the weight factor has the default value of 1. Finally, a subclass of `FreeFlowDecision` must be defined. This subclass must implement the abstract method `createFreeFlowTree()` that constructs the application specific free-flow tree.

The framework's cookbook [34] provides examples of the various hot spots to support the developer with the instantiation of a free-flow tree. [22] describes a supporting modeling language and design process to design free-flow trees with roles and situated commitments.

5 Simultaneous Actions in the Environment

An interesting feature provided by the framework is support for simultaneous actions. Support for simultaneous actions enables to simulate the effects of actions that are conceptually executed at the same time, but physically are performed separated in time, e.g., on a single or sequential processor system. In this section, we first explain the notion of simultaneous actions. Then, we show how simultaneous actions are supported in the framework. We illustrate the explanation with examples from the Packet-World.

5.1 Simultaneous Actions

In the literature, several researchers refer to simultaneously performed actions. Some examples: Allen and Ferguson [5] discuss "actions that interfere with each other" and that can have "additional synergistic effects". Boutilier and Brafman [8] mention "concurrent actions with a positive or negative interacting effect". Griffiths, Luck and d'Iverno [17] introduce the notions of "joint action that a group of agents perform together" and "concurrent actions, i.e. a set of actions performed at the same time". Joint actions and concurrent actions are based on the concepts of "strong and weak parallelism" introduced Kinny [19]. In [20], Michel, Gouaïch, and Ferber introduce the notions of weak and strong interactions that are related to simultaneous actions.

We denote simultaneous actions as actions that happen together and that can have a combined result. To calculate the effects of simultaneously performed actions that physically are performed separated in time, the actions are reified as influences [12]. Support for simultaneous actions requires two mechanisms: first, a mechanism is needed that determines which influences are treated as being executed together; second, a mechanism is needed that ensures that the combined outcome of simultaneously performed influences is in accordance with the domain that is modelled.

Determining Simultaneity. Simultaneity of influences is determined by a synchronization mechanism. Two possible mechanisms for synchronization are global synchronization and regional synchronization. With global synchronization, all agents in the multiagent system act simultaneously. Global synchronization is simple to implement, but the mechanism imposes centralized control. Regional synchronization offers more fine-grained synchronization. With regional synchronization, the composition of groups of synchronized agents—regions—depends on the actual locality of the agents and dynamically changes when agents enter or leave each others locality. Support for regional synchronization can be implemented as a service of the application environment [26,10]. Alternatively, the agents can take care for the formation of regions themselves, providing a fully decentralized solution for synchronization. [29,27] discuss an algorithm for regional synchronization in detail and provides a proof of correctness.

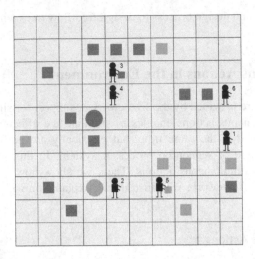

Fig. 7. Example of simultaneous actions in the Packet-World

Imposing Domain Constraints. Domain constraints are imposed through a set of action laws. Action laws determine the effects of a set of synchronized influences on the state of the application environment. As such, action laws impose constrains on the implications of agents' (inter)actions. Figure 7 shows an example of simultaneous actions in the Packet-World. In the depicted situation, agents 3 can pass packets to agent 4 that can directly deliver the packets at the destination. Such packet transfer only succeeds when the two agents act together, i.e. agent 3 has to pass the packet while agent 4 simultaneously accepts the packet. To model the packet transfer, an action law is defined. This definition includes:

1. *The set of influences.* This set consists of two influences: `PassInfluence` and `AcceptInfluence`.
2. *The preconditions.* The packet transfer only succeeds if: (i) both agents have enough energy to execute the transfer, (ii) the locations of the agents match with a chain, (iii) the tail holds a packet and the head does not.
3. *The effects.* Applying the law properly reduces the energy level of both agents, and the packet is transferred from tail to head.

Notice that agent 2 and 5 also form a chain to transfer packets. In this chain however, packets are passed indirectly via the environment, i.e., agent 5 can put packets in between the two agents and agent 2 can pick the packets and deliver them at the destination. Contrary to the *synchronous* collaboration between agent 3 and 4, this *asynchronous* collaboration does not involve any simultaneous actions.

5.2 Support for Simultaneous Actions in the Framework

Figure 8 shows the main classes of the framework involved in the execution of simultaneous actions.

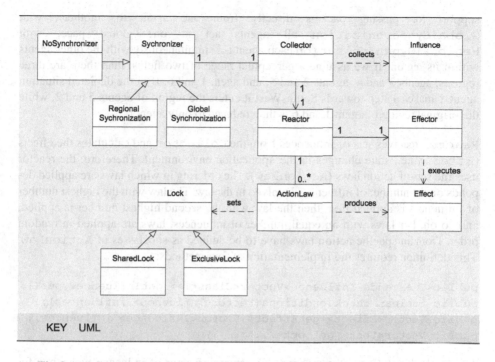

Fig. 8. Main classes of the framework involved in the execution of simultaneous actions

`Collector` collects the influences (`Influence`) invoked by the agents and stores the influences in a buffer. Domain specific influences are defined as subclasses of `Influence`. A simple example is `StepInfluence` that is defined as follows:

```
public class StepInfluence extends Influence {
  private Direction direction;
  public StepInfluence(AgentId agent, Direction direction){
    super(agent);
    setDirection(direction);
  }
  ...
}
```

`Synchronizer` determines when influences are passed to the `Reactor` for execution. With `NoSychronizer` influences are passed one by one; with `GlobalSynchronizer` the set of influences of all agents is passed; with `RegionalSynchronization` the influences are passed to the reactor per region. To form regions, the framework provides a default implementation for locality that is based on the default range of perception. In particular, a region in the framework consists of the set of agents that are located within each other's perceptual range, or within the perceptual range of those agents, and so on. Applied to the situation in Fig. 7: with `NOSynchronizer` all agents act asynchronously (in this case there is no

support for passing packets directly from one agent to another); with
`GlobalSynchronization` all agents act at one global pace; with
`RegionalSynchronization` each agent act simultaneously with the other agents
within its region. If we assume a perceptual range of two fields, than there are three
regions: agents 3 and 4, agents 2 and 5, and agent 1 and 6. If in the depicted situation
agent 1 makes a step towards South-West it enters the region of agents 5 and 2, while
the original region of agent 1 and 6 is than reduced to only agent 6.

`Reactor` receives sets of influences from the `Collector` and calculates the effects
(`Effect`), i.e., state changes in the application environment. Therefore, the reactor
uses the sets of action laws (`ActionLaw`). The ordering in which laws are applied depends on the number of influences involved in the law. The law with the highest number
of influences is applied first, then the law with the second highest number is applied,
and so on. For laws with an equal number of influences, laws are applied in random
order. Domain specific action laws have to be defined as subclasses of `ActionLaw`.
This definition requires the implementation of four methods:

```
public<T extends Influence>Vector<Class<T>> getInfluenceTypes();
public boolean checkConditions(Vector<Influence> influences);
public Vector<Effect> getEffects(Vector<Influence> influences);
public Vector<Lock> getLocks();
```

The method `getInfluenceTypes()` returns a vector of influence types, one for
each influence involved in the law. This method allows the reactor to check whether the
law is applicable or not. For `TransferPacketLaw` that models the rules for agents
to transfer a packet, `getInfluenceTypes()` is defined as follows:

```
public<T extends Influence>Vector<Class<T>> getInfluenceTypes()
{
  Vector<Class<T>> infs = new Vector<Class<T>>();
  infs.add((Class<T>)PassInfluence.class);
  infs.add((Class<T>)AcceptInfluence.class);
  return infs;
}
```

The method `checkConditions()` verifies whether the necessary conditions hold to
apply the law. For `TransferPacketLaw` the conditions are:

```
public boolean checkConditions((Vector<Influence> infs)){
  //the agents must have enough energy
  passAgent=(AgentState)getState().getItem(infs[1].getAgent());
  if (passAgent.getEnergyLevel()<passAgent.tresholdToRecharge())
    return false;
  ...
  //passAgent must hold a packet, acceptAgent not
  boolean hold = false;
```

```
for (Relation rel:getState().getRelations(HoldRelation.class))
{
  if (rel.containsItem(passAgent)) {
    hold = true;
    break;
  }
}
...
}
```

The method getEffects() returns the effects induced by the law. An application specific effect has to be defined as a subclass of Effect. A simple example is AddRelationEffect that is used to add a relation in the state of the application environment. Such relation is used to link the agent with the packet it accepts during a packet transfer:

```
public class AddRelationEffect extends Effect {
  public AddRelationEffect(GridState state, Relation relation){
    super(state);
    setRelation(relation);
  }
  public void execute(){
    state.addRelation(relation);
  }
  ...
}
```

Finally, each action law has to implement the method getLocks(). This method returns the locks on the state elements used by the law. Locks (Lock) avoid conflicts between action laws. To ensure that all simultaneously performed influences are applied in the same circumstances, the action laws produce the effects of influences from the same state of the application environment. However, applying a law may induce constraints on state elements. For example, assume that StepLaw handles the movement of a single agent. If agent 6 in Fig. 7 makes a step to South than agent 1 can no longer step to North. To avoid a conflict between the application of the law for both agents, the first application of StepLaw puts a lock on the field the agent moves to. During the execution of the law for the other influence of the region, the reactor uses the lock to check whether the StepLaw is applicable or not. The framework supports two types of basic locks: ExclusiveLock and SharedLock. An ExclusiveLock on a state element of the application environment excludes other laws to access the locked element. A SharedLock allows other laws to put a shared lock on the element, however, it excludes a possible ExclusiveLock.

Effector is responsible to apply the effects induced by the action laws. Each Effect implements the method execute() that actually performs the effects to the state of the application environment, see the AddRelationEffect above.

Hot Spots. Much of the complexity to deal with simultaneous actions is hidden by the framework core. If the application requires support for simultaneous actions, the developer has to select a particular type of synchronization. This selection has to be specified in the `EnvironmentFactory` definition. Furthermore, the developer has to define application specific instances for `Influence`, `ActionLaw`, `Lock`, and `Effect`, as illustrated above.

6   Failure Treatment in the Framework

Basic failure treatment in the framework is dealt with by Java exception handling. To avoid overloaded code excerpts, we have omitted the exception code in the examples in this paper. As an illustration, we show the exception handling for setting a lock in the `SharedLockType` class.

```
public class SharedLockType implements LockType {
  public boolean canSetLock(LockType currentLockType){
    if (! (currentLockType instanceof SharedLockTypes()) ||
        ! (currentLockType instanceof ExclusiveLockType)))
      throw new IllegalArgumentException
          ("only read and write locks allowed");
    if (currentLockType instanceof ExclusiveLockType)
        return false;
    return true;
  }
}
```

A shared lock can only be combined with another shared lock. The method public boolean `canSetLock(LockType currentLockType)` returns a boolean that indicates whether the type of lock can be set on a given object or not. When the given lock type is not a shared or exclusive lock, an exception is thrown. When there is already an exclusive lock on the object, the lock can no longer be set and a false is returned. Otherwise the lock can be set and true is returned.

7   Applying the Framework to an Experimental Robot Application

As a validation, we have used the framework to develop an experimental application in which two Lego-Mindstorms robots collaborate to organize the supply of products. In this section we give an overview of application. First, we introduce the application based on a simulation, and we explain the setup of the physical system with robots and the environment. Then we show how we have instantiated the framework to develop the application software. We limit the discussion to the agent software.

7.1   Robot Application

Figure 9 shows a schematical overview of the robot application.

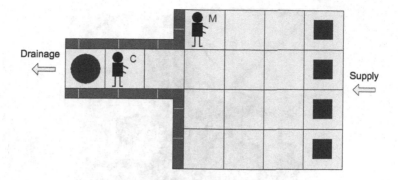

Fig. 9. Simulation of the robot application

The environment consists of two zones: the corridor on the left side in which a non-mobile crane robot can manoeuvre, and the rectangular factory flour on the right side in which a mobile robot can move around. The colored packets on the right side of the factory floor represent products. The circle represents the delivering point for products. The task of the robots is to guarantee a stream of products from supply to drainage.

We have developed the robots with the Lego-Mindstorms packet [3]. Besides building blocks to construct robots, Lego-Mindstorms offers a programmable microcomputer called Robotic Command eXplorer (RCX) to program a robot. To enable the robot to interact with the environment, various sensors (light, pressure, etc.) and actuators (switches, motors, etc.) are available that can be connected to the RCX. Furthermore, the RCX is equipped with an infrared serial communication interface that enables a developer to program the microcomputer. We have used the LeJOS (Lego Java Operating System), as a replacement firmware for the Lego Mindstorms RCX. LeJOS is a reduced Java Virtual Machine that fits within the 32kb on the RCX, and that allows to program a Lego robot with Java [4].

Figure 10 shows one of the robots. Robots are equipped with various sensors to monitor the environment, and they have two grasp arms to pick up packets. The robots can communicate with a local computer via infrared communication.

Figure 11 shows environment with the two robots in action. The robots use light sensors to follow the paths that are marked by black lines.

7.2 Applying the Framework

Due to memory limitations of the RCX, it was not possible to execute the full robot control software directly on the robot hardware. Therefore the robot software is divided in two collaborating programs: one program running on the RCX of the robot that monitors the environment and executes actions, and a second program running on a local computer that selects actions. Figure 12 shows how the robot software is deployed on the various hardware units. The agents use LTDSchedule as scheduling schema. LTDSchedule is a predefined scheduling schema in the framework that successively activates perception, communication, decision making in an endless loop. Perception transforms the data sensed by InfraredSensor into a percept

Fig. 10. A robot carrying a packet

Fig. 11. The environment with the robots in action

(WAStatePercept). Periodically, the RCX sends an infrared message with the current status of the robot (position, hold packet or not) to the agent program on the computer. Infrared communication is handled by IRTower and IRPort on the host computer and the RCX respectively. The decision making modules (CraneAgentDecisionMaking and MobileAgentDecisionMaking) take care for action selection. The action selection mechanisms of the MobileAgent continuously executes a sequence of three roles: LookForPacket, ReturnToCorridor, and PassPacket. When the MobileAgent arrives with a new packet at the corridor, the CraneAgent executes AcceptPacket, it delivers the packet (DeliverPacket) at the destination, and subsequently waits for the next packet (Wait). WAExecution sends the selected actions to the RCX via the

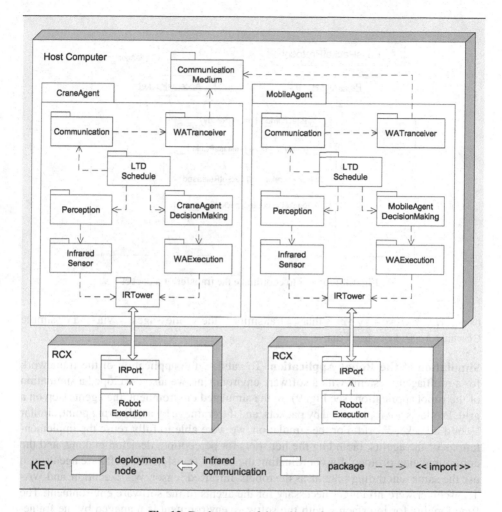

Fig. 12. Deployment of the robot software

IRTower. The decision making modules however, produce high-level actions, such as "drive to the corridor" and "put packet on the destination". When RobotExecution receives such an action, it translates the actions into low-level actions to steer the actuators.

When the MobileAgent arrives with a packet at the corridor, it has to pass the packet to the CraneAgent. To coordinate this interaction, the agents use a PassPacketProtocol that is handled by the Communication module. The subsequent steps of this protocol are depicted in Fig. 13. When the MobileAgent arrives at the corridor it informs the CraneAgent that it has arrived with a packet for delivering. The CraneAgent drives towards the packet and as soon as it is in the correct position, it informs the MobileAgent to release the packet. When the MobileAgent has released the packet it informs the CraneAgent. This latter then brings the packet to the delivering location. To communicate with one another, robots

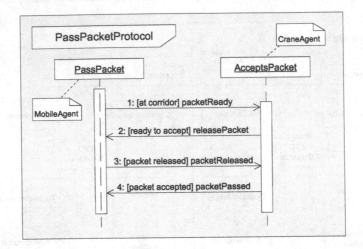

Fig. 13. Protocol to coordinate the transfer of a packet

use WATransceiver that transmits the messages via a simple CommunicationMedium.

Simulation of the Robot Application. To validate the application of the framework for a multiagent systems with a software environment, we also developed a simulation of the robot application (see Fig. 9). In the simulated environment, the agents step on a grid. Products are represented by packets, and the drainage by a delivering point, similar as in the Packet-World. For the simulation, we were able to fully reuse the implementations of the agents, including the hot spots for perception, decision making, and the communication protocol for coordinating the packet transfer. The software agents also use the same scheduling schema as the robots. InfraRedSensor, WAExecution, and WA-Transceiver were no longer necessary for the agents in the software environment. The functionality for interfacing with the software environment is managed by the framework core.

8   Differences with Other Multiagent System Frameworks

Many frameworks and development tools for multiagent systems have been developed, for an overview see for example [2]. We touch on two representative examples and point to the typical differences with the framework presented in this paper.

JADE (Java Agent DEvelopment Framework [7]) is a well-known Java framework for the implementation of multiagent systems that fully complies to the FIPA specifications [16]. JADE comes with a set of graphical tools that supports the debugging and deployment of agent systems. JADE provides advanced support for agent communication in terms of ACL libraries and a distributed communication infrastructure. Support for developing agent internals is rather limited and environment functionality other that message communication infrastructure is absent.

MadKit (Multi-Agent Development Kit [18]) is a modular multiagent system platform written in Java. Agents in MadKit can be programmed in Java, Scheme, Jess (rule based engine), or BeanShell. MadKit comes with a set of features for launching, displaying, developing and monitoring agents and organizations. MadKit provides extensive support for the AGR (Agent/Group/Role) organizational model: agents are situated in groups and play roles [13,14]. MadKit uses the notion of "system agent" to provide support for various kinds of system responsibilities that are typically covered by the application environment in the framework presented in this paper. As most multiagent system frameworks, MadKit is strongly biased towards a message passing interaction model. As such, support for other concerns such as perception and indirect interaction through the environment is limited.

9   Concluding Remarks

In this paper, we gave an overview of an object-oriented framework for situated multiagent systems. The framework targets experimental applications that are characterized by highly dynamic operation conditions and in which global control is difficult to achieve. The framework shows a concrete design of various mechanisms for adaptivity we have developed in our research, including selective perception, protocol-based communication, and behavior-based decision making with roles and situated commitments, and shows its application to an experimental robot application and the implementation of the Packet-World.

The framework releases the developer from many difficult and error prone tasks when developing a situated multiagent system. One important example is control flow (threading) in the agent system that is fully managed by the framework. The only task to derive an application from the framework is to implement the various hot spots and use the available factories to instantiate the application. However, the framework has many hot spots. The large number of hot spots keeps the framework generic, yet the price is more work to implement the application specific parts of the application. The cookbook [34] aims to guide the developer in the development process of an application with the framework. The framework is available for download, see [1].

Acknowledgements

We are grateful to Elke Steegmans for the joint research that has contributed to the framework presented in this paper. We also would like to express our appreciation to Els Helsen and Koen Deschacht for their contribution to the development of the framework and the compilation of the framework cookbook. Finally, we thank the anonymous reviewers for the valuable feedback.

References

1. DistriNet   Framework   for   Situated   Multiagent   Systems   (Delta),   (12/2006). http://www.cs.kuleuven.be/~danny/delta.html.
2. Multiagent system, Wikipedia, (12/2006). http://en.wikipedia.org/wiki/Multi-agent_system.

3. Lego Mindstorms, (8/2006). http://mindstorms.lego.com/.
4. LeJOS, Lego Java Operating System for the Lego Mindstorms RCX, (8/2006). http://lejos.sourgeforce.com/.
5. J. Allen and G. Ferguson. Actions and Events in Interval Temporal Logic. *Journal of Logic and Computation, Special Issue on Actions and Processes*, 4:531–579, 1994.
6. K. Beck and R. Johnson. Patterns Generate Architectures. In *ECOOP '94: Proceedings of the 8th European Conference on Object-Oriented Programming*, Lecture Notes in Computer Science, Vol. 821, London, UK, 1994. Springer-Verlag.
7. F. Bellifemine, A. Poggi, and G. Rimassa. Jade, A FIPA-compliant Agent Framework. In *4th International Conference on Practical Application of Intelligent Agents and Multi-Agent Technology*, London, UK, 1999.
8. C. Boutilier and R. I. Brafman. Partial-order planning with concurrent interacting actions. *Journal on Artificial Intelligence Research*, 14:105–136, 2001.
9. J. Bryson. *Intelligence by Design, Principles of Modularity and Coordination for Engineering Complex Adaptive Agents*. PhD Dissertation, MIT, USA, 2001.
10. L. Claesen. *Regional Synchronization in Situated Multiagent Systems*. Master Thesis, Katholieke Universiteit Leuven, Belgium, 2004.
11. M. Fayad and D. Schmidt. Object-Oriented Application Frameworks, Guest Editorial. *Communications of the ACM, Special Issue on Object-Oriented Application Frameworks*, 40(10):32–38, 1997.
12. J. Ferber. *Introduction to Distributed Artificial Intelligence*. Addison-Wesley, 1999.
13. J. Ferber, O. Gutknecht, and F. Michel. From Agents to Organizations: an Organizational View of Multi-Agent Systems. In *Agent-Oriented Software Engineering (AOSE) IV*, Lecture Notes in Computer Science, Vol. 2935. Springer-Verlag, 2004.
14. J. Ferber, F. Michel, and J. Baez. AGRE: Integrating environments with organizations. In *1st International Workshop on Environments for Multiagent Systems*, Lecture Notes in Computer Science, Vol. 3374. Springer-Verlag, 2005.
15. J. Ferber and J. Muller. Influences and Reaction: a Model of Situated Multiagent Systems. *2nd International Conference on Multi-agent Systems, Japan, AAAI Press*, 1996.
16. FIPA. Foundation for Intelligent Physical Agents, FIPA Abstract Architecture Specification. *http://www.fipa.org/repository/bysubject.html*, (8/2006).
17. N. Griffiths, M. Luck, and M. d'Iverno. Cooperative Plan Annotation through Trust. In *UK Workshop on Multi-Agent Systems*, Liverpool, UK, 2002.
18. O. Gutknecht, J. Ferber, and F. Michel. Integrating tools and infrastructures for generic multi-agent systems. In *AGENTS '01: Proceedings of the fifth international conference on Autonomous agents*, pages 441–448, New York, NY, USA, 2001. ACM Press.
19. D. Kinny, M. Ljundberg, and A. Rao. Planning with Team Activity. In *4th European Workshop on Modelling Autonomous Agents in a Multi-Agent World*, Lecture Notes in Computer Science, Vol. 830. Springer-Verlag, London, UK, 1992.
20. F. Michel, A. Gouaich, and J. Ferber. Weak Interaction and Strong Interaction in Agent Based Simulations. In *Multi-Agent-Based Simulation III*, Lecture Notes in Computer Science, Vol. 2927. Springer-Verlag, 2003.
21. K. Rosenblatt and D. Payton. *A Fine Grained Alternative to the Subsumption Architecture for Mobile Robot Control*. International Joint Conference on Neural Networks, IEEE, 1989.
22. E. Steegmans, D. Weyns, T. Holvoet, and Y. Berbers. A Design Process for Adaptive Behavior of Situated Agents. In *Agent-Oriented Software Engineering V, 5th International Workshop, AOSE, New York*, Lecture Notes in Computer Science, Vol. 3382. Springer, 2004.
23. T. Tyrrell. *Computational Mechanisms for Action Selection*. PhD Dissertation, University of Edinburgh, 1993.

24. D. Weyns, A. Helleboogh, and T. Holvoet. The Packet-World: a Test Bed for Investigating Situated Multi-Agent Systems. In *Agent-based applications, platforms, and development kits*. Whitestein Series in Software Agent Technology, 2005.
25. D. Weyns and T. Holvoet. Look, Talk, and Do: A Synchronization Scheme for Situated Multiagent Systems. In *UK Workshop on Multi-Agent Systems*, Oxford, UK, 2002.
26. D. Weyns and T. Holvoet. Model for Simultaneous Actions in Situated Multiagent Systems. In *Multiagent System Technologies, Erfurt, Germany*, Lecture Notes in Computer Science, Vol. 2831. Springer Verlag, 2003.
27. D. Weyns and T. Holvoet. A Colored Petri Net for Regional Synchronization in Situated Multiagent Systems. In *1st International Workshop on Coordination and Petri Nets, Bologna, Italy*, 2004.
28. D. Weyns and T. Holvoet. Formal Model for Situated Multi-Agent Systems. *Fundamenta Informaticae*, 63(1-2):125–158, 2004.
29. D. Weyns and T. Holvoet. Regional Synchronization for Situated Multi-agent Systems. In *3th International Central and Eastern European Conference on Multi-Agent Systems, Prague, Czech Republic*, Lecture Notes in Computer Science, Vol. 2691. Springer Verlag, 2004.
30. D. Weyns, K. Schelfthout, T. Holvoet, and T. Lefever. Decentralized control of E'GV transportation systems. In *4th Joint Conference on Autonomous Agents and Multiagent Systems, Industry Track*, Utrecht, The Netherlands, 2005. ACM Press, New York, NY, USA.
31. D. Weyns, E. Steegmans, and T. Holvoet. Integrating Free-Flow Architectures with Role Models Based on Statecharts. In *Software Engineering for Multi-Agent Systems III*, Lecture Notes in Computer Science, Vol. 3390. Springer, 2004.
32. D. Weyns, E. Steegmans, and T. Holvoet. Protocol Based Communication for Situated Multi-Agent Systems. In *3th Joint Conference on Autonomous Agents and Multi-Agent Systems*, New York, USA, 2004. IEEE Computer Society.
33. D. Weyns, E. Steegmans, and T. Holvoet. Towards Active Perception in Situated Multi-Agent Systems. *Applied Artificial Intelligence*, 18(9-10):867–883, 2004.
34. D. Weyns, E. Steegmans, T. Holvoet, E. Helsen, and K. Deschacht. Delta Framework Cookbook. In *Technical Report 473*. Departement of Computer Science, Katholieke Universiteit Leuven, Belgium. http://www.cs.kuleuven.ac.be/publicaties/rapporten/CW/2007/, (1/2007).

Author Index

Lecture Notes in Computer Science

For information about Vols. 1–4525

please contact your bookseller or Springer